D1143848

AS WHITE AS SNOW

The *fantastic deliverance of DEBBIE FORREST,*
a desperate drug-addict.

NOEL DAVIDSON

AMBASSADOR INTERNATIONAL
Greenville, South Carolina • Belfast, Northern Ireland

AS WHITE AS SNOW
© Copyright 2005 Noel Davidson

ISBN 1 84030 164 3

Ambassador Publications
a division of
Ambassador Productions Ltd.
Providence House
Ardenlee Street,
Belfast,
BT6 8QJ
Northern Ireland
www.ambassador-productions.com

Emerald House
427 Wade Hampton Blvd.
Greenville
SC 29609, USA
www.emeraldhouse.com

CONTENTS

FOREWORD

During the past twenty years that it has been my privilege to lead the work of Teen Challenge in the UK thousands of broken young men and women have turned to it for help. These are young people whose lives had been totally destroyed by their journey into drug misuse and other life controlling problems. By and large these are men and women who have been rejected by society as having no hope or future purpose in life and who were considered a threat to society.

In Isaiah 45 verse 3 there is a promise made to Cyrus that God would restore to Israel 'the treasures hidden in darkness' that were taken by the invading armies from the Temple. These were temple instruments that were used by worshippers in their praise of Jehovah. The Lord promised that although they had been stolen and hidden away in dark places they would once again become instruments of worship in His service. These treasures are a type of the many young lives that have been created by God for His pleasure, only to have been stolen and hidden in darkness. It is the work of Teen Challenge to invade that darkness to recover those lives and to see them restored to physical, emotional and spiritual wholeness.

One of those treasures is Debbie, whose life has been transformed by the power of God's grace. She represents so many of her generation who fail to achieve their potential because of the devastating effects of drug abuse. Her story is both a warning and an inspiration. Addiction threatened to destroy her life, which was full of so much potential. Like the story of the Prodigal Son, Debbie is a testimony to the amazing love of God that is able to reach a person at their lowest ebb.

It is my hope that this book will encourage others who may find themselves in similar circumstances to Debbie to turn to Christ for His forgiveness and to receive the new life that only He can give.

John E J Macey
Executive Director
Teen Challenge UK

INTRODUCTION

"I'm awfully sorry but Debbie is counselling at the moment," the voice replied, in response to my call asking to speak to a lady called Debbie Forrest. "Perhaps you would like to ring back later."

This exploratory telephone call came after I had been watching the BBC programme 'Songs of Praise' one Sunday afternoon and saw Debbie being interviewed. Her story was so gripping and told with such clarity and sincerity that I turned to my wife and said, "I would like to write that woman's testimony sometime."

Having seen the sign 'Hope House,' in the background of one of the shots I made a few discreet enquiries and was given a contact number for the rehabilitation centre for broken women in south Wales.

A follow-up call 'later' was to bring a similar reply. "I'm sorry but Debbie is counselling at the moment, but if you give me your telephone number I will have her call you back."

Counselling again! There must be a lot of people needing counselling in that place, I thought.

When I did make contact with Debbie some days later she willingly agreed to allow me to write her story. This was not, she was careful to make clear, to draw attention to herself, but in the hope that other addicts may read it and come to Jesus to have their lives turned around just as hers had been.

It was about a year later that I made my first trip across to Wales to interview Debbie and two things impressed me about her during that initial visit. One of these was immediately evident from the moment I met her, the other it took me just a day to discover. The first of these was the sheer vitality of her Christianity. Her eyes sparkled with life as she told me about what the Lord meant to her, and with love when she told me what He was doing in Hope House.

Secondly, as we thought about the possible outline of a book, soon after I had arrived at my destination, I was to be totally bowled over by the depth of Debbie's story. It all began in a turbulent teenage, where dabbling in alcohol and cannabis to mask a sense of shame led to the use of heroine and crack cocaine. That, though, was only the beginning. Things grew worse. When she was a mental and physical wreck, and frequently suicidal, God intervened in her life in a marvellous way. When Debbie started to tell me of the sequence of events following her conversion, I was totally amazed, pausing occasionally to remark, as I wrote it all down, "This is fantastic!"

By the time I was ready to leave for home I realised that the research material I had collected on the story I had just heard would make an absolutely wonderful witness to the power and grace of God, if I could condense it into book form.

Debbie's enthusiasm for the work was infectious from the start, and helped carry me along. The storyline too was so strong that it had me thinking about it, even when I wasn't writing it. It wasn't just a job for me, it was both a pleasure, and a preoccupation.

As with most of the biographies I have written, a number of the friends of the subject have become friends of mine. In this context I would like to thank Richard and Alicia for kindly volunteering to make their home my home on my visits to Wales, Debbie's mum, Eileen, who often charmed me with her culinary skills, and Emily, Debbie's daughter who has been blessed with her mum's sheer zest for life. Look out for Emily and Eileen in the story too!

I feel I ought to end this short introduction by returning to where I began it, in Hope House. More than half of this book relates to Debbie's experiences there, initially as a resident and then latterly as a member of staff. The first time I stepped into it with her, I could understand why she loves it so much. During three successive visits to Wales I have come to know Fiona and Julie, senior staff members along with Debbie, and appreciate the excellent work all three of them do as a team in seeing many young women cleared of their addictions in a caring Christian environment.

It was when I came to meet a few of the residents and hear from them little snippets about their backgrounds that I realised why so much counselling is necessary. And why it can take so long! The book includes some of Debbie's experiences as a counsellor as she set about dealing with people like Alison and Brenda. These young women arrived, as many do, hooked on heroin and crack and with the serious physical, mental and emotional problems that accompany such extreme addiction.

Spending the past eight months researching this book with Debbie, witnessing what God has done in her life and what He is still doing in the work in which she is involved in Hope House for His sake, has reminded me forcibly of one important spiritual fact.

God is not dead, nor has He retired. He is very much alive and at work, 'the same yesterday, today and forever.'

Debbie and I both pray that you will find 'As White As Snow' interesting and perhaps even inspirational to read, and that it will be blessed to the salvation of many souls and the restoration of many lives, for the glory of God.

Noel Davidson
October 2005

1

I WANT TO BE A JEW!

"What you have done is wrong. You have committed a mortal sin. There is a black mark on your soul..."

The nun looked horrified as she gazed down at eleven year-old Debbie Forrest, who was sitting with her head bowed before her, in the chapel of Our Lady Of Mercy Grammar School, in Wolverhampton, England.

Although the nun's proclamation of doom on one of her youngest pupils was delivered in the privacy of the chapel, the episode had begun ten minutes earlier in the convent's walled garden.

It was a beautiful summer afternoon, and when Debbie saw a particular nun, whom she thought might just be sympathetic to what she had to say, pottering alone amongst the plants, she had made her approach.

This came after weeks of delay. It represented the climax to endless attempts to summon up the courage to disclose her dark secret. Debbie had tried on a number of occasions already to report what had been happening to her, but had always drawn back at the last minute. Her inability to adequately express the hurt and sense of shame she was feeling, had held her back more than once. On other occasions it had been the fear of the reaction of others to her story, and the possibility of unpleasant consequences arising from the telling of it, that had kept her lips tightly sealed.

Now though, was the big moment. A spell of fine weather had introduced a certain feel-good-factor to the school environment. All the girls in her form seemed so carefree, dressed in their summer blouses and laughing and joking with happy, shining faces.

How Debbie longed to be like them. If only she could return to being the happy-go-lucky little girl of her early childhood. But she couldn't. A dark cloud had come into her life, and it was gradually settling like sickening smog on her heart and mind, threatening to smother the sunshine of her very soul forever.

She had to tell somebody.

If she didn't she would surely go mad.

This was it. There could be no turning back this time...

Walking sheepishly up to the teaching nun in the garden she had said, "Sister, I have something to tell you."

"Yes, Debbie. What is it?" her teacher had enquired quite pleasantly. The good weather and the imminent approach of the end of term appeared to have put her in quite a genial mood, too.

"I want to tell you what is happening to me at home," Debbie began, nervously. Then, as the nun listened she opened her mouth, and her heart, and let all the wretchedness come flooding out. The truth was that her mother's boyfriend had been sexually abusing her for some time. She hadn't thought much about it at first, but as it had continued Debbie was becoming increasingly disturbed by it. Surely her teachers would be able to help her to do something to have it stopped.

The man kept assuring her that it was normal, but it had to be 'kept as a secret' between them. Debbie's conscience was telling her, however, that it wrong. She had begun to feel dirty and defiled by it.

As Debbie shared this intimate information with the nun whom she had chosen as her confidante, the sister's countenance had changed dramatically. It was as though a sudden and unexpected thunderstorm had burst upon her glowing sunny summer face.

"This is awful, Debbie," had been her instinctive reaction to her pupil's frank disclosures. "We cannot discuss such deeply personal matters out in the garden like this. The other girls might hear you. We must go to the chapel where we can talk about it in private." Debbie hadn't quite figured out whether her tone of voice reflected anger, embarrassment or just plain exasperation, before she gave the curt command, "Come on. You must come with me." With that she had marched off in the direction of the chapel, leaving the even more bewildered pupil to follow a step or two behind, like a chastened puppy.

When Debbie sat down, a few seats from the back of the empty echoing chapel, the nun began to walk back and forward across the front, giving her decision on this 'whole sordid affair' as she had chosen to call it, as she did so. It was clear to Debbie that her confidences had upset her teacher considerably and that the nun's pronouncements did not emanate from any sense of malice, but were the product of a deep and sincere conviction. They were hard to accept, nonetheless.

"It is very wrong of you, Debbie," she declared at one point, "To lead a man astray like this." That had been followed by her stern observations on the eleven-year-old's mortal sin and black-marked soul.

Debbie felt awful. Her stomach was churning and she was having difficulty keeping herself from being physically sick. The colour had drained from her face and her mouth had dried up completely.

"Does this mean I won't go to heaven?" she croaked in a rare moment when the pontificating nun paused for breath.

"Yes, that's exactly what it means," came the instant reply.

The pitiful question had merely opened up another angle of attack for her 'counsellor.' "You will go to hell."

So it was all her fault. She had come for help for she knew that what this man was doing to her was wrong. This was only to be told that she was in some way responsible for it! She felt disappointed at not having been shown any sympathy or offered the slightest support, and both astonished and appalled at having been blamed for something she definitely hadn't started and desperately wished would stop.

And according to this nun, whose spiritual authority she was expected to respect, she was on her way to hell, and that was it. There was no way back.

"Stay there, and don't move," her accuser commanded a short time later. "I must bring someone else in on this." Having said that, in an icy tone chilling enough to freeze Debbie to the seat on a hot afternoon, she disappeared out the door, only to return very quickly with another sister.

The arrival of this second nun plunged Debbie even deeper into despair. Now there were two of them up at the front with their backs to her, nodding and shaking their heads alternately but constantly, and always whispering, whispering, whispering. The only indication she had that they even remembered she was there was when they turned around to regard her with looks of utter disdain. They are probably just checking, Debbie thought, in a flash of beleaguered bitterness, that I haven't turned into a witch, or a demon, or a big ugly frog or something else equally awful and wicked.

It soon became evident that the two nuns were in a quandary. They had possibly never encountered a problem like this before, and didn't know how to react. As they stood before her, still nodding like a pair of clockwork pecking birds Debbie had seen once on a market stall, the pupil lifted her gaze to the statue directly above their heads.

It was of 'the sacred heart of Jesus'. The red heart was supposed to be pulsating with love and mercy for everybody, but especially children. Yes, mercy for children.

'You have committed a mortal sin... There is a black mark on your soul... You will go to hell...' The words re-echoed in Debbie's ears, and bounced about like a superball in her mind.

Can this be mercy? she wondered.

Can this possibly be what Jesus is all about? she pondered.

It didn't add up, somehow.

A succession of even more distressing questions followed. Her heart was already breaking. Her self-esteem was in tatters. And now she felt that her mind was about to explode as she asked herself such things as, 'Does Jesus not actually care for me after all?.. Am I really now an absolute outcast, totally beyond the reach of God's love and mercy?... What is going to happen to me? How can I be accused of committing a mortal sin when I am the one being sinned against?..'

The muted whispers at the front were the only sounds to break the sanctimonious silence of the chapel. The polished wooden seats, the polished wooden floor and the whitewashed stone walls all looked so fresh and clean. Why did she feel so unworthy and so worthless, sitting in such unsullied surroundings?

Gradually Debbie began to divert her attention away from the nuns at the front of the chapel, to all the trappings of ceremonial religion around it. And she was now to discover that she felt strangely distant from it all. The altar, the statues, the huge cross with Jesus on it, the candles and the stained glass windows, all of which had been an integral part of her life up until that moment suddenly seemed that they had been transposed to another planet. They didn't belong in her life any more.

Debbie had grown up in a happy home with her mother and her loving, caring grandparents. The three adults in her life had done their best to ensure that she wanted for nothing. They were particularly careful, especially when she was in her early years, to arrange a party for her at every birthday. One of the features of these occasions was the provision of a variety of brightly coloured balloons, and when Debbie was four or five somebody taught her how to blow up a balloon and then stretch the neck of it to release the air and make a harsh noise as she did so. This left the balloon stretched, limp and soggy.

That was exactly how Debbie felt at that moment. The air had been released from her balloon. There was nothing to keep her up any more. She had ended up crumpled, crushed, useless, limp and soggy. All enthusiasm for formal religion had gone.

When she was younger she and her cousin Stephen had often played 'churches.' It had been a natural extension of innocent childhood. They attended church so often, and held it in such awe and respect, that it seemed only natural to want to weave it into the fabric of their lives. Some boys they knew modelled themselves on their soccer heroes. Some girls tried to imitate their pop-idols. Debbie and Stephen's role models were priests and altar boys.

That desire for, and love of, the church and all it stood for, died in Debbie that summer afternoon. It had been brutally murdered.

When, eventually, the nun who Debbie had first approached told her that she could go, the tormented eleven-year-old rose and walked sullenly out of the chapel. She felt empty and betrayed. Neither of the conferring teachers had told her what action, if any, they were going to take in response to the secret she had plucked up the courage to share with them. Nor did they give her any advice as to what to do, or make any arrangement to meet her again to discuss the matter further.

It was all left up in the air. Debbie thought later that they had probably decided to 'brush it under the carpet.' Unsure of what to do, or say, in such circumstances, they had chosen to blame Debbie for her own mental, emotional and spiritual turmoil and hope that sometime, somehow, it would all just 'dry up and blow away.'

This may have happened with the nuns, but it didn't with Debbie. They could, perhaps, in time, manage to consign the anguish of an eleven year old who had looked to them for help, to the backs of their minds, considering it largely self-inflicted.

Debbie now found herself with a double burden. She was no nearer to a solution for an ongoing problem, but she considered herself very much alone in the world. Everybody and everything had forsaken her, and she was angry with them.

She was angry at the church, which had failed her in her hour of most need.

When the abuse had first begun she had prayed to God that it would stop. And it hadn't. So she was mad at God, as well.

By the time she reached early teenage, Debbie had become very difficult to manage in school. She did well in the subjects she liked, but was extremely disruptive and rebellious in Religious Education classes. She couldn't stomach being taught by nuns who looked and sounded ever so holy, but whom she had come to consider as heartless and unfeeling. This conclusion was perhaps rather unfair, since it was based on her experience with only two of them, but it stuck nonetheless.

Debbie disrupted virtually every RE class she attended, and was disciplined time after time. No matter what the subject of the lesson was, she would find some aspect of it on which to heap open scorn. She laughed at the parables, mocked the miracles and refused point-blank to say, or even respect the prayers.

And she didn't care. What did it matter what she said, or did? Was she not a hopeless case? One of her supposed spiritual mentors had already earmarked her for destruction. So if she was already on her way to hell, why should she ever try to be good?

Before every RE class an irrepressible tide of revolt rose in Debbie. She began, almost subconsciously, to build up a mental store of verbal abuse. If she said anything that made her teachers particularly angry she noted it as worthwhile using again.

She added a new, and as it was to turn out, most effective weapon to her armoury one evening while watching television. The play being screened told the story of a Catholic girl who had started 'going with' a Jewish boy, and graphically depicted the animosity this liaison caused in both their deeply religious families.

This gave Debbie an idea, and on the next opportunity she announced in the RE class, "I don't want to be a Catholic any more. I want to be a Jew."

Possibly only setting the classroom on fire could have caused a more panic-stricken reaction. Consternation reigned. The 'ill-informed' teenager was immediately sent to a senior figure in the convent for counselling. Surely she couldn't understand the implication of what she had just said.

It was true. She didn't understand all the theological issues involved. What she did know, though, was that she had discovered a sore point, a chink in the armour. Debbie, the rebel, had stumbled on a phrase that shot straight 'up the nuns' self-righteous noses.'

So she used it again, and again.

On the frequent occasions when she would be banished from the Religious Education classroom for 'disruptive behaviour,' she would stick her head back in round the door before heading off to her allotted punishment, and leave the class and the teacher with her parting shot.

"I want to be a Jew!" she would yell, and then slam the door behind her.

2

I WOULD LIKE THE PINK ONE!

The abuse continued, and Debbie felt trapped in it.

She couldn't tell her mother about it for her boyfriend was the person responsible, and she didn't want to hurt her. Or she could even suffer at the abuser's hands for 'squealing.'

She couldn't tell her loving, caring grandparents for they would be both shocked and terribly upset by it.

She couldn't tell any of her school friends for they all seemed so blissfully innocent, so clean, and so free. Why burden them with her troubles? The very thought of what was happening to her seemed to drive an invisible wedge between her and them. She felt so dirty, but would it do any good to pollute their pure minds? All Debbie wanted to do was sit in the bath for as long as she could, scrubbing at herself in an effort to cleanse what she felt was her defiled body.

She had once plucked up the courage to tell her teachers about it and they hadn't believed her, choosing rather to blame her for it. So they were definitely a lost cause.

Nothing worked. And she was so miserable. The feeling of guilt and the sense of having been somehow publicly tainted, tormented her day and night. Debbie became so obsessed with this perception of personal impurity that she began to believe that people were stopping to stare at her in the street. They weren't, but she imagined that they were.

Her abuser came up with one solution to help negate her nagging conscience.

It was, of necessity, initially only temporary, but if indulged in frequently, temporary could become semi-permanent. In the short term, however, anything was better than nothing.

His answer was to ply the twelve-year-old with alcohol. It began one day when she had protested that she didn't 'want to do this any more.' He offered her a glass of wine, assuring her that if she drank it she would 'feel more relaxed.'

Debbie drank it, and then another one, and another, until her brain became sufficiently fuddled not to care what was happening to her. At last she had found a vehicle through which she could block out all the mounting horrors in her life. The man recognised that he had hit upon a way to counter her resistance and so he always came to the house equipped with a bottle of something.

It wasn't long, though, until Debbie was drinking every day. It was such a comfort, for when she drank she didn't feel ashamed. Her senses were stupefied and her conscience anaesthetised. It felt great. Alcohol allowed her to block out the constant self-reproach.

By her early teens, Debbie had become very much 'a loner.' She felt that she didn't fit in anywhere, or with anybody, except with her nana, her granddad and her mum. This sense of isolation stemmed from her conviction that the church had let her down, God hadn't helped her in any shape or form and school was boring but bearable. That was, of course, except for the RE classes, where she considered it her duty to actively oppose 'self-righteous prudes polluting people's minds with pious platitudes.'

On the way home from school Debbie often bought herself two cans of cider, and had them drunk before reaching the house. That helped her prepare for a less conscience- stricken evening, as she tried half-heartedly to struggle through a few homeworks, and face what might happen to her before bedtime.

Late one afternoon, Debbie's uncle Vic spotted her meandering aimlessly home, with a can of cider in one hand and a lit cigarette in the other. Debbie saw him too, but ignored him, hoping that he hadn't noticed her, but she was soon to discover that he had. Within days her mum said to her, "Debbie, your uncle Vic was here this morning and told me that he saw you smoking a cigarette and drinking a can of cider on the street the other day."

"On no, mum! It couldn't have been me!" the straight-faced, playing-innocent daughter exclaimed in mock disgust. "It must have been somebody else! All the girls at our school look nearly the same in their uniforms, you know."

Mum wasn't totally convinced, but left it there, only to have her suspicions aroused again, six months later. That was when she was summoned up to the school to be informed that Debbie had been found with a one-litre bottle of Bacardi white rum in her possession.

That was easily explained away, too, when mother confronted daughter on the issue. She just happened to be caught with the bottle of rum before she had been able to pass it on to one of the other girls in her class. This girl had asked Debbie, who looked older than she actually was, to go to the off-licence and buy the bottle of Bacardi as a present for her grandfather's birthday. Or so the story went!

Debbie had by then begun to derive a peculiar sense of satisfaction, living within the web of indignity and duplicity that so often threatened to close in around her, strangling her completely. She had at last managed to achieve something, even if was only deceiving her mum and grandparents, the people who loved her most.

One of Debbie's favourite places to spend a Saturday morning was round at her grandma Forrest's little terrace house, which was just a short walk from where she lived. The growing girl's uncle Keith lived two doors down from this other grandma, and she made a point of paying him a visit at every possible opportunity.

There was a specific reason for this.

Uncle Keith made his own wine, beer and cider. There was always something fermenting or brewing about his place. An added bonus for Debbie was that the end product of his endeavours was always clearly to be seen and available to be sampled. Her uncle kept a big flagon of cider beside his chair and when no-one was looking Debbie lifted it to her head and had a long slow swig of it. The longer the swig the longer she would be able to keep her chastening conscience at bay.

All the paraphernalia for Uncle Keith's particular pastime was kept in the cubby-hole below the stairs and Debbie was constantly mesmerised by it. The complicated set-up reminded her of the picture on the cover of a book called 'Charlie and The Chocolate Factory,' which she had read when she was much younger. It showed an endless stream of scurrying bubbles chasing each other through a maze of tiny tubes and then drip, drip, dripping into queer shaped vessels of various sizes.

Debbie's uncle was pleased that she showed such an interest in his hobby and one Saturday morning he asked her, "Would you like to try your hand at making some wine, Debbie?"

"I would like to, but I'm not sure that I could," his niece replied. She certainly didn't feel up to creating a crazy complex of bottles and bubbles like his.

"Don't worry about that," uncle Keith volunteered cheerily. " It's easy. Let's go down to the chemist's shop and you can choose a kit. It will have everything you need in it, and I will help you set it up."

Having made their way down to the little shop at the end of the road, Uncle Keith directed Debbie to a section clearly labelled 'Home-Brewing Kits.' The shelves were divided into 'Beer' and 'Wines.'

Uncle Keith was in his element. Having explained the different processes involved in using some of the packs, he pointed to a shelf where wine-making kits in a variety of colours sat waiting to attract some curious customer's attention.

"Any of those would be simple enough to start with, Debbie," he announced with the air of an expert. "Choose whichever one you like."

It didn't take Debbie long to make up her mind. One particular kit had caught her eye while her uncle was in the middle of his introductory pep-talk.

"I would like the pink one," she said.

"That's a good choice, Debbie," her uncle declared, with a reassuring smile. "That will make a lovely sweet wine."

They weren't long back to the house until they began setting up the winemaking process. For the next few weeks Debbie made frequent visits to her latest project to check on its progress at the various stages. The family encouraged her in this latest enterprise for they were pleased to see Debbie actually interested in something. It made a change from sitting in her room on her own for hours on end.

With all the stages complete, Debbie was rewarded, under Uncle Keith's supervision, with twelve bottles of sparkling red wine. She was proud of her achievement, as indeed were the family, referring to this end product as 'Debbie's wine.'

Since everyone recognised it as hers, and since it was approaching Christmas, Debbie decided that she would make sole use of the wine. Her idea of celebrating the festive season, and obliterating everything else, was to drink every last drop of all twelve bottles, over a four-day period, herself.

This 'celebration' was to have an appalling outcome.

After her mad drinking binge Debbie felt so rotten that she didn't drink any more for days. This, in turn, led to her becoming violently ill, and her sickness culminated in a horrifying experience.

That was when Debbie, who was still in early teenage, was subjected to her first attack of delirium tremens, a psychotic condition induced by withdrawal from alcohol.

She lay in her bedroom in the dark, petrified. Her nightwear and bedclothes were soaked in sweat and her body shook uncontrollably.

These physical symptoms, although very distressing in themselves, were mild compared to the hallucinations that followed. These were utterly terrifying.

Debbie saw herself transported out of her bedroom into a cold, dank, castle dungeon where she lay motionless on a stone table. She was surrounded by a succession of monks wearing black hoods where they should have had heads, and who walked around her paralysed body in a solemn procession, chanting. They had no facial features whatsoever. No eyes, no nose, no mouth, nothing but those bizarre black hoods, out of which came this endless ominous chant.

Slowly the scene changed. Debbie was still laid out on the cold slab but now a rabid Alsatian dog, with froth dripping from its mouth kept jumping up at her. It was jumping, jumping, jumping and trying to bite her, but she was powerless to move out of its way no matter how hard she tried. It was coming to get her. Any minute now those frightening rabies-infected jaws would close on her leg, and if that happened she would soon be ...

It was horrendous.

Debbie's loving 'nana' realised that her young granddaughter was having what she understood to be 'awful nightmares' and stayed by her bedside throughout the night. When Debbie, who was wide-awake, and often wide-eyed in sheer fright, was compelled to cry out in terror, 'nana' would squeeze her sweaty hand just a little bit tighter and whisper over and over again, "Don't worry Debbie. It will be all right. Everything will be all right. Everything will be all right..."

They were comforting, reassuring words at the time.

The only problem was that they were to prove untrue.

When Debbie was well enough to go back to school, and return to what for her was 'normal life,' she discovered that everything hadn't changed to being 'all right.'

Everything continued to be all wrong.

3

IT'S BILLY-WHIZZ!

Debbie had caught the last bus home. She had been out in Wolverhampton town centre with a few other girls and since they all lived on different bus routes, she was returning alone. Her mum and she had just recently moved out from 'nana and grandpa,' and she was travelling back to the flat they now shared, some distance from their former home.

It was well after eleven o'clock and there were very few passengers on the bus, so Debbie had her favourite seat, the long one right across the back, all to herself. This was only to be until the bus reached the next stop, though. She had just settled down and was about to light a cigarette when she heard a cheery voice call, "Hello there, Debbie!"

Looking up she saw John, a friend from school who had just hopped on, making his way down the almost empty bus towards her. Our Lady of Mercy Grammar School had amalgamated with a top boy's Grammar School about a year before, and although John was a year ahead of Debbie in the new school set-up she knew him for they lived near each other.

The two teenagers sat chatting and smoking as they travelled home together. Debbie always enjoyed talking to John. He had a bubbly personality and was one of those people who could chat animatedly about almost anything.

When they reached their stop John and Debbie alighted and started walking towards their homes. As the bus pulled away they were left in a deserted street and when John had checked around that no one was about, he stopped at the end of a dark alleyway. Taking a step or two up the alley to be out of the glare of the streetlights, he said, "Hi Debbie, would you like some of this?"

As Debbie stepped over beside him she saw that he had pulled a small plastic bag, containing what looked like a white powder, out of his pocket.

"Some of what?" Debbie wanted to know.

"Some of this," John went on, opening the bag he was holding in his left hand with the deft fingers of his right.

"Well... I mean... what is it?" Debbie sounded rather hesitant. She wasn't sure what the stuff was, and had no idea how to take it, or buy it, or do whatever it was that John expected her to do with it.

John tried to be reassuring. He had a warm smile that seemed to split his face from ear to ear, and he used to its best advantage that evening.

"It's nothing to be scared of," he told her, with one of those charming, innocent smiles. "It's billy-whizz."

"And what's billy-whizz?" Debbie enquired.

She was still on the defensive and couldn't resist blurting out the question she had been struggling with ever since John had slid the plastic bag from his pocket.

"Is it drugs?" she asked, looking him straight in the face. She was trying to ignore the encouraging, but perhaps somewhat exaggerated, smile, and see if she could trace the truth in his sparkling eyes. It was impossible, so she would have to rely on what he told her.

"No. It's billy-whizz. It's stuff like sherbet. You just lick your finger, stick it in the bag, and lick your finger again, the same way you do with sherbet."

John then proceeded to give a demonstration. Licking his finger with a lot more pomp and ceremony than such a commonplace act would normally require, he jammed it into the bag, and having checked that a quantity of its powdery content had stuck to his finger he licked it slowly and with simulated pleasure.

"Go on, Debbie. Have a go! I guarantee that it will make you feel good!" he promised. John was laughing now, and if a lick of billy-whizz made somebody feel as happy as he appeared to be, it might be worth trying.

Although her mum's boyfriend had disappeared off the scene when they moved to the flat, and the trauma of the persistent sexual abuse had stopped for Debbie, her sub-conscious being had been indelibly scarred. Alcohol helped block out the pain, but if she could actually find something to reverse the process and make her feel happy again, that would be an unbelievable bonus.

Debbie trusted John. He was an intelligent lad from a very good family. Surely, she reasoned, he wouldn't be involved in anything that was wrong. And if what he was telling her was true, and it would make her feel good about herself, why should she not have a try, just one little dip, of this billy-whizz stuff...?

She put a finger in her mouth and held it there a moment in solemn contemplation. Then she pushed it down timorously into the bag John was holding up to her. Withdrawing her finger she found that it was covered with the powder which her friend claimed would work wonders for her. Debbie completed the cycle, as instructed by her grinning tutor, by returning her finger to her mouth and licking it comprehensively.

"Ugh!" was her instant reaction. "That doesn't taste a bit like sherbet!" The powder was bitter and clung stubbornly to the inside of her mouth despite all her efforts to swallow it.

"Don't worry," John tried to console her. "It might taste rotten for a minute or two, but it will be worth it. You will feel great later on."

They had been talking as they walked along, and had by that time reached the spot where they had to go their separate ways.

"I hope you are right, John," Debbie declared, rather uneasily, as they parted. "Goodnight."

It came as something of a surprise to Debbie to discover that John had, in fact, been right. The teenager was less than an hour into the flat when she livened up considerably. She was possessed with an unmistakeable zest for getting things done and even though it was after midnight she set about tidying her bedroom, something her mum had been asking her to do for weeks, but she could never 'be bothered.' With the bedroom all spick and span she then sat down to write two letters. This was another task she had been 'putting off' for a long time.

If billy-whizz was drugs, and John had been rather hedgy about that when she had asked him about it, then drugs couldn't be all that bad after all. She wondered what everybody was making such a fuss about. Debbie would certainly be prepared to give anything that made her as happy and enthusiastic about everything as she did that night, another go. How could anybody say that something, which could give her that positive sense of well-being, was wrong, or even worse, harmful?

Soon after this John invited Debbie to join him and a number of his friends going out to the 'Northern Soul' nights. These music and dance sessions were held in some of the northern cities of England. Some of John's group of friends had driving licences and old cars, which they had no trouble in packing full with young people from Wolverhampton for a trip to Leeds or Wigan, Blackburn or Manchester on a Saturday evening. When they arrived at the dance venue, wherever it happened to be, they would have some 'magic powder' and dance through until Sunday morning. Debbie loved this. Although only fifteen years of age she fancied herself as one of the world's greatest dancers and would stay on the floor for as long as the music lasted.

It was a superficial, false environment. Everyone was on a drug-induced high, but Debbie enjoyed the experience immensely for two reasons. She was able to forget all her past miseries while swirling and twirling and whirling the night away on the dance floor. A second bonus was that she felt at home and accepted in this scenario. Although most of 'the weekend crowd' were older than Debbie, she was good company and an accomplished dancer and John and his friends had welcomed her as one of them right from her very first outing.

Debbie soon began to look forward to every weekend, but the intervening weeks were still a problem. She reckoned that her only hope of enduring the humdrum routine of successive unhappy schooldays lay in boosting herself with an excessive intake of alcohol. There were times when she arrived home from school in the afternoons and drank her way through what homeworks she considered it worth the effort to even attempt, ending up totally befuddled by bedtime.

Soon after Debbie became an accepted member of 'the gang' going to the 'Northern Soul' music and dance nights, she became friendly with Jim (not his real name). This handsome, well-dressed young man took an immediate interest in Debbie from the first night they met. The charming, vivacious teenager appealed to him, and although he was quite a few years older than her, Debbie was attracted to him as well. Jim and she were both quick-witted and intelligent and it seemed that there was an immediate, invisible bond forged between them.

In a matter of months Jim and Debbie were seeing each other twice or three times every week. This new friendship helped Debbie to feel really 'grown-up.' She now had a good-looking boy-friend who had his own car and she was made to feel 'special' for she usually got to sit in the front beside him on their weekend adventures.

One evening Jim had taken Debbie, and a close friend of hers, a girl called Shani, plus a few others to a party in the Royal

Hospital in Wolverhampton. As the evening 'warmed up' Debbie saw Shani sitting with a group of lads in the corner, smoking.

"Come on over and smoke a joint with us, Debbie," her friend called.

"Do you mean cannabis?" the cautious Debbie enquired.

"Yes. That's what I mean," Shani replied. "Don't tell us that you are one of these stuck up prudes that is afraid to try cannabis. You will probably be telling me it's bad for me or something."

"You should know me better than that, Shani. I'm no goody-goody," Debbie countered defiantly. Was she not 'a big girl' now, an integral part of this 'really cool' crowd, and game for anything?

Within minutes she was sitting with the group and discovered to her slight surprise that one of the prime movers in the joint-smoking cell was her boy-friend, Jim. He showed her how to roll a 'spliff' and she began to smoke it.

The effect was wonderful. Soon Debbie began floating away in her mind. The boring cares of this life had been left far behind as she found herself drifting around in a distant happy-go-lucky land where nothing really seemed to matter all that much any more. Everything was a huge joke, and she began to laugh heartily when someone made even the most inconsequential remark. Debbie found this compulsion to giggle most gratifying. She was making up for lost laughs. Growing up had been neither a bed of roses nor a bag of laughs for her.

It wasn't long until Debbie began to crave her regular 'joint' and Jim seemed always both willing and able to help her satisfy her growing addiction. 'Going-out together' during the week often meant sitting in the car in some isolated spot, drinking and smoking cannabis.

On other occasions, when one of 'the crowd' knew that his or her house was going to be free, John, Jim, Debbie, Shani and others from time to time, would congregate in that home. There they would while away the evening watching a Richard Prior video, drinking and smoking cannabis together.

One evening Debbie's mum had been out and Debbie had invited her friends round for a party. The revellers had dispersed about half-an-hour before mum was due to arrive back and Debbie set about tidying up the living-room.

Unfortunately she missed a block of cannabis resin that someone had left on the mantelpiece during the evening session.

As soon as Debbie's mum entered the room she walked straight across to it, as though attracted by a magnet.

"What's this?" she asked her daughter who appeared totally absorbed in the magazine she was reading.

"I don't know," Debbie lied with an air of innocence.

"It's drugs, isn't it?" mother persisted.

"I told you I don't know what it is," Debbie insisted, trying to look surprised that such a strange substance should somehow turn up on their mantelpiece. "What do drugs look like anyway, I would like to know?"

With that Debbie rose from the couch where she had been sitting and stretched out her hand and said, "Here, give it to me until I have a look at it!"

She then took the small brown block of stuff from her mother, and turned it over and over while moving it across lightly from one hand to the other, pretending to give it a thorough examination.

"It looks like a lump of dog-pooh to me!" she concluded at length. Then without waiting for any response from her suspicious mother, she held it up to her nose.

"And I tell you what, it even smells like pooh too!" she exclaimed. "We can't possibly keep that thing in the house any longer!"

That was Debbie's cue to stride out the back door and dump the offending block of such a foul-smelling substance in the outside bin. She then returned into the kitchen and made a great show of washing her hands thoroughly, as though very anxious to ensure that she hadn't been in any way tainted by handling that awful stuff.

Little did Debbie's mother know, but the bin was not to be the chunk of cannabis resin's final resting place. That small block was worth about fifty pounds, and the next time she was out of the house Debbie descended on the outside bin, and retrieved it!

She and her mates had another party, and smoked the evil-smelling lump of 'dog-pooh,' until it was finished, two nights later in John's house!

4

RISING STAR

After leaving school at sixteen Debbie had two successive jobs, neither of which afforded her active mind the sense of job satisfaction she had expected. She was constantly looking for employment in which she could feel fulfilled.

One of her earliest ambitions had been to become a nurse, and she took the first step in achieving that aim when she was accepted for training in Wolverhampton Royal Hospital in May 1983. She enjoyed the training programme, in both its study and practical aspects, right from her very first day and made many friends during her three years of training. The work was interesting, although also often tiring, but Debbie sought to compensate for the rigours of the course by continuing to smoke, drink and dance with an increasing number of her acquaintances, as study schedules and duty rosters allowed.

Debbie qualified in 1986 and she had been so impressive during training that she was immediately appointed to a nursing position in the hospital's coronary care ward. She loved her work with the patients on the ward, and relished her free-time, which she used to the full to enjoy a hectic social life with her circle of friends, both new and old.

There were very few things for which Debbie would even consider resigning from her career on the coronary care ward, but one of these exceptions occurred in 1988. Debbie found that she was expecting a baby and so decided to give up her work, rather than applying for maternity leave.

Little Emily, Debbie's lovely baby daughter, was born on March 5, 1988. Her birth gave her proud mum, her loving grandmother and her delighted great-grandparents, untold joy. They were to watch each stage of her development through infancy with endless pleasure.

When Debbie phoned her dad, with whom she had occasional contact, to tell him that he had become a grandfather, he was completely taken aback. It just happened that he had also been born on March 5, though many years before, and so when he realised that it was his daughter on the other end of the line he immediately enquired, "Hello, Debbie. Have you phoned up to wish me a happy birthday?"

"No," Debbie replied. "I have phoned up to tell you that I have had a baby. You are a grandfather now!"

"What!" her father yelled back. Debbie was left to wonder whether this one-word response to her exciting news had been a spontaneous expression of irritated surprise rather than an outburst of irrepressible excitement. At least he had been told, and as the realisation of the relationship dawned upon him, he would doubtless continue to show an interest in his growing granddaughter.

When Emily was just three months old, Debbie learnt that a vacancy had arisen for a nurse to do night duty on the coronary and intensive care wards in the Royal Hospital. With her mum having volunteered to look after baby Emily, whom everybody adored, Debbie submitted an application, attended for an interview and was appointed.

It was exacting, but nonetheless rewarding work for the young mother. The energetic Debbie appreciated the challenge of it and continued to do her 'nights.' Her ability and dedication were recognised when she was promoted to senior staff nurse status.

She had been in this position for a year when she saw a job, which would afford her a more regular work pattern, advertised. It was as a Practice Nurse to a group of five GP's and the prospect of daytime hours, Monday to Friday, appealed to Debbie. This would save her mum having to be responsible for the care of Emily throughout the night.

Debbie was interviewed for this position and offered the job. When she took up her new post she discovered that there was much work to be done, not only with the patients but also in the updating of the equipment. During her first week in charge she told someone that the Treatment Room was like an exhibit from the British Museum. Immediately Debbie began to prioritise, and within six months she had seen most of the more antiquated equipment replaced and all the patient medical records computerised. This meant that all in the group practice had easy access to basic information about the patients they were treating, thus facilitating both the speed and effectiveness of the care being offered.

The more efficient organisation of the available resources meant that additional money began coming into the practice, and Debbie turned her attention to exploring ways in which this could best be used. It was ironic that one of the goals on which she decided to focus was the reduction in the level of smoking amongst the practice patients.

Debbie, who was still smoking regularly, but never in or near her workplace, had pledged herself to advising others to give it up!

When she had set up a programme to target all the smokers in the practice Debbie's work in establishing the project was commended by the Smoking Cessation Board of the Health Education Authority. This public recognition of her campaign led, in turn, to Debbie being invited to become a member of the committee responsible for writing a book entitled, 'The Smoking Epidemic.' It was hoped that this publication would be produced, with statistical updates every five years. Its aim would be threefold. Initially it would highlight the advantages of a non-smoking lifestyle, secondly it would outline, in some detail, the dangers of smoking, with the final emphasis being on the urge to abandon the habit, and suggesting means by which this could be achieved. It was planned than this concluding section should contain information on an extensive network of practical help available to those willing to attempt giving up smoking for good.

The committee meetings for the compilation of the book took place in London and Debbie enjoyed her all-expenses-paid trips down from Wolverhampton to attend these. When the book was finally published all the co-authors were invited to the nation's capital for an official launch.

On the night before that prestigious occasion Debbie had been invited to stay over at the flat of one of the senior members of the editorial committee. During their conversation that evening Debbie and her host had been reflecting on the phases in the production of the joint publication, and speculating on its possible impact on the great smoking public. Then, with all the formal business out of the way, Debbie's well-heeled host asked her if she would like to 'share a joint' with him!

Thus, on the eve of the launch of a book, to which they had both contributed in all seriousness, on the horrors of smoking, two of the co-writers sat in a comfortable London flat smoking cannabis and discussing amiably everything under the sun except their habit!

As the smoke curled up and Debbie's mind relaxed into its drug-engendered hollow happiness, she began to laugh. Is this not utterly ridiculous? she thought. What total and absolute hypocrisy.

"And we will both look ever so concerned and sound ever so convincing tomorrow!" she quipped to her host, who was in the process of preparing a second 'spliff.' With that they had a good laugh together, completely unconcerned.

Another of Debbie's ongoing projects as Practice Nurse was geared towards the treatment of asthma. She decided that she needed to demonstrate that the money earmarked for the treatment of this often-distressing condition was being properly used.

Her first step in this process was to devise a system for determining the degree of acuteness of the asthma in individual patients. To do this she created a list of four possible symptoms, namely, nighttime cough, shortness of breath or wheezing, symptoms after exercise and chest infections. 150 patients on her treatment list was give one of these appraisal forms on which he or she was asked to record the frequency and intensity of the given symptoms as they occurred over a twelve-month period.

The information thus obtained provided Debbie with a valuable database from which to make assessments and administer inhalers especially suited to the individual needs of the patient. This survey had a number of other beneficial spin-offs, one of which was that it justified its overall aim in proving that the money designated for asthma treatment was being used to maximum advantage. A second was that it showed one particular inhaler, though more expensive than its rival products, to be also appreciably more effective in the treatment of the condition.

The pharmaceutical company that manufactured the recommended inhaler was, understandably, pleased with the findings of Debbie's research initiative. When their quarterly figures revealed that her practice was the top prescriber of their product in the West Midlands, senior representatives from the company began calling to see her. Having studied the outcome of the investigation she had undertaken they started sending Debbie to courses and seminars on the treatment of asthma, as their representative.

In a follow-on from this Debbie was asked to visit other GP practices across central England to report on the reason for, and structuring of, the asthma survey she had conducted. An important part of these talks was the climax in which she drew attention to the positive results that one specific inhaler seemed to produce in a majority of the cases under review!

Early in 1994 Debbie left her position as Practice Nurse to take up an appointment with a leading pharmaceutical company as their Respiratory Care Advisor. Her main role in this position was to visit GP practices and hospitals and contact those responsible for the treatment of asthma, never failing to highlight the effective nature of the company's special inhaler.

Debbie was on the up and up, and fast. The speed of her transformation from coronary care nurse to suave business woman had taken everyone, and not least herself, by surprise.. The company had now provided her with a green Vauxhall Cavalier sports car with a sunroof and car phone. She and Emily were soon able to move out into a beautiful house on their own. It was all wonderful

Another aspect of her work, and one that she particularly enjoyed was the organising of seminars in Hoarcross Hall and some of the other top hotels in the Midlands. Doctors and senior practice nurses would be invited to these sessions, plied with an abundance of high quality food and wine, and made to feel very special.

They were special, too, as far as Debbie's company was concerned, for they were in a position to prescribe drugs and inhalers for the treatment of asthma. At some stage in the two- or three-day programme Debbie would teach her carefully-pampered guests how to conduct an asthma audit, and give them statistical evidence why they should carefully consider her company's product.

These occasions were invariably productive, and Debbie continued to expand her base into other regions beyond her local area. She was now really enjoying life to the full. She had money, a posh car, and a lovely home. There was no problem satisfying her addictions either. Debbie could drink as much she would ever want, usually at the company's expense, and one of her chief delights was to return to her luxury home in the evenings and settle down to smoke a long, slow 'spliff,' before going to bed.

Her success as a saleswoman had catapulted her up the social and financial ladder, three or four rungs at a time.

Debbie loved her work. It had become her billy-whizz.

The black shadows of her tortured teenage had paled into insignificance in the light of the progressive lifestyle she was generating all around her. She had become a rising star.

And the only question that remained was, where was she going to end?

Had she the potential to graduate from being a star in one galaxy to becoming a sun, the controlling force, in a little universe of her own?

That remained to be seen.

5

LIT UP LIKE SELLAFIELD

The conscientious Respiratory Care Advisor met many different people and made numerous telephone calls in the course of any single week in the pursuit of her blossoming new career. When the pressure of the week was over, however, there was one call Debbie was careful to make every Friday night, without fail.

This was not to a prospective customer but to an old drug dealing acquaintance. Or if he wasn't available, his girlfriend would take Debbie's 'order.' She needed to buy some cannabis to see her over the weekend and for her 'nightcap' before bedtime for the coming week.

Debbie was the kind of buyer the dealer liked to have 'on his books.' As an up and coming businesswoman she was under constant pressure and had come to rely on her regular 'joint' to keep her on a 'performance high.' Having a buyer in this position had an added bonus for the dealer. His 'client' had loads of money to spend and always paid 'up front.'

Some Friday evenings Debbie would say, "I'll take an ounce tonight." Other times she would only want half-an-ounce and on rare occasions she would say, "I'm O.K. this week. I'll be in touch again next Friday."

Having developed an acute business mind, with her continued involvement in the competitive world of marketing, Debbie gradually began to question if there wasn't a cheaper way of fuelling her dependency on cannabis. What if she could grow a few plants herself? Would that not be a less expensive means of getting her hands on some top quality 'gear?' And perhaps she could even start selling it as well. If the user could become a grower, then the grower might even become a small-time dealer. And Debbie knew what kind of money some of those guys were making.

It was a project worth considering.

Debbie made a few discreet enquiries in Wolverhampton's shady underworld and was eventually put in touch with a man who 'kept a few plants.' When Debbie called him she discovered that she already knew him, and he invited her to 'come round and have a look at my set-up.'

She was eager to take him up on his invitation and when she did, found it fascinating. This grower had converted a spare room into a cannabis garden. He had two huge lights and twelve plants. The heat in the room was overpowering and the plants appeared perfectly healthy.

He recommended a book to Debbie and gave her a contact number in Amsterdam from which it could be procured. Since cannabis is not classified as an illegal drug in Holland, Debbie was able to send for the book called 'Hydroponics,' and have it sent to her without any trouble.

When she had studied its contents carefully Debbie made contact with another grower in Doncaster and ordered one hundred plants of a top-cropping strain known as 'Super Skunk.' No dozen plants for her, either! If Debbie was going to do it, then she was going to do it right!

Her next trip was to a hydroponics shop in Leicester, where she was able to purchase six lights and a quantity of rock wall, the medium in which to plant them. All that remained now was for Debbie to make the run to Doncaster, collect her order and set up her cannabis production line in a carefully blacked-out upstairs room of the house in which her mum was by then living. Emily stayed with her grandma when her mum was at work so Debbie was able to feed and water her plants when leaving her little daughter off, and collecting her again later in the day from, 'gran's.'

The cannabis room had to be kept at a constant high temperature to make the plants grow quickly and come into bud early. Being the only room in the house that was always kept locked and designated as 'strictly out of bounds' to little Emily during the day it presented a challenge to her childish curiosity. She would take every possible chance she could to sneak into the steamy, stuffy atmosphere if her mum should happen to leave the door unlocked.

On one such day of carelessness Debbie was joined by her daughter who enquired, "Mummy, what are you doing in here?"

"I am growing some tomatoes, pet," came mum's lie in reply. How could she tell her seven-year old daughter the truth?!

It is not the leaves of the cannabis plants that are smoked, but the buds, and after almost four months of constant care, 40 of the plants were ready for cropping. This was Debbie's first 'harvest' and her 'Super Skunk' buds made very agreeable 'joints.' Or at least so the producer-cum-user tried to convince herself.

The venture had been a success. When she had cropped all her plants it would be time to scrap them and order more. Debbie's active mind was constantly at work, examining the possibilities for expansion. Perhaps next time around she could… or she should… or she even most definitely would…

All her plans to develop her spare bedroom 'hothouse' hobby into a lucrative market enterprise skidded to a sudden halt, however, in September 1994.

Debbie was driving along in her flashy car, between appointments, when the car telephone rang. She picked up the handset and the man at the other end of the line enquired if he was speaking to Debbie Forrest. When she had confirmed her identity, the mysterious caller continued, in a very solemn tone, "This is a detective-sergeant from Wednesfield Road Police Station in Wolverhampton. We have your mother here in custody. Your daughter is also in custody. We have seized your cannabis plants. Could you please come along to this Police Station immediately? We plan to hold your mother and..."

Many of Debbie's friends and acquaintances, including a number of her cannabis-cultivating contacts, had the number of her car phone, and she assumed it was one of them playing a practical joke on her.

"Aye, very funny!" she interrupted the caller in mid-sentence.

"Try pulling the other leg! It has bells on it!" she went on to chuckle, light-heartedly. And with that she switched off the handset and returned it to its cradle.

Moments later it rang again.

When Debbie answered it the second time, and recognised the same voice, she was about to retort, "Oh no! Not you again!" when something stopped her. It was the even more sombre tone, and unmistakeably resolute attitude of the caller.

"I repeat, this is a detective-sergeant from Wednesfield Road Police Station in Wolverhampton," the mystery man had begun once more. "And I would like to assure you, that this is not a joke. I am deadly serious. We have your mother in custody. Your daughter is also in custody. They will be held here until you come. We have also seized all your cannabis plants. They are here, too, waiting for you. Please drive round here as soon as possible."

"Right," Debbie stammered, the possible ramifications of the situation already flooding in on her. "O.K."

When she replaced the handset, and attempted to return her left hand to the steering wheel, she discovered that her arm had begun to shake. The strength had drained out of her legs, and the colour had drained from her face. Five minutes earlier she had been a confident young businesswoman, on the way to her next appointment. Now she was a pale, powerless blob of flesh and bone on the way to a police station. And she felt that she was going to be sick.

It was bad enough the police apprehending her. But what business had they holding Emily and her mum? She had let them all down. And what if her employers found out? Where would that leave her? The more she thought about it, the sicker she became.

She pulled up outside Wednesfield Road Police Station in her green Cavalier sports. As Debbie locked it before going in she took one long hard look at it. What was going to happen to her, or it, or her mum and Emily, in the next few hours, or days, or weeks? She would soon be in a position to find out. And she wasn't looking forward to it, either...

As soon as she entered the reception area of the Police Station, the duty constable called her in through a door into the back offices. When she was being led down a corridor to an interview room, Debbie's heart missed a beat or two and her stomach started to turn over yet again.

From the moment she had entered the station she had been playing the bewildered young innocent woman role, appearing confused at all the fuss. This stance was going to prove difficult to maintain, however, for there, lined up in rows, and in individual plastic bags, each one of which had been duly sealed with evidence tape, were what appeared to be all of her remaining uncropped cannabis plants.

She was followed into an interview room by a WPC who ordered her to undress completely. As a suspect on a drugs charge Debbie had to submit to a total body search. She had no option but to comply with this command, although she found it a most humiliating and degrading experience. When she was allowed to put on her clothes again she was directed to a holding cell where she found the detective-sergeant who had made the telephone call summoning her to the station, waiting to interview her.

Having gone through the preliminaries of identification, and then outlining the possible offences with which she could be charged, the officer remarked, trying to sound ever so matter-of-fact, "You know you will have lost your job."

Debbie felt overcome by a rising anger, which, although directed at the detective, actually had its origins in a mounting awareness of her own crass stupidity.

"How could you possibly know that?" she countered, curtly.

"Well, you see, we had to make contact with the company you work for to find out the number of your car phone," was the officer's perfectly reasonable to him, but instantly repugnant to Debbie, explanation. "They were obviously interested to find out why the police were so anxious to speak to one of their most-respected representatives and so we felt that they ought to be informed that we were planning to apprehend you on a drugs charge."

When he had finished obtaining all the information he needed from Debbie, the detective asked her if there was anything she wanted to say.

"No, not really," she replied. Logical reasoning was beyond her at that moment. Then her maternal instinct took over. "All that I want to know is, what is going to happen to my mother and little daughter Emily? Are you planning to keep them in here?" she enquired anxiously.

"Oh no," the sergeant told her. "Don't worry about them. Now that we have you here, they will be taken home safely."

As he was leaving the cell, where Debbie was to be 'held in custody until bail could be arranged,' the officer turned to her and said, "I have just one more question for you. Why would a nurse, with a promising career ahead of her, want to be growing drugs?"

"How would I know?" Debbie replied, shrugging her shoulders in despair. It was a telling question, and one that she had suddenly begun to ask herself over and over again, in light of all that had happened in the past few hours. The truth was that she had always assumed that the police would never discover what she was up to. She was too clever for them. Or so she thought. She would always remain 'one step ahead of the game.'

Now they had caught up with her, and she was facing the possibility of spending a night in their holding cell. Perhaps they weren't that stupid after all.

The arresting sergeant was about to turn away for the final time when Debbie delayed his departure, if only for another moment or two. She had suddenly remembered that she too had another question to ask. Not that the answer could have any bearing on her situation now, but she would be intrigued to know the answer to it.

"Before you go," she said, "there's just one more thing I am curious to know. How did you ever track me down? Did somebody grass on me?"

"No," came the investigating officer's reply, which was to be delivered with a satisfied smirk. "Nobody grassed. But your house was lit up like Sellafield. Nobody could miss it. And certainly not if you happened to be passing in a surveillance helicopter!"

This declaration was followed by a short, self-satisfied laugh, and then the key turned in the cell door.

Debbie was left alone with her thoughts.

And she had a lot to think about.

6

SORT YOURSELF OUT

Later that evening Debbie was formally charged with her offences. When they were read out to her she immediately thought, 'I could go to prison for this.' It was not a pleasant prospect. She felt awful.

The lustre had disappeared from her glossy lifestyle, all in the course of one afternoon and evening. Everything had suddenly turned tacky, tawdry, tarnished.

Debbie was to be arraigned on two charges, both of them serious. She would stand trial accused of 'the production of a controlled class B drug, namely cannabis,' and also 'the possession of a controlled drug with intent to supply.' Soon after these indictments had been made against her, the former up-and-coming businesswoman with the once-upon-a-time promising career ahead of her was released on bail. She would be summoned to attend the local Magistrate's Court in due course, she was told.

What, though, was there left for her to do in the meantime?

One of the first phone calls she took next morning was from the pharmaceutical company with whom she had been employed. Their message was simple, and hardly surprising. The detective back in Wednesfield Road Police Station had forewarned her that it was on its way. Thus it didn't come as a shock to her to be informed that she was being 'suspended until further notice.'

In the wake of her summary suspension Debbie spent the remainder of that frustrating, nauseating day engaging in alternating flurries of aggressive self-examination, futile anger and pointless self-pity. She owed those whom she loved an apology, she felt, for the disgrace she had brought on them all.

With Emily out at school Debbie had time to spend moving from room to room of the comfortable home she had rented for the two of them in a quiet suburb of the city. It was a case of, 'look your last on all things lovely every hour.' There could be no doubt but that their days in it were numbered. How could she possibly afford to continue paying the rent, having been deprived, in the course of one critical twenty-four hour period, of her entire source of income, legal or otherwise.

Later that afternoon she was sitting watching TV for something to do, when the local news bulletin came on. The leading headline of the day was, 'Police in Wolverhampton have made a significant drugs haul. Cannabis plants, valued at £64,000 have been seized in a house in the city. We are joined on the line by Detective Sergeant...'

Debbie switched off the set at that point. She couldn't bear to hear any more. Imagine! Being headline news, but for all the wrong reasons. At least they hadn't disclosed her identity. If she could just lie low, perhaps nobody would ever know...

And £64,000! That maddened her! They had obviously counted her precious plants and valued them at about £1000 each. She had never expected to make that amount out of them. Somebody, somewhere, had got his or her sums wrong. If only she hadn't been caught. But she had, and that was all that mattered.

Three days later she received a letter from her employers. It was short and businesslike, notifying her of the date that had been set for the review of her position within the company. Debbie read it over a few times, trying to find any possible crumb of comfort in it. There was none. She phoned her area manager and asked, "Is there any point in me coming down for the hearing?"

"No," was the immediate reply. "I can't see that it would be worth your while. Since you are still on probation the hearing will not take long, and I doubt if your input would make any difference to the outcome. We will be letting you go."

Although Debbie had been bracing herself for this moment, ever since the night in the police station, and following her subsequent suspension, the news of her dismissal sounded so stark, so cold, so numbing, when the area-manager spelt it out in such uncompromising terms.

He hadn't finished yet, either.

Having given Debbie a moment or two to stagger under the impact of that stunning blow, the area manager then went on to deliver another. Just to make sure she was down and out for good. The firing, with its resultant humiliation, had to be utter and complete. There could be no way back.

"I would like you to meet me in the car park at the Novotel on the Wolverhampton ring road on...' he went on, in what was an order, made to sound like a request, and giving her a date and time. "I will expect you to have your car ready for collection that day, along with your laptop, all your presentation material and equipment and everything else belonging to the company."

When the morning of the handover came Debbie was mortified. She was embarrassed to meet anyone from the company she had started to represent so successfully and which she tried to deceive so selfishly. She stood with tears streaming down her cheeks as the Cavalier sports car, which had been her pride and joy, her symbol of success, was driven away, out of the car park, onto the ring road, and out of her life. Forever.

Devastated Debbie cut a forlorn figure as she crossed to the front of the hotel to find a cab to take her home. She was twenty-nine years old, with a six-year old daughter. She had just lost her job and probably all she had to look forward to was a lengthy prison sentence.

The future looked unbelievably bleak.

So she went home and smoked a 'joint' of cannabis. It was, she reckoned, the only substance that could keep her sane. It was her sole solace in a world that was caving in around her relentlessly. Otherwise she would go mad.

Her situation was soon to become even more distressing, for when her landlord heard that she had lost her job he asked her to leave the beautiful home which Emily and she both loved so much.

When Debbie was summoned to attend for trial, not at the Magistrate's, but at the Crown Court, she realised that she could be in big trouble. The moving of the hearing from the local to the more senior Court could only be interpreted as an indication of the prosecution service's perception of the extremely serious nature of the case.

On the morning of the trial Debbie again resorted to smoking cannabis. She was on her way out to be tried for growing the drug, and of possessing it 'with intent to supply.' In other words, of being 'a dealer.' And yet so compelling was her addiction that she had to use some to calm her jittery nerves before going to court.

Appearing before a judge in the Crown Court to answer a serious drugs charge was a lot different to appearing before a group of doctors and nurses answering questions about asthma inhalers. It was a strange, formal, unnerving experience.

Debbie had an excellent barrister to represent her, and his advice was, 'leave everything to me. I will call you when it is time for you to speak.'

The court preliminaries left Debbie cold. They were taken up with the judge and the barristers for both sides following routine court procedure. This seemed to require them to engage in an exchange of incomprehensible jargon spoken with incredibly posh accents.

When the charges were read out, Debbie had no difficulty understanding them, however. She knew what they meant, and what catastrophic consequences they could have for her, in days to come.

The defendant was then expected to answer the charge, and when Debbie was asked, "How do you plead?" she took her barrister's advice. He had told her that her only chance of being shown any leniency from the judge was to plead guilty, and say 'sorry.'

"Guilty, my lord," Debbie replied, in a croaky voice. Her whole mouth had suddenly gone completely dry. "And I want to add that I am sorry for what I have done," she went on.

Debbie didn't find it hard to say sorry. For that is exactly how she felt. Sorry for the mess she had made of her life. Sorry for letting her mum and daughter down. Sorry for losing her job. Sorry that she had to be asked to leave her lovely home. Sorry that she couldn't kick her habit. Sorry that she was going to have to find the finances to fuel it somewhere else. Sorry, sorry, sorry…

Having looked at her, and listened to her, the judge realised that Debbie had lost her home, her career and more importantly, her self-respect. It would seem that almost everything she had ever had to live for was gone. He recognised two commendable qualities about the pathetic young woman arraigned before him, however, despite the dire straits in which she now found herself. The first was her genuine contrition and the other her obvious potential to rise to higher and better things. When it came to passing judgement on her, the moment that Debbie had been dreading, many, and most certainly the defendant, were surprised at the sentence she was given.

"In view of the plea made by your counsel, and having spoken to you myself, I am giving you an absolute discharge," he pronounced. "Go and live your life right. Go and sort yourself out. And I trust never to see you back here again."

This unexpected reprieve gave Debbie another chance, but where did she even begin to avail herself of it? For days after the trial her only trips out of the house were to purchase the absolute necessities for her daughter and herself, and to pay occasional visits to her 'nan' and granddad who had been extremely supportive of her throughout the roller-coaster ride she had come to call 'Life.'

One morning she had smoked a joint of cannabis to bolster up her confidence sufficiently to allow her to go down to the local corner shop to buy bread and milk. As she was approaching the shop the words on the newspaper billboard outside it stopped her in her tracks. They just seared straight into her brain. The wording on the billboard poster was simply duplicating the banner headline of a leading national tabloid.

It read, 'Wolverhampton Nurse on Drugs Charge.'

Debbie dithered. Should she go into the shop or not?

What if the people in there knew that she was the 'Wolverhampton Nurse' on the board outside and the paper inside? No, they wouldn't. Surely they couldn't.

Not wanting anyone to see her looking sorry for herself in the street, Debbie finally entered the shop, bought the items she most needed and headed for home again, with all due haste.

For the second time in her life Debbie was beset with an overwhelming sense of shame. 'Wolverhampton Nurse on Drugs Charge.' How those words cut and stung. What ignominy! What disgrace! It was different this time around, though, for now she could not blame her utter self-abhorrence on anyone else. What had happened to her had been entirely of her own making. And she must live with the consequences.

Debbie and Emily had been forced to move into the only accommodation the out-of-work mother could afford, was a small terraced house in what was generally reckoned to be 'the worst end' of Wolverhampton. Unemployment rates were high there, and so were the crime rates. Drug dealing and prostitution were the pastimes, or the 'professions', of a fair percentage of the people.

The judge had been sympathetic in his judgement, and sincere in his injunction to 'go and live your life right.'

How Debbie would love to have been able to do just that.

She longed, more than anything else, to have the ability to 'sort herself out.'

But she couldn't do it.

Probably not there.

And certainly not alone.

She would most definitely need assistance.

Who, though, would have either the power, or the patience, to help her?

7

BYE-BYE BABY

Jim, perhaps?

Debbie hadn't long moved with her daughter into their next home on the less salubrious side of the city when a note was pushed below the door. It was from Jim, who had a brief message for his former girl friend.

'I'm out of prison. Ring me at this number,' was the terse instruction it conveyed.

Perhaps someone just released from jail on a drugs charge wouldn't be the person the local Health Advisory Board would recommend as a lifestyle counsellor, but Debbie rang him very soon, nonetheless. It seemed the natural thing to do.

She was lonely, and felt forsaken. Most of her erstwhile business and nursing friends had long since either fled or faded out of her life.

She was depressed.

She was unemployed. Her conviction on a drugs charge meant that she would never nurse again.

The dark grey clouds closing in around her were quickly turning jet black.

Then, in the midst of all the encircling gloom, she had this note from Jim. And whatever his faults, deep down she liked him. She always had, from the first day they had met. Jim had been left behind in his seedy underworld while she had been enhancing her career. He had been in jail while she had been wining and dining in top hotels. Now, though, her plane had been shot down, her soaring had ceased, and she had hit the ground with a splat. Her parachute hadn't even opened.

And now Jim was keen to make contact once more.

Why shouldn't I ring him? she had reasoned.

Debbie was well aware that Jim understood her. They had been soul mates. And not only did he know her, but he knew the scene in which she was now living 'like the back of his hand.' It was his 'patch.' Some of the counsellors Debbie had come across in her working days were genuine people but they lived in comfortable homes, drove air-conditioned cars and operated out of plush offices. They didn't really relate to where she was at. Jim did, though.

One of his first questions on taking Debbie's call was, "Can I come round to see you?"

Having told him that she would be glad to meet up with him again, Jim lost no time until he was at Debbie's door. Being reunited was like a ray of light in a dark world for both of them. They had so much in common, and so much to talk about. It was early afternoon and not the best time for all the catching up they had to do. Emily would soon be coming home from school and would need some attention. Jim recognised this, when Debbie told him all the latest about her daughter, and so left with the promise, "I'll be back later on tonight."

As they sat talking during their second meeting of the day, much later that evening, with Emily in bed, Debbie helped herself to a 'draw' of cannabis. Jim, on the other hand, seemed to have moved on to 'higher things.' While she had begun to smoke her cannabis he was still in the process of preparing himself a heroin 'spliff.'

With all the catching-up complete, Jim, who was a known dealer in the district, and fancied himself as an authority on the subject, began comparing the 'positive' effects of various drugs on the user, while drawing slowly on his homemade heroin roll-up.

When Debbie had finished her cannabis joint, Jim leaned across to her, and offered her his heroin spliff. "Here, have a pull of this," he encouraged. "It's the best pain-killer in the world."

If this drug was all Jim had cracked it up to be, Debbie thought that there could be no harm in giving it a try. So she did, and fell in love with it straight away.

It made her feel unbelievably peaceful. A restful glow replaced the restless gnawing in her innermost being. The fear, anxiety and self-denigration that had returned to haunt her over the past few months all seemed to melt away, like a snowman in the sun, soon after she had taken it.

The pace of Debbie's life, which had slowed almost to a stop after her trial, was suddenly to speed up again dramatically, after her introduction to heroin.

Jim moved in to live with her inside a week of them meeting up again, and one of the first lessons he taught his new 'partner' was how to make her own heroin spliffs.

For the first few weeks it was great. Debbie had an easy, relaxed relationship with Jim, and he was able to supply all the heroin they needed, to keep them 'floating.' The drug seemed to Debbie, just as cannabis had done more than ten years before, like the answer to all her problems.

She was determined, though, not to become addicted to heroin. 'If I just take it for a few days, and then go off it again for a few days, I should be O.K.' she kept trying to reassure herself. Jim supplied a number of addicts and they were dreadful looking sights. Deathly pale, skinny as though they never ate anything, and some of them were all covered in sores. There was no way that she was ever going to allow herself to end up looking like that. At least, not if she could help it.

The problem was, however, that she couldn't help it.

Within a month she had toned down her approach. Her determination had become dulled and the focus of her argument altered. She still maintained that she didn't want to become addicted to heroin, but not with the same fiery intensity as she had done at the first. Now, with the drug having already begun to take a hold on her mind and body, despite all her efforts to persuade herself that it hadn't, she had started to say things like, " I don't want to become a heroin addict, but even if I do, what would it matter? Who cares about me anyway, when all's said and done? What have I left to lose?"

This attitude gradually gave way to a total abandon, an inability to reason about anything. All that was important in her life now was getting heroin. However it came, or from wherever it came had ceased to matter to Debbie, her body was craving, crying out for it, so she had to have it.

She had become a heroin addict.

When Jim showed her how to use foil to 'chase the dragon' she began doing that, and found it more effective. That, though only lasted a while. There was another way, the ultimate way, of getting the drug into, and through, her body, to give maximum and almost immediate effect. That was by injecting it directly into a vein.

Needles were readily available, free of charge, from the chemist's across the road, and Debbie was soon injecting, not only heroin, but also a frightening cocktail of drugs. Someone had told her that if you mixed heroin, crack and ecstasy and shot them straight into the vein it would give you 'a super high.' Having become, by that time, totally oblivious to anything but the need for, and hopefully increased thrill from, the next 'fix,' Debbie began concocting her own personal powerful 'mixes.'

With regular shots of such potent drugs it wasn't long until all the veins in Debbie's arms and legs had collapsed. Her limbs had become ugly and swollen. The next stage was to begin injecting into her neck and her groin. She had been told by some of Jim's drug-shooting acquaintances that if she did this the high would be fantastic and almost immediate.

It might have been fantastic in the sense that it made Debbie feel as though she was been wafted away to some beautiful, sunny, carefree land. None of the worries that surrounded her in life bothered her there. It was true, too, that it was almost immediate, but in an entirely different way. Within minutes of having injected her homemade cocktail of drugs into the neck or groin, Debbie's mind may have been floating, but her body was lying unconscious on the floor.

To help fund her addiction Debbie began to help Jim sell drugs. This could mean driving to different locations to collect, or distribute, heroin, cocaine, cannabis, ecstasy, anything. If it made money Jim was at it. And if he was at it, so was she.

Jim had watched Debbie's rapid deterioration from occasional cannabis user to heroin addict with little concern. He was a junkie too, and to a junkie another junkie was just another junkie. The degree of addiction or physical and mental degeneration wasn't an issue. It was all part of the environment.

There was one man, however, who was watching Debbie's decline with increasing anxiety. He was Emily's father. Although Emily lived with her mum, Kevin, her dad, had continued to keep in regular contact with them, taking his daughter for outings on agreed weekends.

As he observed, with dismay, Debbie's increasing dependence on hard drugs, he began to wonder about Emily's welfare. Was this woman, who had once been a dedicated and caring mother, still fit to be looking after his child? Questions arose in his mind. Was she being adequately fed? Was she being taken to school every day? What would happen to her if Jim was out of the house and Debbie was out of her mind?

He determined that he needed to do something about it. He had just been married for less than a year and was in a stable relationship. His new wife and he were in a position to offer Emily a place in a loving home. The only question was, when should he approach Debbie about the matter? How long dare he allow the present state of affairs to go on?

Matters came to a head on the morning of the school trip.

Kevin had paid for Emily to go on an outing with the school and had arranged to collect her on the morning of the trip and take her to join the others.

The only problem was, though, that Debbie had been up late the night before washing and ironing her daughter's clothes. It had been the first time in the whole day that she had even felt able to do this. And her late-night stint was to have a knock-on effect.

Next morning, when Kevin called at the house to collect Emily, and knocked at the door, no one answered.

Debbie had slept in.

When Emily wakened her with the news that her dad was at the door, a frantic rush ensued. Debbie found it hard to focus on the job in hand. Her mind was splitting into fragments, darting from one task to another, but not performing any of them properly. While she was endeavouring to check that Emily had everything she needed, Kevin was standing around, looking anxiously at his watch, his patience stretched to the limit.

Emily was ready at last, and there followed a hurried drive round to the school, only to discover that they were too late. The coach had left a short time earlier. They had missed it!

A member of staff explained to them that they had waited as long as they possibly could, but then assuming that Emily wasn't going to make it, had gone. Anxious that his daughter should not miss out on her trip, as a result of her mother's inability to have her ready in time, and having learnt the route the coach would take, Kevin set out to follow it. After a nerve-racking chase he eventually caught up with the coach at its first stop in a motorway service area, and Emily joined the group. It hadn't been the most relaxing way to start her school trip!

A few days later Emily's dad appeared round at the home his daughter shared with her junkie mum and Debbie's drug-dealing partner Jim

The concerned father was gracious, but very firm. Although worried primarily about the welfare of his little eight-year-old daughter, he had enjoyed his once-upon-a-time relationship with Debbie, and was prepared to show her genuine consideration as well.

"I have come to take Emily to live with my wife and I, at least for a while, Debbie," he told her, when he considered that the time was right to state, in no uncertain terms, the purpose of his call. "You are in no fit state to look after her in the way that both you and I would like to think she would be looked after. You know that, and so do I."

"You didn't ask me if you could," Debbie replied, trembling. She knew that what he was saying was true, but her mind was in such a fragile state she was struggling to come to terms with it. Her drug-splintered mind could barely cope with the concept of what this was going to mean for all three of them.

"I'm not asking you, Debbie. I'm telling you," the single-minded dad persisted, with a gentle determination that was compelling, but frustrating. Why could he not just yell and shout, and bang things and throw things, like some of the men Debbie had already encountered in recent days? This quiet resolution was hard to resist.

Having given the confused mother a few moments to appreciate that he was really in earnest, he went on, "Now do you want me to help you get her things ready? I am not leaving here today without Emily."

When Debbie realised that he was determined to take their daughter with him she packed some of Emily's clothes into what few bags she could find. Tears had begun to stream down her face as she was doing this, and Kevin said at one stage, possibly by way of consolation, "You know, this could be a good thing for you, Debbie. At least it will give you an opportunity to sort yourself out. You need treatment. You have to return to being the Debbie I once knew. And when that happens we can reconsider the situation."

It was obvious that Emily's dad was truly perturbed by Debbie's distressing state of both mind and body, but the words 'sort yourself out,' sounded depressingly familiar. Where had she heard them before? It had had been in the Crown Court, nine months ago.

Her life now, though, was in a far bigger mess than it had been then.

Sorting herself out was something she had even stopped thinking about.

How could it ever be possible?

In half-an hour they had collected all that Emily would need for her new life with Kevin and his wife. The sensitive dad promised to bring her back to spend an occasional weekend with her mum, when she was well enough to care for her, and then he made towards the door. He went out and packed Emily's bits and pieces into his car and then returned for his daughter.

Emily hugged her mum, then took the hand her dad was holding out to her, and walked out with him on to the pavement.

Debbie watched the car until it disappeared at the end of the street and came in and shut the door. She collapsed backwards on to the second step of the stairs and sobbed and sobbed for a very long time.

In those wild early days on heroin she had become more and more addicted to the drug, telling herself all the while that she had nothing left to lose.

She knew now, however, that she had.

And she had just lost it. Or her.

Emily, her only child, had gone.

8

RUN FOR YOUR LIFE

There was nothing left to live for now.

Having been relieved of her sole interest in life, that of caring for her daughter in so far as she had been capable, Debbie began to spend the greater part of every day in bed. She had probably been up most of the night before, either using, or dealing, in drugs, and so wasn't fit to do anything else.

Not that there was anything else to do anyway.

She didn't have any friends any more.

The only people to come to the door were junkies like herself, wanting to buy drugs. Debbie's only excursions out of the house were on the rare occasions when she felt like shopping for food and on the times when she drove to Birmingham to pick up another large consignment of heroin.

Her misery mounted day by day as she and Jim began to quarrel aggressively, and these spats, which were increasing in frequency and intensity, often ended in physical violence. Jim insisted that Debbie was not allowed to take any drugs for her own use, unless she had the money to pay for them herself. "I have been a drug dealer for twenty years," he told her more than once, "but I have never come across anybody with as bad an addiction as you. You are a disaster. But remember, you had better be paying for all this 'gear' you are using."

If Jim ever suspected that Debbie was sneaking some of their stock to use on the sly, an ill-tempered bust-up would occur. Although he had once been a normal, rational man, and in his lighter moments could still be interesting company, Jim's twenty years in the drugs scene had caused him to lose all reason, and concern for anybody but himself, in his constant battle for self-preservation. The drug barons amongst whom he operated could be merciless men.

There is a saying amongst drug-dealers that 'you never get high on your own supply.' Debbie's live-in boyfriend reminded her of this often, in their confrontational sessions. "If we don't have the money to pay these guys because we have used all our own stuff then they won't shoot you. They will shoot me! So you'd better make sure you have enough to pay them when they come looking. Understand?!" he would tell her in no uncertain terms.

Such outbursts could be accompanied by an arm twisted up Debbie's back until she squealed, or a stinging slap on the face that brought tears to her eyes. It wasn't all one-way traffic, however. Debbie, often high on heroin, usually fought back, 'giving as good as she got,' kicking, clawing, and punching.

One of Debbie's best customers for drugs was Della, who lived just across the street. Debbie sold Della, a well-known prostitute in the city, heroin and crack on a regular basis and they often chatted to each other, when making the transaction.

"You know, Debbie, I can make my money a lot easier than you. And what's more, I'm not going to get the 'bird' (prison sentence) that you are going to get if you are caught at this," Della said to her supplier more than once.

What she said was probably true, but Debbie invariably told her, in reply, "I couldn't do it, Della. I just couldn't do it."

"You could, if you really wanted to. If you were as desperate for money for a fix as I am many a time, you could, Debbie," Della kept encouraging her. Debbie always maintained that the drugs were bad enough but she wasn't up for 'the game.' It wasn't her scene.

Or so she thought, until a series of circumstances one Sunday afternoon led her to change her mind, in a fit of pique.

Della had arrived over to the house to buy some drugs, only to catch Jim and Debbie in the middle of a blazing row. Although the thumping and punching, kicking and mauling had been curtailed in the presence of 'a valued customer,' the war of words continued, unabated. This was conducted at the tops of their voices and liberally laced with expletives.

When she had exhausted her store of insults to hurl, Debbie, in blind rage, opted for what she knew Jim would consider the ultimate obscenity. "Come on, Della!" she shrieked. I'm going out on the beat with you!"

"You are not!" Jim yelled, trying to restrain her.

"I most certainly am!" Debbie retorted, having struggled free from him, and dashed out to the front door. "Come on, Della," she went on to scream. "Hurry up!"

Probably considering it the best way to defuse the situation, Della did as she was told. When Debbie saw her safely out on the pavement, she slammed the door behind them with such venom that every window in her tiny terrace house vibrated.

As they walked down the road towards Della's 'beat' the experienced prostitute gave her friend a crash course on procedure. When she had gone into some detail about what to say, and what to do, to satisfy her client, Debbie began to feel increasingly repulsed. Della was aware of a growing edginess in her attitude and a mounting sense of revulsion, possibly a throwback to her childhood experiences, in the questions that she asked.

"You don't have to do this, you know, Debbie," Della declared at one stage, slowing almost to a stop, conscious of the fact that they would soon be arriving at the spot where she would be considered 'on duty.'

That statement confirmed in Debbie's mind something she already knew. She didn't have to do it, and come to that, the more she heard about it, and the more she thought about it, the more she realised that she didn't actually want to do it. Debbie had only come out with Della to get one up on Jim, but was now forced to admit to herself that it had been a step too far. So she made up her mind accordingly.

When Della stopped at the street corner, which marked the border of her 'beat,' to wait for the first car to pull up, Debbie just kept on walking. She didn't stop for a moment in case a prospective 'client' might mistake her for one of Della's associates.

Her granddad's house was just about half-a-mile away and Debbie kept on walking until she reached it. She talked to her granddad for nearly an hour and before leaving asked him for the loan of forty pounds. Granddad had always continued to be kind to Debbie, despite her chequered career, and feeling distinctly sorry for her, lent her the money.

Debbie had her loan request very carefully worked out. Forty pounds would buy enough drugs to last Jim and her for the remainder of the day, so she went to an accomplice and picked up some. Body and mind were by then screaming out for a 'fix,' so she took some to keep her going, and then began the walk back towards her own house with what was left of her purchase in her pocket. She was sure that Jim would have cooled down by then, and the heroin she was bringing home should surely please him. They could share it later that evening.

When she arrived back at the house, Debbie was to receive a nasty shock, however. Jim was clearly not in the mood for sharing anything. Some of his cronies had phoned with 'a bit of news' for him, and another who had called at the house to buy some drugs, had told him the same thing in person. They were all certain that they had seen Debbie out with Della, 'on the beat.'

What they obviously didn't know was that Debbie hadn't stayed with Della, 'on the beat.'

Nor was there any time to explain.

Jim had flipped. He'd gone completely 'bonkers.'

The minute Debbie entered the house he dashed straight across and reached for her. His returning girlfriend had just begun to say, "Jim, I borrowed some money and bought us some..." when she stopped mid-sentence.

She realised instinctively, and immediately, that she had entered a danger zone.

Having grabbed Debbie by the hair Jim dragged her round the room, knocking, or kicking over anything that happened to cross his path. He had a wild, mad, crazed look in his eyes. It was obvious that he had worked himself into such a distracted state that he had lost all sense of reason.

"But Jim, I didn't..." Debbie started to howl, only to be given a smack across the mouth with an open hand.

"Shut up, you liar!" came the hysterical response. "I have had three or four of my mates on the phone, or even at the door to tell me that they saw you! Are you trying to tell me that they are all liars just like you?"

Debbie pleaded for mercy, but it was pointless in the face of such irrationality.

She tried to fight back, but felt powerless against Jim's almost superhuman frenzy-fuelled strength.

Soon large lumps of Debbie's golden hair were lying around in the living room, but that didn't put her jealous attacker off in the slightest.

Every time a handful came out Jim merely grabbed another one and pulled even harder, while trailing Debbie around more ferociously.

With the downstairs wrecked, Jim then started dragging the distraught Debbie up the stairs, banging her head fiercely against the wall, every time they went up another step. Every crashing contact of her forehead against the wall was accompanied by a torrent of verbal abuse.

"Here take that, you dirty whore!" was a common one.

"Are you not ashamed of yourself, you tart? For if you're not, you will be when I have finished with you!" was another.

When they reached the top of the stairs Jim steered Debbie, by the hair, into a bedroom. "Come in here! I have something to show you!" he shouted in her ear, and then gave a sinister, cynical laugh.

Debbie had some lovely clothes, which she had kept in that bedroom. A number of them were mementoes from her out-and-about-on-business days, and although she had lost so much weight that they didn't fit her any more, she occasionally tried them on. It was a means of escape, a ticket for a trip on the time machine, back into the pleasant land of Prosperous Past.

Now all Debbie's clothes had been pulled from the wardrobe and were strewn across the floor. They were crushed and crumpled as though Jim had been walking over them and possibly even throwing or kicking them about. He had been doing all those things… and more.

The smell of urine on material in an enclosed space was nauseating.

He had urinated all over them as well.

"Oh, no!" Debbie wailed.

"Shut up I told you!" her drug-crazed partner yelled in return. "I have to teach you a lesson!"

It was then that he hit her really hard.

Pulling her head back by the hair with his left hand he smashed his right fist into the centre of her face.

Blood spurted everywhere.

The pain was excruciating.

Debbie's nose was broken.

She put her hand up to her face and drew it away again, covered in blood. Her upper lip had already been bleeding from the smack it had received downstairs, but now her face was a smeared, swollen, bloody mess.

The wall, the floor and her clothes were all spattered in her blood.

When she staggered back against the wall to steady herself, Jim was still spewing out his tirade of terrifying threats.

"Don't you dare go down those stairs you slut!" he warned her. "For if you do I am definitely going to kill you!"

With the mood he was in, Debbie had no cause to doubt that he meant it.

She lay half slumped against the wall, considering her next move. She knew she daren't even attempt to go down the stairs. There were times recently when she had thought that death would represent a welcome release from the turbulence of life, but even in that context she hadn't considered being murdered as a serious option.

Jim had backed off. Perhaps he thought that Debbie had learnt the lesson he had been intent on teaching her, or perhaps he had taken a moment to contemplate what further torture he could inflict on the battered body by the wall.

Debbie didn't know what he was thinking. She didn't care, either.

All she knew was that she had been granted breathing, and thinking, space.

She was in unbelievable agony, and her mind was in a whirl, but her subconscious survival instincts warned her that she must get out of that house as soon as possible. But how? It would be fatal to even attempt to go down the stairs.

Her only alternative was to make her exit from an upstairs window. It would be dangerous, but worth the risk.

If she killed herself in the process, they could call it suicide.

If she allowed Jim to kill her, they would probably call it murder.

A few minutes later, Debbie made a dash for it.

The suddenness of her action caught Jim by surprise, and by the time he had caught up with her she had run from the front bedroom where they were, into the little back room. She pushed up the sash window and swung herself out into a sitting position on the windowsill. Jim struggled desperately to pull her back, but couldn't quite manage it.

Then she jumped.

The small enclosed yard was ten feet below her, and she landed in a dishevelled heap on the concrete. She was already so traumatised that she didn't even feel the impact with the ground. Nor was she in the slightest bit hurt. At least her jump hadn't added to her already dreadful physical distress.

She had made it.

Debbie scrambled to her feet, and crossed quickly to the door out into the back alley. She slid the bolt, and bolted. Out through the door she sped, down the alley, out into the street, and away.

She knew that she had to run as fast and as far as she could. If Jim came after her, and caught up with her, she would never run anywhere again.

It was shortly after six o'clock on a sunny Sunday evening and a number of very presentable people, possibly on their way to a church service, stopped to stare at the fugitive.

What a shocking sight it was, too.

A young woman with her eyes swollen and red from crying, set deep in a face swollen and red from a punching, running as hard as she could. Her hair was sticking out all over, as though she had just had an electric shock, and her clothes, which were splattered with blood, looked decidedly bedraggled.

The fleeing figure didn't care how long they stood. Or how hard they gaped.

She just kept running and running and running. Away and away and away.

Debbie was running, literally, for her life.

9

PLEASE DON'T LET MY MUMMY DIE

Later that night she was back.

Having run until she hadn't another breath left, Debbie was forced to stop for a rest. When she did so, and discovered that she was out of danger, she began to consider what to do next.

It came as no surprise to her to realise that she didn't have a lot of choice. She felt that she daren't go near anyone she knew in her current hideous-looking condition. There were hostels and help-lines for people in her predicament, but she hadn't a clue how to contact them. And even if she did, she was still quite sure that Jim would seek her out, and then 'sort her out,' once and for all.

Debbie ambled around the side streets of the city for hours, trying to avoid people as much as possible. She soon began to feel sick with pain and exhaustion. Every step had become a nightmare for every aching limb and joint seemed to want to give up. Her abused, bloodied body was in need of urgent pain relief. Her fractured mind was screaming out for the obliterating effect of heroin.

Her own street was empty and silent when she arrived back in it, after eleven o'clock. Slowly, apprehensively, she turned up into the alley, and then through the yard and pushed the back door. It was still open.

Jim heard her come in, and when he saw the state of her, said nothing for a few minutes. Eventually he stood over Debbie where she had flopped down, with her head buried in her hands.

"So you're back," were his first words.

"Yeah, I'm back," Debbie replied, wondering what he would do next.

Drug-dealers aren't noted for their habit of saying 'sorry,' and Jim didn't say it that night. He did, though, prepare her some 'medicine,' the panacea for all ills for a junkie. Having put some heroin into a syringe he urged her, "Here. Have that. It will help you."

Debbie guided the needle skilfully into a vein in her neck and injected the drug. By the time she would have cleaned up her blood-smeared face, the pain of body and anguish of mind would have begun to ease. For a while at least.

A few days later, when Jim and she were sitting together in the house on one of those increasingly rare occasions when they were both in a fit state to conduct a rational conversation, Debbie told him what had actually happened on Sunday afternoon.

"Although I said I was going 'on the beat' with Della, that was only to wind you up," she explained. "I couldn't do it. I couldn't stomach the thought of it."

"Oh, is that right?" Jim retorted. Sounding only half-convinced was one way of saving him having to apologise for the violent punishment he had meted out.

Debbie was soon forced to change her mind, and overcome her inhibition about 'working the streets,' however. Despite what she had said to Della, and Jim, her circumstances were soon to create a compelling need for money. Big money. And quick.

Jim had told her that she had one of 'the worst habits he had ever seen.' It was true. Debbie had to have her drugs, hard drugs in big quantities, whatever the cost. And the cost was huge. By that time she was spending £100 a day on heroin and £1500 a week on crack cocaine.

There was only one way she knew to make that kind of money.

In quiet desperation, she contacted Della, who understood her situation perfectly. She had been forced to go out onto the streets in order to satisfy her heroin addiction.

Della gave her drugs supplier a refresher course on all the information they had covered in the introductory session that ill-fated Sunday afternoon, but it wasn't a problem to Debbie second time round. She could cope with the prospect of 'going on the game' O.K. Necessity had overcome modesty or morality or whatever it was that had held her back before. It was her only hope. There was another factor that helped her make up her mind, too. Since half the people in the shadowy underworld where Jim and she did business believed that she was a 'hooker' anyway, why not just go out there, live up to their expectations, and be one?

Her big chance came one evening when Jim was away on a 'buying trip,' and wouldn't be home that night. And she was in dire need of money.

It was after midnight when she slipped out of the house into the deserted street and down to Della's 'beat.' Her 'tutor' had given her permission to ply her 'patch' any time she felt like it, assuring her that nobody would say a word to her.

For a while everything was extremely quiet, almost eerie. It was cold out there and Debbie wondered how long she would have to wait until 'a client' came along. Della hadn't been very clear about that. Debbie had mixed feelings while waiting, and walking, and waiting...

On the one hand she needed the funds and had been telling herself since leaving the house that 'it would be no big deal' and when it was over she would have all the money she wanted to buy all the drugs she needed for at least a day.

There was, though, at the back of her mind, a secret hope that nobody would want her 'services.' Then she could tell Della that she had stood out there for more than an hour and got nothing but a foundering. It would be almost a relief to that last lingering shred of reticence if nothing were to happen.

Then, just when Debbie was seriously considering turning and heading for home, it did.

A large car pulled up beside her and the driver leaned across, opened the front passenger door and spoke out to her. Debbie crossed to the car, spoke into it, and then stepped into it. She had begun life as a prostitute.

Her life on the streets was to be short-lived, however. It only lasted for six months, for by that time nobody wanted her. Debbie had ceased to be desirable, even to the least demanding of clients any more.

The once attractive businesswoman had deteriorated to such an extent that she now looked like some grotesque stick insect. Her pitifully thin arms and legs protruded pathetically around the edges of whatever clothes she could find to fit her. The days of designer fashion were long since gone. Debbie now procured her outfits by paying shoplifters in heroin and crack cocaine to bring her tracksuits and jeans for nine and ten-year-olds out of some of the chain stores. On the rare occasions when she felt well enough to leave the house she invariably wore two pairs of trousers to bulk herself up a bit.

Since she was sick virtually all the time she spent most of the twenty-four hours of every day in bed. Her body and face became covered in sores. Jim was constantly taking her to the hospital with some complaint. Every treatment was a nightmare. The infected black cysts, which grew on the insides of her eyelids, were extremely painful to have removed. Since her body was full of heroin the local anaesthetic was totally ineffective so Jim had to hold her down physically while the doctors removed the offending cysts with no pain relief of any kind.

Debbie was a mental wreck as well. She couldn't bear to be without the numbing effect of hard drugs, even for the shortest of periods, for without it her mind was in a whirl. It felt as though her brain had all the stability of a jellyfish, sloshing about in her head. It could never come to a concrete decision about anything. Even the simplest of choices had become major issues. She couldn't think. She couldn't remember. She couldn't prioritise.

All the joy had seeped slowly out of her life. Debbie Forrest, who had once been the 'life and soul of the party' wherever she went, didn't laugh any more now. She didn't even smile. She didn't cry either though. She had sunk to such a low ebb that she had actually lost the power to care.

What did it matter if she lived or died? Life had become little more than a living death.

Communication with the family had totally broken down. None of them came to see her, and she had no interest whatsoever in going to see them.

That was except for her mum and Emily. Kevin still brought their daughter on short visits to Debbie and it was on those occasions that the eight-year old began to realise that there was something terribly wrong with her mum. Every time Emily saw her, she appeared to be even gaunter looking.

Desperate to do something to help her, but not quite sure what, she began to pray. Emily had never been to church in her life, but she had heard in school about praying so she decided to try it. She had no idea who she was praying to, but she just began by saying, each night before switching out her light and going to sleep, 'Please help mum get better. Please.'

Her big prayer opportunity came one Saturday evening when Debbie's Aunt Maureen called round at Kevin's house to take Emily out. As they were driving away Emily's great-aunt asked her, "Would you like to come to church with me this evening?"

Emily nodded, not quite sure what to expect.

When she entered the Church of St. Joseph with Maureen the evening sunlight was glinting through the stained glass windows and Emily felt a sense of tranquillity. This is a good place, she thought. Maybe I can find help for mum here.

She watched others picking up small white candles from a box on the floor, lighting them, and kneeling down, presumably to pray.

"Can I do that, too, Aunt Maureen?" Emily enquired.

"Of course you can, dear. I will put something in for you," and with that she dropped a coin or two into another box.

Emily then picked up her candle, lit it, and knelt down.

She still had only a vague perception of God, but although rather hazy about who she was praying to, she was perfectly clear in her mind as to what she must pray about. It had become the overriding concern of her life for the past few months.

"Please don't let my mummy die," was her earnest request. "Please don't let that awful stuff kill her. Please save her. Please don't let her die. Please. Please. Please..."

10

THE MAN IN THE STREET

Although her daughter was praying that her life would be preserved, Debbie, who was totally unaware of Emily's passionate pleadings, had other ideas.

She had become tired of rising out of bed, which she only did when she couldn't avoid rising out of bed, to be confronted by an image of a corpse in the mirror. Death was staring her in the face every time she dared look at herself. Why, then, she began to think every day, if I am so close to death, can I not just go the whole way?

Life continued to be one endless round of wretchedness.

Death, she reckoned, probably wouldn't be any better. Nor, though, could it be any worse. It wasn't particularly that Debbie wanted to die. It was just that she didn't want to live any more. There was no point in life, and there was no other way out.

While the prospect of death had become an option in Debbie's mind, the spectre of death had begun to creep closer to her in a physical sense, as well. Jim and she were as busy as ever, dealing away in hard drugs, and like any business enterprise, when one of their regular customers stopped calling to pick up his or her usual 'order' they chased them up.

'What happened to Sammy?" either of them would enquire of an accomplice.

"Oh didn't you hear about Sammy?" would come the typical reply. "Sammy's dead. He was found lying out at the back of a pub one night."

Or they would ask somebody who had called to collect their weekly supply, "What ever happened to Sally? She used to be a friend of yours did she not? It's just that she hasn't been round to pick up any 'gear' for a long time now."

The same type of question would often evoke the same type of response. It would be something like, "They had to force their way into Sally's place last week and they found her lying dead in the hall."

The people that Jim and she were supplying with drugs were dropping off one by one, killed by their addiction. Debbie had no conscience about this, though. Rather, in a certain sense she envied them. Lucky so-and-sos, she used to think, to have escaped out of this ghastly rotten world.

Then, right in the middle of her muddle of misery, she was asked to assume responsibility for calling on her granddad, five days a week. Her 'nan,' whom she had loved so much, died, but before passing away asked her junkie granddaughter to promise that she would 'make sure granddad was well looked after.' Debbie's mum, who worked, could attend to his needs at the weekends, leaving Debbie to call with him every morning from Monday to Friday, and bring him what he needed from the shops.

Jim was glad that Debbie had been accorded this task, feeling that it would give her a focus in life, 'something worthwhile to get up for.' Debbie, on the other hand, didn't really want anything 'to get up for.' All she wanted to do was lie in bed. 'Getting up' just meant yet another haunting face-to-face with the corpse in the mirror.

"I'd rather be sick here than over there," she would tell Jim when he insisted that having to go out to see her granddad every morning was 'really a very good thing.'

One Friday morning Debbie was performing what had become for her this unbearable chore. She was walking through the town of Bilston, where granddad lived, on the way back to catch a bus to return to his house with the shopping. Fridays meant two things. For one, granddad usually wanted more stuff then than any other day of the week. It was also market day in Bilston so there were many more people around than the reluctant shopper would normally encounter on her daily trudge through the streets.

The bags were heavy and Debbie was tired. She was not only physically exhausted at having to match her emaciated frame against the weight of the bags, but she was also mentally and emotionally at the end of her tether. This wearisome cycle of futility, which consisted of rising out of bed, being sick, shooting-up on heroin or crack, going shopping for granddad, being sick again, shooting up on heroin or crack again, going to bed again, only to have to rise again to begin the whole pointless process all over again, had just become too much.

This wasn't living. This was barely existing. And it couldn't go on.

Struggling back in the direction of her bus stop Debbie cut a solitary figure in a melee of chattering shoppers. As she negotiated her way out of Bilston's outdoor market and up towards the Town Square, she made a critical decision.

It was time to put an end to it all.

This was definitely going to be the day.

Granddad didn't know it yet, but somebody else would be buying his cheese from one stall, his sausages from another and his fresh vegetables from yet another, next week. She wouldn't be there.

Walking along, head down, arms and legs weak and shaky, Debbie decided not only on the certainty of her deliverance by demise, but also on the method of it. She had a gram of heroin at home. She would mix this up on a spoon, put it into a 2ml syringe and 'hit' it into her groin. That, plus the heroin level already in her body would knock her out totally, completely and forever. She would drift away into oblivion and this sad, sick, stupid world, could just rumble on however it liked without her. It had nothing left to offer her, and she had no desire to languish one minute longer in it.

As soon as she had resolved to take her own life, Debbie felt an uncanny peace flood into her heart. Only a few more hours and the agony would be ended. Suddenly the bags didn't even seem heavy any more. It was like her first heroin trip. The pressures and anxieties had all instantly evaporated into the buzz of Bilston on market day, and her mind was floating, floating, floating away.

For the first time in many months Debbie had something in prospect to which she could really look forward. Even it was death by overdose.

She was so engrossed in her ultimate 'release' that she didn't realise that she was being watched. Derrick Cole from the Open-Air Mission had just finished preaching in the Square to the many people walking and standing around, and had begun to distribute tracts to anybody who would accept one from him.

Two men had gone past him, talking away loudly but totally ignoring the proffered tract, when he lifted his eyes to suss out his next possible contact and saw a phantom-like figure coming towards him. Her face was painfully thin, her eyes were sunk in hollow black sockets and her straggly straw-coloured hair looked as though it hadn't been brushed for days. It was a pleasant late summer day but this woman looked as though she had all the clothes she possessed piled around her scrawny body.

As she drew closer and lifted her face momentarily to see where she was going, Derrick was immediately arrested by her expression. She had a vague, faraway, extra-terrestrial look about her. It was as though she didn't, or at least soon wouldn't, belong on this planet.

Debbie was plodding onward, still preoccupied with her perception of a final freedom from all the cares of earth, when she was conscious of a man stepping across into her path.

It was Derrick. Something had told him that it was now-or-never with this person. If he didn't speak to her today, he would probably never have another chance.

"Young woman, I have a message for you," he began, with a warm smile. "It is that Jesus loves you, and He has a plan for your life."

Those words stopped Debbie in her tracks.

She was surprised initially that someone would even bother to speak to her about anything. The people standing about in twos and threes in the square were discussing everything from the vagaries of the weather to the fortunes of Wolves, the local football club, but nobody ever stopped to chat to her. She often felt like an outcast, an 'untouchable.'

This man, though, had not only spoken to her, but there was something about what he had said, and how he said it, that she found instantly compelling. It came across as if he had just been on the hotline to heaven and this 'message' had been delivered as top priority for her. It sounded incredibly credible, somehow.

Derrick then struck up a conversation with Debbie, and as she recounted some of the highs and lows of her life to date, to him, carefully stopping short of her resolution of five minutes before, the street evangelist felt genuinely sorry for her. He then seized the opportunity to explain in more detail the meaning of the message he had for her. Jesus loved her so much, he said, that He had come to earth, to die on a cross to bear all the punishment for her sins. If she would only believe on Him, He would forgive her sins and make her a completely new person.

It all sounded wonderful to Debbie, almost too good to be true.

Her sins all forgiven. Debbie Forrest 'a new person.'

How could that ever happen?

After they had spoken for a few minutes Debbie said that she 'must be off' or she would miss her bus back to granddad's.

Before leaving, however, she had something to ask of Derrick, and it was a request that took him rather by surprise.

"Will you pray for me, please?" she begged, softly. Debbie knew about prayer, for Jim's grandmother, who was a Christian, had told him often, much to his annoyance, that she prayed for him every day, along with his junkie girlfriend and partner-in-crime.

"Of course I will pray for you, Debbie," Derrick assured the forlorn-looking scrap of humanity before him, but he had mistaken the urgency of her plea. What he had meant was that he would add Debbie to his 'prayer-list' and 'remember her,' along with dozens of others, in his regular daily prayer times in the weeks to come.

That was not what Debbie had intended, though.

"But what I mean is, will you pray with me NOW?" she persisted.

"Of course I will pray with you now," Derrick went on, using virtually the same words, but feeling somewhat chastened that he hadn't understood the plea of Debbie's anguished soul straight away.

The bustle around them was forgotten as Derrick and Debbie stood together in the corner of Bilston Town Square with their heads bowed, and the street evangelist prayed for the heroin addict. Derrick knew to keep it short and simple. This girl wouldn't understand church jargon. What she needed was God's hand in her life, and that is what Derrick asked his Heavenly Father for, in language that she would understand.

His prayer, in essence, was for three vital elements. He asked God, 'in His boundless love and mercy,' to preserve Debbie's life, save her soul, and use her for His glory.

When they had finished, Derrick assured Debbie that he would continue to pray for her. She, in turn, thanked him for talking to her, and hurried off to catch her bus.

Debbie had a lot to think about now.

Having gone through the daily ritual with granddad, of what she had bought where, and how much it had cost, she set out for home.

By the time she had arrived back at her own house, the one gram of heroin in the 2 ml syringe had been forgotten. Her mind, which less than an hour earlier had been totally fixated with her impending death, had now been overtaken by what the man in the street had called God's plan for the rest of her life.

The only problem was that she didn't have a working relationship with God, or Jesus, or who ever it was that had dreamt up this marvellous master plan.

So how could she possibly know what it was?

At least Emily's prayers had been answered and she was still alive. That was always a start, and perhaps the Supreme Designer would reveal His blueprint for her, to her, sometime, somehow, somewhere.

He would have to be quick about it, though.

For if He wasn't she would be dead, killed by her addiction like all the rest.

11

THE TAMBOURINE CHURCH

Winter had closed in, adding its increased greyness by day and blackness by night to the ceaseless gloom of Debbie's life, when she had to endure what for her was the ultimate in anguish. That was a drugs-reduced weekend.

Jim had taken himself off for a few days and this meant that Debbie's intake of heroin and crack had to be curtailed. She had learnt from bitter experience that it would be dangerous, for a number of reasons which Jim still spelt out to her periodically and emphatically, to 'exceed the stated dose', at any time, but particularly when he was away.

There was, however, a positive spin-off from Jim's absence. This was that Kevin had allowed Emily to come and stay with her mum over Saturday night and all day on Sunday. Anxious to enjoy every moment of her daughter's visit, as far as was physically, mentally and emotionally possible in her fragile state of mind and body, Debbie determined to limit her use of drugs over that precious twenty-four-hour period.

Debbie did all in her power to maximise the bonding of mother and daughter in their brief times together. If Emily ever indicated that she would like them to do something or go somewhere together her mum would make every effort to ensure that her wish was granted. On that Sunday, December 8, 1996, however, Emily made what to her mum sounded like an unusual, and almost unfeasible, request.

It was still early in the morning when Emily said, "Please Mummy, will you take me to church today?"

Debbie was stunned into silence for a second or two. What did she say to that?

I can't go to church like this, she thought. Church is for respectable people with good jobs, fancy cars and happy families. It's no place for drug dealers, dropouts and the living dead.

"Oh no, pet," she replied after a short pause. "Church is just for good people. Nobody would want to see the likes of me at church."

"No, mummy, that's not right," her daughter persisted. "Anybody can go to church. It's for everybody."

"But look at me, Emily," her mum continued. "I am in such a state that I couldn't go out anywhere, not least to church. Everybody would be looking at me. And what's more, you would probably be ashamed of me."

"No, mummy, I would never be ashamed of you," the nearly-nine-year-old protested. "And you said that you are not fit to go out anywhere. I know, though, that if I had asked you to take me to the cinema or a shopping centre you would have taken me. So why won't you take me to church? Please."

"All right then," Debbie conceded at length. "We will go to that big Church of England down the road, just for you. It is the nearest one to us, so it shouldn't take us long to get there."

When she had made her pitiful personage as presentable as possible Debbie set out with her daughter to church. This was to be her first time back in a church since her childhood, which she recalled occasionally, but only as one haunting, unending nightmare.

There was no one about to greet them as they entered the building, so Debbie and Emily pushed open a heavy wooden door at one side of the vestibule and walked apprehensively down the aisle. They chose a pew about one-third the way in from the back, and began to look around.

It was obviously a very old church. There were a number of Gothic arches down each side and the walls all seemed to be of stone. Strained winter light filtered in through a series of stained glass windows illustrating Bible stories, only a few of which Debbie recognised. The pews were of a dark polished wood and the hymn books in the little wooden racks in front of Emily and her mum looked as though they had been there since the church was opened two or three hundred years before. The binding was discoloured and fraying at the edges and the pages were faded and stained.

The church felt cold. It was a large draughty place, and would have been most difficult to heat. Emily held her arms in close to her chest in an effort to keep warm and Debbie wasn't long in until she wished that she had worn four sweaters instead of just the two that she had pulled on and then covered with a padded anorak to try and disguise her shapeless stick-like frame.

The chill of the church building was nothing compared to the chill demonstrated by the church congregation, however. The few others already seated, waiting for the service to commence, stared at this wretched woman who seemed to have blown in off the streets with, amazingly, an attractive, healthy-looking eight-or-nine-year old girl in tow.

Debbie and Emily felt very isolated, and yet recognised at the same time, to their extreme embarrassment, that they were very much the centre of attention, as they sat close to one another in the pew.

No one came near them and nobody ever seemed to think of speaking to them, yet every eye in the church was riveted on them. It wasn't that they glanced across and then glanced away again either. They just gaped and gazed and gawked. By the expressions of shock and disdain on their faces it seemed as though they thought that Debbie was in some way defiling their super-sacred building.

Although accustomed to being treated like an outcast by society in general, Debbie felt the shame of the situation especially keenly that morning for her daughter's sake. 'Poor Emily,' she thought. 'She so much wanted to come to church and all these very respectable and self-righteous people are treating her like an alien. And it's all because of me. She is suffering this public disgrace because of the look of the phantom she calls her mum.'

Emily didn't feel disgraced, though. She felt angry. 'Poor mum. I know what those people are thinking,' she said to herself. 'They are thinking, what's that scraggy drug addict doing in here? Well she's my mum, and she's here because I wanted to go to church. Oh mum, when this is over I am going to have to tell you how sorry I am for forcing you to come here to have all these men and women stare at you as if you were dirt.'

The start of the service offered mother and daughter some welcome relief. It was then that the curious congregation redirected their attention from the interlopers in the anoraks beside them to the man in the robes before them. The pressure was off, at last.

The service seemed to drag on for ages. The words of the hymns were strange and were sung very slowly, and with little feeling. Debbie and Emily were not surprised that they didn't know, or relate to the hymns. Neither of them had sat through a church service for years, so how could they?

It was the ups and downs of the congregation that left them confused, and occasionally flustered. At some stages the people in the pews sat and chanted their responses, at others they knelt on little cushions and chanted their prayers, and when it came to singing the hymns they stood up. There were times when the two bewildered visitors weren't quite sure whether they should be sitting, standing or kneeling. This meant that they were invariably two or three seconds behind everyone else when making their move.

Finally it was all over and time to go.

The vicar was in the foyer as they went out. He nodded briefly across in Debbie and Emily's direction as they passed him on their way to the outside door, and said with a wan smile, "Thank you for coming. Good day."

As they walked the short distance back to the house, Debbie felt a certain sense of satisfaction, almost of closure, on two counts. Not only had she been kind enough to respond to Emily's request and take her to church, but that would probably also be the last time she would have to do such a thing. Emily would definitely never want to go to a place of worship again. It was in a certain sense gratifying to know that church was now all done and dusted. An experience like the one they had just had would surely have knocked the thought of church, and religion, and God out of her head for good.

Debbie was wrong, though. It hadn't.

It was after dinner when Emily made her second plea of the day. Debbie's mum had joined them for their midday meal, and thinking that she would have an ally in 'nanny,' Emily tried another time.

"Mummy, please will you take me to church this evening?" she asked. "I want to go to church again."

"No, Emily. We have already been to church today, darling, and you know that we didn't like it. We don't need to go twice in one day, anyway. It's only very religious people who go to church twice on a Sunday," Debbie replied at once. She was surprised at her daughter's recently acquired obsession with going to church, and keen to trot out every possible excuse to dampen down her strange desire. Surely it must only be a fad, a peer-pressure thing. It could be extinguished if she sprayed it gently with the prospect of futility and the fear of fanaticism.

Emily was not to be put off, however. "When I asked you to take me to church, mummy," she began to explain, "I didn't really mean the church you took me to this morning."

Her mum was puzzled at this. Was one church not something the same as the other? "If that church wasn't the right one, which one did you want to go to?" she went on to enquire.

"I wanted to go to the tambourine church farther down the road," the undeterred daughter continued. "You know, the one with the big cross on the outside of it. I was passing it one evening and the sound of the music coming out of it was really great. I'm sure the people in there would be friendly. I just know they would. Please, mummy, will you take me down there tonight?"

Debbie soon capitulated. "All right, dear, I will," she found herself submitting, contrary to her own personal preference, for the second time in the same day. She loved her daughter so much and realised that she had her heart set on visiting 'the tambourine church' as she called it. If she said, 'No,' Emily would probably keep on asking all afternoon in an attempt to make her change her mind, so it would afford them both a couple of peaceful hours just to say 'Yes' in the first place.

"I just hope it is warmer and more welcoming than that other church we were in this morning," Debbie added, conscious of the need to qualify her switch from initial reluctance to half-grudging assent.

Emily could scarce contain her excitement. "It will be. Of course it will be!" she exclaimed. Not content with just the two of them going, as they had done in the morning, she then turned to Debbie's mum, who up until that moment had been a silent listener to the discourse between mother and daughter, and asked, "What about you, gran? Will you come with us, too?"

Nanny wasn't hard to persuade. If Emily wanted it, she would do it, if at all possible.

"Yes, love, I'll come too," she promised, aiming a reassuring kiss at her granddaughter's glowing cheek.

12

IT MUST BE O.K.

Since mother and grandmother had agreed, with varying degrees of enthusiasm, to take Emily to her 'tambourine church' that evening, the only problem remaining was to know what time the service began. The general consensus of opinion was that it would be 'around six o'clock' and so they decided to make their way down there for 'just before six.'

It was early December and a bitterly cold evening. There had been a number of short snow flurries during the day and there was still snow lying on the pavements as they set out. Emily didn't appear to feel the cold, though, as she strode on a few steps ahead of her mum and gran, turning round every now and then to make some comment to the wrapped up ladies bringing up the rear.

When they reached the church it was closed.

Debbie had been secretly hoping that it would be, for it gave her the chance to put her opt-out plan into action. "That's a pity," she began, trying to sound sorry for Emily's sake. "We don't know what time the service starts at and we can't stand about here all evening. We will freeze to death. My toes are numb already. We should just go back home again. We can always return some other time."

Emily was having none of it.

"There!" she cried, as though in triumph, pointing to a notice board encased in glass and fixed to the front wall of the building. "It says here, 'Gospel Service. 6. 30 pm.' That's not long to wait."

"Not long!" her mum blurted out in reply. "That's more than half-an-hour! I am already frozen to the marrow! What will I be like in half-an-hour?"

It was true, too. Although Debbie had piled on her new Sunday-go-to-church outfit, long skirt to her feet and two sweaters with anorak over, she was already shivering and her teeth were chattering.

Nanny sensed a mounting conflict of interest between her daughter and her granddaughter. She was anxious not to be seen to 'take sides,' and so came up with a compromise solution. "Let us wait for another ten minutes," she suggested. "And if nobody has turned up by that time we will decide what we are going to do then."

Debbie and Emily both agreed that it was a sensible proposition and pulled their clothes tightly in around them in preparation for their ten minute endurance test. They didn't have to wait their self-allotted time, however, for in less than five minutes a little man appeared. He walked up to the door of the church and produced a long key from his overcoat pocket.

Immediately aware of the shivering trio beside him he greeted them cheerily. "Oh hello. Are you new around here? Come on in and get yourselves warmed. I'm the pastor here, and I'm really glad to see you," he said, questions and invitations all tumbling out and over each other in a torrent of genuine welcome.

As soon as he had opened the door and ushered Emily, and her mum Debbie, and her mum Eileen, all inside, the pastor switched on the lights in what was obviously the large room in which the service was to be held. Walking on ahead of the three, who weren't quite sure of what to do next, or where to sit, he dragged three chairs across to a radiator, saying as he did so, "Come on over here and warm yourselves. You must have been frozen standing out there waiting. It will be a minute or two yet before anybody else arrives. Some of our folks leave it until nearly the last minute before they turn up!"

He then went off to make final preparations for the start of the service, leaving Debbie and her mum and daughter to hold their hands and feet up to the radiator by turns in an attempt to restore the throb of life to those numbed extremities.

It was comforting to feel heat return to their bodies, and even more reassuring to feel genuinely welcome. The pastor's earlier greeting had a relaxed sincerity about it that had made them feel instantly at home, and as other members of the congregation began to arrive their reaction to the trio that had appeared unexpectedly in their midst was exactly the same.

Everybody, both young and old, came across to speak to their thawing-out visitors.

"It's great to see you," an elderly gentleman said. "You are very welcome." His wife nodded her head so vigorously in agreement that her white hair flopped and her glasses nearly fell off.

"I take it this is your first time in our church," a much younger Indian lady with sparkling dark eyes and a perfect mouthful of shiny white teeth observed as an opener. She then went on to say, "But whether it is or not we are delighted to have all three of you with us."

And so it went on.

As they came in, the congregation greeted each other with unmistakeable warmth, and then came over, either singly or in small groups, to welcome Debbie, Emily and Eileen. Never in her long-gone nursing or business careers had Debbie ever seen such a multiracial gathering of patently happy people all in the same place at the same time. There seemed to be at least one representative of every ethnic group in Wolverhampton present. It looked from where the three ladies were sitting that people from every colour and culture in the world, whether Indian or West Indian, Chinese or Mediterranean, and ranging in age from under nine to over ninety, had come in through the doors behind them. What Debbie found utterly amazing was that they were all mingling and chatting away with each other, and their English friends, in one big unrehearsed demonstration of mutual contentment. They gave the appearance of having been really glad to get there. It was as though it really meant something to all of them.

It was immediately obvious to Debbie that these people possessed some secret formula for living that neither she, nor the people with whom she had been associating for the most of her life, had ever discovered. This was manifested in an inexplicable combination of sincerity and transparency. As they came and looked her in the face and said, 'I'm glad to see you,' they sounded as though they really meant it. The colour of their skin was irrelevant, for it was the look in their earnest eyes that convinced Debbie. These people were clean, untainted, through and through. They had no second, ulterior agenda, nothing to lie about, nothing to hide. It was a long time since anybody had looked Debbie in the face and been so totally genuine.

The fact that she had all the appearance of a malnourished scarecrow didn't seem to make the slightest bit of difference to them, either. It didn't matter that she had to wear two sweaters and an anorak to make her look as though she had the body of a woman. Nor did they appear to notice the over-generous application of make-up on her face to cover the yellow skin and the unsightly scabs.

Debbie was quite convinced that the words 'disgusting drop out' or 'despicable drug-addict' didn't belong in their vocabulary. It struck her that they were glad to accept her, sorry specimen of humanity that she was, as a valued addition to their Sunday evening congregation.

When it became clear that the service was about to begin, Emily, and the two older women whom she had coerced into coming along with her, left their haven of heat at the radiator and moved their chairs back into one of the rows facing towards the front. This afforded Debbie a brief opportunity to survey her surroundings.

The floor was covered in a green carpet, the congregation were all seated, not in pews as in the few churches Debbie had already been to in her turbulent life time, but on individual padded chairs, and the heat of the air certainly contributed to the warmth of the atmosphere.

There was a big map of the world on the wall just over to her right. White strings radiated from pins in the centre of it to pins all around the edges of it. The perimeter pins served a dual purpose, for in addition to being the destination of the divergent strings they had also been used to affix photographs of smiling people to the wall as well. The three-word title of the chart revealed its purpose. It invited anyone who was sufficiently interested to 'Pray For Us.'

As she allowed her eyes to scan around the walls Debbie was struck with the simplicity of the décor in the large meeting-room. It was so uncluttered compared with other churches.

Where were the candles? Where were the crosses? Where were the images of Jesus and the Virgin Mary? Where were the stained glass windows?

Turning her attention from the walls to focus on the front of the church presented Debbie with another problem. There were three men up on the platform and it seemed that all three of them were preparing to take at least some part in the proceedings, One was the little man who had welcomed them so warmly when he had found them out shivering on the doorstep, the man who had called himself the 'pastor.' Was that something like a vicar or a priest?

There was a West Indian man and a Punjabi man up there as well, though. What were they all going to be doing? Why were none of them wearing robes? Or even a round collar? This was all so different. What would the service be like?

Having taken stock of the front and sides of the church interior, Debbie turned half-round in her chair to find out how much of the back wall she could see. What clues might it afford to the nature of the service soon to commence?

Over by the door there was a poster advertising the Sunday
School Christmas Carol Service, which was due to take place in
two weeks time. Whoever had made the poster must have had
an ample supply of coloured foil. Three, what were obviously
supposed to be kings wearing long robes and shiny, overly-
pointy crowns of different colours sat stiffly on stiff-legged
camels. They were all gazing towards a cluster of distant flat-
roofed buildings. The night scene was illuminated by a large
silver star, which was shedding shafts of glistering light from
the top right-hand corner down across the sleeping town.

When she had finished admiring the poster Debbie had to
turn almost right round to read the words emblazoned across
the back wall. They constituted the only item of the church's
wall displays that she hadn't yet seen, and when she looked at
them she was to find that the words of the text on view up there
set her wondering, wandering mind strangely at ease.

Someone had cut out a series of huge gold letters and stuck
them to the wall. The arrangement of the letters was significant,
however, for they spelt out, with an elegant authority, 'JESUS
CHRIST IS LORD.'

If they worship Jesus Christ in this place, Debbie assured
herself, it will be all right. It must be O.K.

13

GRACE THAT BLOWS ALL FEAR AWAY

When the service began it was a complete change from anything Debbie, Emily or Eileen had ever been used to before. Their only experience of church up until that moment had been in a very formal tradition. They were accustomed to large, architecturally elaborate buildings bedecked with religious icons, in which an austere God was worshipped by means of a series of rituals and ceremonies.

This, though, was entirely different.

The West Indian man on the platform welcomed everybody warmly, including particularly 'our friends who are with us for the first time this evening.' He then announced the first hymn, which he invited everyone to 'sing heartily to the glory of God.' Debbie didn't know the words but she couldn't fail to recognise the enthusiasm with which the congregation responded to the chairman's request. The room reverberated with the sound of spirited singing and lively music, including the accompaniment that had attracted Emily, the tambourines.

After the singing was finished the West Indian man prayed, and his prayer was another eye-opener to Debbie, her daughter and her mum. This man was talking to God as though he knew Him personally, and so expected his prayers to be answered. He wasn't creeping timidly, almost apologetically, into the presence of some distant deity, hoping to be granted a hearing. His prayer was a confident, but respectful approach, like that of a son to a father whom he held in high esteem, but in whose company he felt extremely comfortable.

Before the end of that prayer Debbie had learnt three things about God. They came, not as a list of lesson points, one, two, three, but as an overall impression of the power of a Divine Presence. She would happily acknowledge that God was real, God was in this place, and God was in these people.

It was then the turn of the Punjabi man to address the congregation. His job seemed to be to make the announcements, for he talked about a whole range of other meetings and activities due to take place in the church 'in the run-up to Christmas.' Debbie could understand about the Sunday School Carol Service, for she had already been made aware of it by a set of camel-riding kings, and could envisage it, but she wasn't so sure what form a 'mid-week Bible study' or a Luncheon Club, might take.

Having completed his list of announcements, the church secretary introduced the two girls who were going 'to come forward' and lead them 'in worship.' With that, two young women, one English and the other West Indian, stepped up on to the platform and took a microphone each. They then invited the audience 'to stand and join us in praising the Lord in song.'

As Debbie stood with the others, watching as the words of the first song were projected onto a screen at the front of the church, she was touched. The infectious commitment of the congregation, not only to the music, but also to the content of the pieces, made a stunning impact on her.

The service had only been going for fifteen minutes and nobody had yet read the Bible or preached a sermon, but before she had heard the people all around her sing the second of their 'worship songs,' Debbie had made a further potentially life-transforming discovery. It had come dawning into her distressed soul, like the rays of the rising sun cracking open a bank of grey cloud, over a grey sea, to usher in the light and warmth of a new day.

Having come to a realisation of the reality of an all-knowing, all-loving God, Debbie had come to recognise, from the radiant attitude of those around her, that it was possible to have a meaningful and interactive relationship with Him. This was not confined, as she had once imagined, to holy men, like pastors or priests. Ordinary human beings like herself could make an individual approach to God, and live having Him as the vital controlling force in their lives.

She, Debbie Forrest, could come into personal contact with Almighty God, and actually know Him!

This was mind-boggling!

The words of the third piece in which the two vivacious young ladies with the mikes led the congregation had a profound effect on Debbie. As they were sung with such feeling she was overcome with the message they conveyed. It was as though God had chosen to speak directly to her. She stumbled to get her mouth around the words and her mind around their meaning…

'Lord I lift your Name on high,
Lord I love to sing your praises,
I'm so glad You're in my life,
I'm so glad You came to save us.

You came from heaven to earth to show the way,
From the earth to the cross; my debt to pay,
From the cross to the grave; from the grave to the sky,
Lord, I lift your Name on high.'

By the time one of the girls at the front had raised a hand in the air and called out, "Again!" tears had begun to trickle down Debbie's face. It was the words, 'From the earth to the

cross; my debt to pay,' that were getting to her. That was what
the man in Bilston market had told her. He had said that her sins
could be forgiven, for Jesus had come from heaven to earth to
die on a cross to bear the punishment for them, and God
wouldn't punish two people for the same set of sins.

'My debt to pay.' That was it again, in a nutshell.

The congregation launched into singing the chorus a
second time and by then Debbie felt that she was breaking up.
It wasn't with the mind-splintering chaos of heroin, however,
but with the emotional impact of the concept that none less a
personage than the Son of God Himself should come from
heaven to earth to die on a cross for her. Just for her, and her
sins, and she had plenty of them!

It's not a bit of wonder these people around me are lifting
their hands in the air as they sing, 'Lord, I lift your Name on
high,' she thought. Why wouldn't they after all? They know
Him, and love Him, and want to thank Him, and praise Him, on
and on and on.

Debbie was glad when the piece was finished, for all she
wanted to do was sit down and bow her head in contrition. That
wasn't to be, though. At least not just yet. Some of the more
elderly people around the church had dropped silently back on
to their seats, but a further call from the front meant the
majority of the congregation remained standing.

'Just one more,' the West Indian lady proclaimed in a voice
that implied she had no desire to stop at all, but recognised that
she and her companion were merely the supporting cast. The
star item, the preaching by the pastor, was billed for later in the
programme. "Let's sing, 'Jesus, what a beautiful Name,'" she
announced.

A new set of words flashed up on to the screen and the first
bars of another tune were played, as though to welcome their
arrival.

As the congregation began to sing them Debbie stood
holding on to the chair in front of her for support. Her arms and
legs had begun to tremble. She couldn't utter a word. She was
stunned into silence, rendered speechless, by what she was

seeing before her and hearing beside her. Everyone was singing, with reverent appreciation,

> Jesus, what a beautiful name,
> Son of God, Son of man,
> Lamb that was slain,
> Joy and peace, strength and hope
> Grace that blows all fear away,
> Jesus, what a beautiful name.

> Jesus, what a beautiful name,
> Truth revealed, my future sealed
> Healed my pain
> Love and freedom, life and warmth,
> Grace that blows all fear away,
> Jesus, what a beautiful name.

The last line but one in each of the verses they had just sung seemed to pop up in power to Debbie. 'Grace that blows all fear away.' She had spent her life in fear.

There had been the fear of death, and by contrast the fear of continued life, and what it might bring.

There had been the fear of failure, and the fear of being found out.

There had been the fear of rejection, and even the fear of rising in the morning, to face the mental turmoil and physical torture of another day.

Fear. Fear. Fear. Her life had been lived in a constant state of dread.

Now these people were singing so wholeheartedly about, 'Grace that blows all fear away.'

When they came to the last verse Debbie was weeping openly. Why Emily had been so insistent that they should come to this 'tambourine church,' or why the singing of a few 'worship songs' had such an overwhelming effect upon her, she could not explain. All she knew was that it was happening.

It seemed that some Mighty Power, outside of herself, was at work in her mind, her body, her emotions and her spirit all at once, triggering a reaction over which she had no control. She was being carried along on a tsunami of supernatural sensation.

Virtually every word of that closing verse stuck in her heart. It was hard to see the screen through her tears, but she could hear those beside her as they sang,

> Jesus, what a beautiful name
> Rescued my soul, my stronghold
> Lifts me from shame,
> Forgiveness, security, power and love,
> Grace that blows all fear away,
> Jesus, what a beautiful name.

With the singing over it was time for all those still standing in the congregation to resume their seats, and Debbie flopped, rather than sat, down. She covered her scrawny face with her scrawny hands. They had just been singing about a number of things that Debbie had always longed for in her life. She wanted to be lifted from her shame. That yearning had been with her since childhood.

Then there were the four blessings she had never really known. Forgiveness for her sin. Security in life. Power to overcome evil. A sense of being deeply and truly loved.

Jesus, according to what they had just been expressing in the words of the modern hymn, could give her all of these. The pastor had taken the platform and was announcing his text for the evening, but Debbie didn't hear what it was. She was in a world of her own.

Bowing her head, she prayed. She wouldn't even have recognised it as a prayer at the time, for in her case it represented the impassioned plea of an anguished soul. Her earnest petition embodied some of the sentiments of the previous two hymns in one way another.

'Thank you Lord for coming to earth to die on the cross for me, to take away the debt of my sin," she began, both eagerly and earnestly.

"Lord, forgive me. Come into my heart and life," she went on to plead. "Give me Your power. Show me Your love. Make me Your child. I want to love You and thank You for all You have done for me."

The service was proceeding. The pastor was speaking, but Debbie heard little of what he was saying. She had just had a most wonderful experience.

Having poured out her heart to God she now felt a sense of tranquillity, the like of which she had never known in her entire life up until that moment, flood over her.

Debbie was saved.

Emily looked across at her mum. Her face was smeared and streaked with tear-soaked make-up, but yet she looked less tense and more relaxed that she had ever seen her for years. It looked as though she had been enveloped by an unmistakeable peace. She knew assuredly, and immediately, from the look of enlightenment that had spread over Debbie's face, that her prayers had been answered. Her mum was definitely not going to die.

At the close of the service the kind people of the church came across again, in friendly groups, to the three visitors, whom they had welcomed so warmly at the beginning, and whom they couldn't help but notice had been visibly moved by the service.

"I have just asked Jesus to come into my life," Debbie confessed to a number of them, smiling happily. A great weight had lifted from her heart and mind, and she was sure they would be pleased to hear about it.

They were thrilled, but only to be left totally astounded at what happened next.

"And so have I," Emily said. "When the pastor was speaking I trusted in Jesus too."

Debbie's mother, who had been standing quietly to the side, as some people were speaking to her daughter, then stepped forward and witnessed to having had the same experience. "During the service I also committed my life to God," she told them with just the hint of a tremble in her voice.

These confessions of faith caused the church members to embark upon an impromptu session of praise to the Lord. The women of three generations had come into their evening service unexpectedly, and all three of them had accepted Jesus as their Saviour, at different stages of the meeting, and prompted by different things that were said or sung!

It was a miracle! And what the genuinely delighted church members didn't know was that Debbie and her mum and daughter had been within minutes of turning to go home, even before the service began.

When the thanksgiving session was over, and after they had been invited by almost everyone to 'come back again next week,' Eileen, Debbie and Emily headed off out onto the snow-covered pavement to return home. Not one of them even felt the cold now, however.

A new sense of unity had descended on the group. Despite the age difference, and despite the emotional differences, which had once existed between both mothers and their daughters, they now had a common bond between them.

They were all daughters of the Living God, through faith in His Son, Jesus Christ.

On arriving home they sat and talked for hours.

This was something that Debbie hadn't done with her mum since early childhood.

And this was something that Emily hadn't been able to do with her mum since early childhood either.

There was so much to talk about, not least of which was each of their individual experiences of that evening. They were happy together for the first time in years, bonded invisibly, but eternally, in Christ.

It was almost two o'clock in the morning when Debbie retired to bed, and as she did so she felt unusually secure, wrapped around by the comforting love of God.

When she had asked Him to forgive her sins and endue her with His power, He had done that. He had answered her prayer and created a clean, a pure, heart within her.

The only problem was that it was a new heart in an old, battered and drug-addicted body.

How was Debbie going to cope with that in the days to come?

14

BIG DEAL

For the first week it was marvellous. Debbie knew that something momentous had happened within her. Her attitude had completely changed. Instead of considering the next drugs deal, or planning for her next 'hit', she focused her mind on trying to remember the words of the worship songs that had such a profound effect on her the previous Sunday evening.

They floated around in her head, in a glorious Hallelujah Chorus of praise. She was combining words and lines to express her untold gratitude to God, thinking things like,
'Lord I lift Your Name on high,
    Jesus, what a beautiful Name,'
Or...
'Lamb that was slain, my debt to pay,
Son of God, You showed me the way,'
Or...
'Grace that blows all fear away,
I'm so glad you're in my life.'

Every line, every thought, every word became an instrument with which to worship the Lord, who had suddenly become so precious to her. As days passed her desire to know more about Him intensified. She was aware that she was only paddling in the shallows of the ocean of God's love. There was so much more to learn about Jesus, and this new life and peace she had found in Him. She looked forward with eager anticipation to the following Sunday night.

Before leaving the previous Sunday evening she had promised the kind people down at the Apostolic 'tambourine' Church that she would come back. That promise had been made when on a spiritual, rather than a drug-induced, 'high' but as the week went on, she realised how important it was to her.

Debbie, Emily and Eileen went early for the service that evening and sat soaking up the atmosphere as others began to arrive. It was exactly the same as it had been the previous week. People came across to greet them with genuine warmth. They were not now welcoming a set of strangers in from the street, but two women and a girl whom they knew to be Christians like themselves. These were people whose lives had been touched by the power of God.

There was one person, however, whose welcome was to prove of lasting significance to Debbie, because she had put some thought into their meeting. This was a West Indian lady with braided hair who had come prepared to augment her greeting with a practical gift.

Debbie felt her heart melt in the width and warmth of her sunny smile as she said, "Here you are, Debbie. I feel that you have had big problems in your life and I have been praying especially for you all week. I hope you don't mind but I thought that I ought to buy you a Bible. Make sure you read it, for it is God's Word and it will help you in your Christian life."

With that introduction she placed a small, carefully-wrapped package on Debbie's lap. The new convert felt the tears well up in her eyes for the second week in a row, and the service hadn't even started yet! What kind of love would make this lady, whose name Debbie didn't even know, think about her, pray for her, and go out and buy her a Bible?

The service was exhilarating. Singing those worship songs that had brought her face to face with the claims of Christ on her life the previous week was like a satisfying meal to her spirit-filled God-hungry soul. And she hung on every word of the sermon. It was so refreshing to hear a passage from the Bible read and expounded. She could identify with it. She just wanted to learn more and more about it.

The kind lady, whom she was to discover was called Lynne, had given her the chance to do just that. When Jim was in the house the TV was kept blaring away all the time, whether anyone was watching it or not. Debbie had been quite happy with this background diversion before she had been given her precious little black Bible, but now things were different. As soon as Jim left the house for even the shortest of periods Debbie would have the TV off and be into her Bible.

All she wanted to do was read it and read it. She had no idea what would be the most appropriate place to read, so she read it anywhere and everywhere.

One evening she began to flick through the Book of Isaiah and was arrested by some words her eyes locked onto at the beginning of chapter 43. They seemed to pop off the page as though highlighted in bright red block capitals. They said,

'Fear not, for I have redeemed you;
I have called you by your name;
You are Mine.'

This was overwhelming. Debbie found that the person making this decree was 'the Lord who created you.' And He was telling her not to fear. Here was the 'grace that blows all fear away' concept all over again.

Why should she fear, anyway? It said that God had redeemed her. Debbie had to go to the dictionary for that one. She looked up the word 'redeem' and was astounded to discover that it meant 'to buy back, to set free, to free from sin.'

Here was the idea of 'my debt to pay,' all over again. God, in the person of his Son, Jesus, had actually bought her back and set her free from sin!

Nor was that all! The Lord, who created her, had not only redeemed her but He had called her personally, by name, to be His child.

'You are Mine,' it said.

It was mind-boggling. Debbie Forrest, cannabis-cultivator, heroin-addict, drug-dealer and erstwhile prostitute was now a child in the family of Almighty God!

Wow!

Her hands trembled as she read on,

'When you pass through the waters, I will be with you,
And through the rivers, they shall not overflow you,
When you walk through the fire, you shall not be burned,
Nor shall the flame scorch you.
For I am the Lord your God,
The Holy One of Israel, your Saviour…
Since you were precious in My sight,
You have been honoured,
And I have loved you;
Fear nor, for I am with you;'

Debbie wept as she read these words. They seemed more wonderful than anything she had ever read in her life. As she considered all the alcohol-alleviated self-abhorrence of her teenage years, and the subsequent downward slide into drug-engendered desperation, and then the fantastic pledges that these verses contained she was utterly flabbergasted.

'You were precious in My sight… You have been honoured… I will be with you.'

It sounded incredible, but she had found it in the Bible, and Lynne had said that the Bible was 'God's Word.'

These words and promises of Isaiah chapter 43 became Debbie's spiritual focus for days to come. Every time she lifted her Bible she turned to them and read them, before turning anywhere else. She would often copy the passage out on to a sheet of paper and attempt to memorise it, claiming it for her own. She appeared almost afraid that it would somehow escape into oblivion and cease to afford her its current level of consolation.

A few days after having discovered her keynote verses Debbie was travelling down to Aberystwyth in Wales to see her father, and was amusing herself by reading them in the Bible, then closing the book, and writing them out from memory. It seemed that every time she had done so, for the past sixty hours or so, she had unearthed another gleaming spiritual gem in them.

The lady sitting across from her in the carriage was intrigued. What kind of a strange carry on is this, she must have wondered. Eventually, unable to curb her curiosity any longer, she enquired, "Excuse me, but if you don't mind me asking, what is that you are doing?"

Debbie looked up from her activity, mildly startled. "Oh, I'm writing out some lovely verses. I am trying to learn every word of them. They are what God says in the Bible," she replied, all in one excited breath. She had just commenced her third transcript so she thought for a moment and then, recognising that she could probably spare one, went on, "Here, would you like a copy?"

The woman appeared a little taken aback as a writing-pad page, covered in close, neat script was pushed across towards her. She reached out and took it, nonetheless.

Then, after having read it down twice, she muttered something about it being 'very nice,' folded it over once and consigned it to the depths of a rather posh-looking handbag with a definite click.

It would be a pity, she reckoned, to offend this very friendly religious freak. Who knows but perhaps she had learning difficulties, or maybe she was just going through an Adult Education Programme and had only recently learnt to write. Whatever her problem, writing out the same words out of her book over and over again was a harmless activity, and she seemed to be deriving a tremendous 'kick' from it.

Soon, though, Debbie's mind and body began to scream out for a return to their old source of 'kicks.'

A struggle ensued.

Sinister, faraway voices, deep in her head, were calling out for a 'fix.' These became gradually more insistent and more compelling. The body, which had become accustomed to its daily dose of drugs, had begun to rebel at this sudden shutdown in supply.

Debbie tried to stifle this renewed craving through prayer, crying, in every sense of the word, to God for help. She tried to shout down the continuing clamour in her mind by quoting her favourite verses.

It worked for a while. There would be a period of relative calm, then she would wake up with a start in the middle of the night and the voices were there again. Hammering away in her head, coaxing, cajoling, compelling… 'Just one hit… A single spliff… It won't do you any harm, just this once… You have the 'gear' here in the house…You can still read your Bible if you like…'

 On and on it went.

Debbie was distraught. This had never happened to her before. A month earlier if she had wanted a 'fix' and could pay for it, she had it, and that was it. No question. Now, though, this new life she had received the night she was saved, was battling fiercely against the suggestion of any return to her former habits.

It felt as though some enterprising promoter had decided to stage the world wrestling championships in the middle of her brain.

'I have called you by your name, you are Mine,' the voice of her spirit was saying.

'If we don't get a shot of heroin or crack to keep us going, we will drive you crazy in a day or two. Just you wait,' the tormenting voices in her head would reply, instantly and insistently.

At last, one agonised evening, Debbie succumbed.

She mixed up some crack cocaine on a spoon, transferred it into a needle and injected it into her neck. All through this process of preparation she felt strangely detached from what she was doing. Something within her didn't want to be involved in it, and yet her eyes and her hands continued carrying out all their necessary functions in spite of this inner reluctance. Debbie had no enthusiasm for what she was doing but felt forced into it by the endless voices that claimed her mind was about to be swamped in a sea of insanity, and that a 'hit' of cocaine would launch a lifeboat.

Ten minutes after injecting the cocaine Debbie had to lie down. Something weird was happening to her. Her face had turned ashen white. The only colour left on it was in her lips, which had changed from being red to an unnatural dark blue. Her hands and feet felt extremely cold and when Debbie looked down at her hands she discovered that her fingernails had also turned blue.

The most frightening aspect of this sudden seizure, however, was the pain and tightness in her chest. It felt as though it was being pumped up with a bicycle pump and would explode at any minute.

Debbie recalled her short career as a coronary care nurse. She had listened to a lot of heartbeats in her time, but had never come across what was happening to her own heart at that moment. It appeared to be quivering rather than beating, vibrating rather than pulsating.

She had caved in and opted for a shot of cocaine to stop her from going mad. Now she was gripped with a sense of blind panic. 'I am going to die here,' she thought. 'And I don't want to die. I love Jesus, but I have gone and messed everything up all over again. Why can I never do anything right?'

Since her conversion, nearly three weeks before, Debbie had found solace in prayer. The people in the church had emphasised the importance and the privilege of 'talking to God' at all times, about everything. So it was to God that she turned in her moment of torment and failure.

Lying on top of her bed, with her mind in a spin and her body in shock, she cried out in anguish, "Lord, if You can keep me from dying here, I will serve You forever."

It was a massive commitment, but that was the deal.

Having made that vow, Debbie lay panting for breath, and when that passed she remained there motionless, for she was almost afraid to move, in case she would be struck down dead.

When an anxious hour or two had dragged by, the pain in her chest began to ease and what for her was 'normal colour' returned.

The trauma had passed.

God had spared her life. He had kept His part of the bargain.

Now all that remained was for Debbie to keep hers.

15

AMPLIFIED MEANS LOUD!

Debbie dearly wanted to keep her pledge. The forces of evil, though, that had controlled her every movement for so long, were loath to release her into the service of her new Master.

It became a constant, frustrating battle. She tried repeatedly to rid herself of the trappings of her former life, but found it unbelievably difficult.

Her mother and father, both living in separate locations, offered to help. On more than one occasion Debbie went down to stay with her mum, who had moved in with her granddad, so that she could be out of the drug-centred environment in which Jim and she lived. There she would shut herself off from the world, and immerse herself in the study of the Bible.

This worked for a short period. Then after a while her seemingly insatiable addictions would raise their ugly heads and doggedly demand satisfaction once more.

There were other times when she determined to lock herself away and put herself through the mental and physical torture of 'cold turkey.' Debbie longed to have her life completely cleaned up, so that she could 'serve the Lord forever, 'as she had promised, with her entire body, mind and spirit.

In an attempt to achieve this aim she made two separate journeys down to Wales. There she asked her dad to isolate her in his cottage and only bring her food every now and then.

Debbie was determined to break the strong ropes that were binding her to her addictions. But couldn't. Both times in Wales she thought she had succeeded, but when she returned to her old haunts in Wolverhampton was soon back to her old habits.

Since the night of her conversion Debbie had found it simple to stop swearing. Her language had become influenced by the beautiful words she had begun to memorise from the Bible. The enslavement to drink, drugs and cigarettes were turning out to be much harder to abandon, however. They had been more than an added extra in her life for the previous number of years. They had been her staple diet.

Despite the war being waged within her, Debbie seldom missed a Sunday service at the Apostolic Church. She loved to worship the Lord, and looked forward to being in the company of the people there, for she had always found them to be very understanding.

In the summer of 1997 the ladies of the church invited Debbie to join them in a weekend retreat for women in Staffordshire. She was pleased to be asked and immediately accepted, glad to be able to shut herself away, not to endure 'cold turkey,' but to enjoy Christian fellowship, for a few days.

Debbie was delighted to find that she was sharing a room with Lynne who had given her the Bible that she had come to cherish. Lynne had always shown her genuine love and concern, assuring her at every opportunity, "I remember you in prayer every day, Debbie."

During the course of the weekend Debbie met a number of other Christian ladies, and two of them, Pat and Hazel, made a point of ensuring that the struggling convert felt welcome and wanted.

When Hazel heard Debbie's story she took her into a room late on the Saturday afternoon saying, "I have something I would like to show you."

When Debbie had sat down on the chair to which her new friend had pointed casually, at the end of a table, Hazel produced a book, which she was handling with great respect. She set it down in front of Debbie, who, on catching a glimpse of the word BIBLE on the cover, enquired, "Another Bible. And what's this one?"

In her relatively short Christian career she had already encountered, or had recommended to her, the Authorised Version of the Bible, The Revised Standard Version of the Bible, The New International Version of the Bible, the Woman's Devotional Bible, The Spirit-Filled Bible, The Living Bible and the New American Standard Bible. There seemed to be dozens of different Bibles. Why, she often wondered, could there not be just ONE Bible in the English language? It would make life so much easier for floundering, detoxing, new believers.

"That's the Amplified Bible," Hazel explained.

"Amplified. What does that mean," Debbie was anxious to know.

"Amplified just means 'loud,'" Hazel replied.

Debbie raised her eyebrows quizzically and made no further comment. Certainly God had spoken to her clearly through the Bible Lynne had given her before Christmas, but she was curious to know why anybody would need a 'loud' Bible. Perhaps there were a lot of deaf Christians about…

Her reverie was interrupted when Hazel reached across and pulled the hard-backed Bible towards her. "There is a Psalm I would like to share with you," she said, as she flicked over the pages. After a short shuffle back and forward through the middle of the book she found the Psalm she was looking for. It was number 103.

"Just listen to this," she invited, and began to read,

'Bless affectionately, gratefully praise the Lord, O my soul;
And all that is deepest within me, bless His holy name!

Bless affectionately, gratefully praise the Lord, O my soul,
And forget not one of all His benefits...'

Recognising that Debbie was straining across to see, as well as hear, what she was reading, Hazel paused, then slid the Bible back over to the obviously eager young woman and said, "Here, Debbie. Would you like to read it yourself? Perhaps you could read it out to me."

Debbie ran her finger down the margin of the page until she came to where Hazel had left off, and began to read the next verse aloud,

'Who forgives every one of all your iniquities,
Who heals each one of all your diseases,
Who redeems your life from the pit and corruption...'

As she spoke these words Debbie's voice began to crack and falter. This Psalm was having an Isaiah 43 effect on her. Every phrase contained an exquisite description of God's love and mercy. All her sins forgiven, all her diseases healed. Her life bought back and set free from corruption.

Debbie had been transported into adoring wonder mode once more.

Having basked in the beauty of those precious truths for a moment she read on and came across another set of words that completely took her breath away...

'Who beautifies, dignifies, and crowns you with loving-kindness and tender mercy...'

She didn't even try to stumble on any further. Instead, she stopped and went back to savour these concepts a second time,

'Who beautifies... dignifies... and crowns you...'

These were inspiring words. Read slowly they hung in the air, entered the ear and charmed the heart.

Debbie, who was engaged in a soul and strength-sapping struggle with addiction and still looked gaunt and strained, had been beautified!

Debbie, who had lost all sense of personal dignity and self-esteem as an abused child, had been dignified!

Debbie, who had more convictions and court appearances on drugs charges than she even cared to count, had been crowned… 'with loving-kindness and tender mercy…'

It was too much. Debbie broke down and wept.

Hazel and she sat there for more than half-an-hour as Debbie lingered over Psalm 103, basking in the beauty of its images.

The caring lady may have got her meaning of the word amplified somewhat mixed up, but the passage which she had felt constrained to bring to Debbie's attention, had certainly spoken 'loudly' to her.

Debbie left that weekend with a dual determination. She was definitely going to break with drugs once and for all, and she was going to read her Bible even more.

The spiritual impetus that the weekend had given her helped in her battle with addiction. She went through 'cold turkey' yet another time and stayed drug-free for more than three months. That was her longest period ever without a 'fix' of any kind and in that time she enjoyed reading the scriptures and praying to God.

Then, just when she thought she was clear, clean and free she slipped up again. It was the same old story. The voices in her head, the craving, the capitulation, and back to square one.

This constant, on-off, forward-and-back encounter with drug-dependence continued all through the winter and into the following spring.

Her friends down at the Apostolic Church could see what was happening in Debbie's life and were consistently supportive. They recognised that she was trying desperately to live the Christian life, but couldn't. She was like a bird chained to a perch, flapping frantically in its inborn desire to soar and be free, but unable to do so because of a binding restriction. Her soul had been saved but her mind hadn't yet been totally transformed, or her body cleansed from drugs.

One Sunday morning in May 1998, as Debbie was leaving the church, the pastor gave her a piece of paper, with the comment, "I have just heard of a place that could possibly help you, Debbie. It is called Hope House and it is in South Wales. A Christian group called Teen Challenge runs it. All the details are there, on that bit of paper. You might want to get in touch with them some time"

Debbie thanked him very much, folded the sheet of paper in two, and slipped it into her Bible. 'It was very good of the pastor to think of me,' she mused on the way back home. 'They are really interested in me, all those people in the church. I must give that Hope House place a ring one of these days and see what they have to say. It would be great if they could help me.'

That was her intention.

On arriving home, though, she became involved in other things and forgot all about it.

16

YOU HAVE TO GO, DEBBIE!

A few weeks later, one Sunday in the middle of June, Debbie arrived in from the morning service in the Apostolic Church. She had been particularly moved by the pastor's message that day and began telling Jim about it enthusiastically. While doing so, however, she was busy rolling herself a heroin 'spliff.'

Her boyfriend was listening to what she was saying, and watching what she was doing, and her actions didn't seem to match her words. They didn't belong together, as far as he was concerned.

"God doesn't like it you know, Debbie," he began. It was time, he felt, to express his feelings on the matter. Despite all the rows and arguments they had been through, Jim loved Debbie, and knew the struggle she was having. He had often sat discussing issues from the Bible with her long into the night, and yet there were other times when she had asked him to bring her some drugs to keep her from going mad.

"Doesn't like what?" Debbie enquired, feigning ignorance. She had a fair idea what was coming.

"You ought to know by now that you can't mess with God," Jim went on. "Are you a Christian or not? That is what you have to decide. Going to church, and then coming home to sit there and tell me about the love of God for a sinful world and smoking a spliff at the same time. One night last week you were trying to read me something out of the Bible and you had to blow the ash from the crack pipe you had been using off it before you could open it! It doesn't add up."

He was right. Debbie knew he was right. She had been living a double life, but had also been battling unsuccessfully to do something about it. It was most disheartening, and to have Jim point out what she already knew, merely served to 'rub salt into the wound.'

"So what do you think I should do then?" she cried out in utter exasperation. "It's impossible. You know that I'm trying. And what's more, God knows that I'm trying. I have gone through 'cold turkey,' I think it must be about fourteen times now. And I keep slipping back."

"I don't know what you should do. All I know is that you can't go on being a hypocrite. Make up your mind. Are you a Christian? Or are you a junkie? You are either one or the other, but you can't be both," Jim replied, matching Debbie's understandable frustration with his own uncompromising conviction.

Debbie sat in silence for a few minutes and then remarked, not to anybody in particular, but as though thinking out loud, "I wonder if that place in Wales would be able to help?"

"What place in Wales?" Jim asked. "What are you talking about?"

" I have just remembered that one Sunday around a month ago the pastor gave me some information about a centre in Wales. He said it was for women with addiction problems, and that I should think about getting in touch with them some time. I have the name and telephone number on a piece of paper he gave me, here in my Bible," Debbie explained.

She then reached across to where she had left her Bible down, amidst all the clutter including packs of syringes, on the table, when she had come in from church. Picking it up she leafed through it until she came across, and then pulled out, a flattened, folded-in-two sheet of paper.

Opening it up she read out, "Hope House. Teen Challenge. There's a telephone number here too."

Jim, who had been lolling in one of their few chairs, sat up straight, as though startled. "Teen Challenge. Did I hear you say 'Teen Challenge' there?" he enquired eagerly.

Not quite sure what had sparked off this unusual interest in her normally fairly matter-of-fact boyfriend, Debbie repeated what she had just read out a moment or two earlier. "Hope House. Teen Challenge. That's what it says here. I think Hope House must be the name of the place and Teen Challenge is probably the group that runs it."

"You mean Teen Challenge. THE Teen Challenge!" Jim had become instantly and uncharacteristically animated. "Are you talking about the Teen Challenge of 'The Cross And The Switchblade'? Do you mean David Wilkerson's Teen Challenge?"

Debbie was suddenly all at sea. She had never heard of Teen Challenge before, not to mention David Wilkerson, whoever he was, or 'The Cross and The Switchblade,' whatever it was. "I haven't a clue what you are talking about, or what Teen Challenge it is," she replied. "All I know is that they have this place in Wales. And it's a rehab centre for women, and it's called Hope House."

Her last few words had been lost on Jim. He didn't appear even to have heard them. While Debbie was speaking he had jumped up and begun rummaging through a pile of books in the corner. Jim read a lot, but as Debbie and he didn't have money to spend on luxuries like bookcases when you had to budget for the necessities of life, like cannabis and cocaine, all his reading material lay in various straggling heaps on the floor.

"Here it is! I've found it! I was sure I still had it!" he exclaimed after having made one untidy pile into three smaller, but equally untidy, piles. A collection of paperback books with faded covers had just finished sliding about, around his feet.

Jim took two steps across to where Debbie was sitting, clutching his unearthed treasure. When he held it up in front of her face she discovered that it was a book. The cover was a golden colour, with what looked like a city skyline at sunset, in the background. There were what were obviously meant to be a pair of crossed daggers in the foreground.

The title of the book was, 'The Cross and the Switchblade.'

The author was David Wilkerson.

Holding the book with his hand clasped around the back of it so that Debbie could get a full view of the cover, Jim waved it gently to and fro in front of her before launching into another vigorous enquiry. "Could you possibly mean this Teen Challenge? 'The Cross And The Switchblade' Teen Challenge? I read this book in prison, Debbie, and it is powerful. Could this place in Wales be part of the same outfit?"

"I don't honestly know," Debbie told him hesitantly. She was rather bewildered. It was most unlike Jim to become unduly excited about a book, especially one he hadn't even seemed interested enough in to tell her about before now.

"Well, can you find out?" he persisted.

"Yes. I suppose I could ring the number on the page here," Debbie replied.

"Do it then," Jim instructed. It was clear that he was keen for Debbie to pursue the subject. "Go on. What is keeping you? Ring them now."

Recognising that she had nothing to lose, and the prospect of perhaps having something to gain, from doing as was urging, Debbie picked up the telephone and dialled the number on the piece of paper she still had in her hand.

A woman's voice answered, quoting the number she had just called.

"Hello," Debbie began. "Is that Hope House?"

"Yes," the voice replied. "It is. How can I help you?"

"I have a question," Debbie went on, looking across at Jim who was following her every word intently. "Are you the same

Teen Challenge as the David Wilkerson Teen Challenge? I have a book here called, ' The Cross And The Switchblade.' Are you part of the same organisation?"

"Yes, we are," the lady's voice assured the interested caller, and her even more interested boyfriend.

"Thank you very much, that's all I need to know in the meantime," Debbie said and switched off the phone.

Jim looked her straight in the eye, before she had been given the slightest chance to give her own reaction to this recent information, and said, "You have to go, Debbie. You have to go!"

"It would probably be a good idea," Debbie agreed. "But I'd like to know a bit more about the place before I sign up."

The prospect of finding help in Hope House was always at the back of Debbie's mind in the next couple of months, especially as she kept recalling Jim's painfully accurate description of her position.

'You can't go on being a hypocrite,' he had said.

'Are you a Christian or junkie? It's about time you made up your mind,' he had advised.

In August, Debbie had the idea to do some personal research into the location of Hope House and what actually went on there. She had gone down to spend a few days with her dad in Aberystwyth, and discovered that by taking three separate bus journeys she could reach the village of Gorslas, where the Christian rehabilitation centre for women was situated.

She found Hope House easily, and when inside knocked on the door marked, 'Manager.'

A lady opened the door and greeted her with a friendly, "Hello. Lovely to see you. And what can I do for you?"

"My name's Debbie Forrest," the visitor on the reconnaissance mission volunteered. "I am a Christian, but I still have a problem with drugs. My church recommended that I should contact you. I am on holiday in Wales and I thought I would give you a call."

"That's great," the welcoming lady at the door of the office replied. "I'm Audrey Rankin, the manager here. Come on in for a chat."

She then showed Debbie to a seat, and returned to her position behind a desk before continuing, "It was good of you, Debbie, to make all that effort to look us up. Now tell me a bit about yourself."

Debbie didn't find that difficult. She liked this woman, Audrey, immediately and instinctively. There was something genuine about her gentleness, and yet it was also clear that she carried with her an admirable aura of authority. It was difficult to explain the effect she had on Debbie, but the desperate to detox Christian crack-addict was instantly at ease with her.

They both sat back and Audrey listened intently, commenting only occasionally, while Debbie told her story. And what a story it was! A distressing childhood, a rebellious teenage, a promising career cut short by a cannabis conviction, the descent into drugs, salvation, struggling… and now here.

When Debbie had finished Audrey said, "You have come to the right place. We can definitely help you."

"Thanks," Debbie replied. "The pastor back at my church in Wolverhampton said you probably could."

With the details of this prospective new resident firmly implanted in her mind, Audrey then asked, "Would you like to have a look around, Debbie?"

"I would love to," came the rapid response. That was, after all, one of the main reasons why she had come.

"Well, just leave your handbag there on your chair and we will take a walk and let you see some of the rooms," Audrey said. She was afraid that someone, stepping in from the big outside world as Debbie had done, could be carrying either drugs or cigarettes in her bag, and could be asked, or tempted, to share them with the girls on her programme.

The manager appreciated would-be entrants who appeared eager, and the two of them set out on what for Debbie was to be her fact-finding tour of Hope House. She was shown the dining-room, the classrooms, the bedrooms, and the chapel. There were young women engaged in a variety of activities around the house, but it was what was going on in the common room that made a lasting impact on her. There a group of young women had been paired off with a basin between them and a towel each and were washing each others' feet.

"We are doing this as a one-off practical example to illustrate what Jesus taught about serving one another in John's Gospel," Audrey explained, aware of Debbie's fascination with this, what she considered rather unorthodox activity.

When they returned to the office for Debbie to pick up her handbag before setting out on her three-bus return to her dad's, the manger had something else to give her. It was a copy of the Hope House rule book. She passed this on with the comment, "You might like to have a read at that later, Debbie. It tells you a bit about how we operate, and the standards we expect."

Debbie thanked her and they said 'Goodbye' to each other. Audrey's last words before they parted were, "There will be a place for you here at any time, Debbie. Just give me a ring a day or two before you want to come and I will make sure you get a bed."

It was unusual for Audrey to make such an outright promise to anyone, but just as she had made an instant impact on Debbie, so, in almost the very same way, Debbie had impressed her in a strangely inexplicable way.

As she watched the thirty-three year old receding down the short drive towards Church Road, her strawberry-blonde hair bouncing in the summer sunlight, Audrey muttered softly to herself, with heaven-sent intuition, "I'll see you again, Debbie. You'll be back. It was God who sent you here, and He has big plans for your life."

Debbie didn't share her confidence, however. By the time she had boarded the third bus she had already been through the Hope House rule book twice, and come to her own conclusion. This might be a Christian establishment but it sounded like a very strict regime to her.

No smoking… no swearing… no alcohol… no drugs… no dyed hair… no body piercings… no phone calls for the first month…

It wasn't all 'no' however. What could she actually do if she went there? Answer, she could go to lessons in the morning, a work programme in the afternoon, lessons again for an hour in the evening, and chapel twice in the day, first thing in the morning and last thing in the evening. And then, just to crown the day, she could put her light out at half-past-ten!

For someone used to her freedom, it all sounded a bit much. Debbie had seen a programme on TV a few months earlier about American 'boot-camps,' and her mind had turned immediately back to it as soon as she had begun reading the rule book.

This place had, she presumed, devised these extreme rules for extreme addicts, but she was surely not that bad.

Jim had told her that she definitely ought to go there, and Audrey sounded as if she would definitely like her to go there. She was sorry, though, but they were both in for a big disappointment.

She would not be going there.

Hope House was definitely not for her.

At least certainly not yet.

17

ONE AWFUL BIG MISTAKE

It was just after Christmas, 1998, and life had become decidedly bleak.

Debbie wasn't attending church regularly as once she had done, and although still reading her Bible at home, was gaining little from it. The promises that had once thrilled her soul seemed now nothing more than mere words. She had lost all zest for praising God for His goodness.

Just after ten o'clock one cold, wet morning in late December, Debbie had left Jim in bed to go out to a telephone kiosk and order some crack cocaine. She knew the dealer's number off by heart, but she also had the Hope House number in her pocket. Although she had decided during the summer that Hope House was probably not for her, as the winter had settled in and the light of her Christian life had disappeared with the darkening days, Debbie began to consider it again. So she carried the number about in her pocket. This afforded her a sense of ultimate assurance. It was like knowing there was a lifeboat to jump into if the storm wrecked the ship.

Debbie was feeling particularly low that morning. She felt physically ill, mentally depressed, socially isolated and spiritually detached. Nothing was right in her life.

Having ordered the crack from a dealer who lived nearby, Debbie agreed to wait in or near the telephone 'box' for a short time until her order was delivered. It was a raw morning, and since there were few others around she decided to shelter in the stale-smoke-laden atmosphere of the kiosk.

That was when she made up her mind. She would ring Hope House to see if they could take her. 'Even I am miserable, what difference will it make?' she thought to herself. 'I might as well be miserable there as miserable here.'

When the phone rang in Hope House Audrey lifted it. She rarely took telephone calls direct, but the girl whose job it was to answer the phone was otherwise engaged, and Debbie was delighted to hear a voice she recognised.

"Hello, Audrey," she began, not quite sure how best to word her request, having left it for five months since their last meeting before renewing contact. "This is Debbie Forrest. Do you remember me? I called to see you last summer."

"Yes of course I do, Debbie. How are you?" Audrey's response was reassuring, and she didn't sound at all surprised to take her call. It sounded as though she was just waiting for Debbie to ring. As though speaking to this bewildered junkie was the most important thing she had planned to do that day.

"I'm not very well, to be honest with you," Debbie replied. 'In fact I'm in bad shape and sick, sore and tired of all of this. I was wondering if you would have a place for me in Hope House sometime, the sooner the better?"

"Of course we would," Audrey answered without even stopping to think about it. "I told you last August that we would always find a bed for you, and I meant it. When would you like to come?"

Faced with such an immediate and unconditional offer Debbie decided to play for time and give herself another few days in which to come to terms with the idea. "Sometime in the next week or two, if that would be O.K.," she said.

"That will be fine," Audrey told the disconsolate Christian with the devastating drugs problem. "Come in on Monday the tenth of January."

With the day arranged for Debbie to be admitted to Hope House Audrey rang off with a cheery, "Looking forward to seeing you again soon, Debbie. We will be praying for you in the meantime. God bless you."

When Debbie told her mum and some of their friends from the Apostolic Church that she had finally contacted, and been accepted by, Hope House they arranged to drive her down from Wolverhampton to south Wales.

They set out on the long trip one morning during the first week in January and as they were travelling through an isolated part of the Brecon Beacons the car broke down. As they were considering how to resolve this challenging situation one of the men from the church remarked to Debbie's mum, "It looks as if the devil is determined to keep Debbie out of Hope House!" Eileen and Debbie both agreed with him, but they would have to make some alternative arrangements. It was by then late afternoon and darkness had already begun to drop, like an icy black blanket, over the encircling mountains. The only solution they could think of was to phone Debbie's dad, and ask him if he could come and take his daughter the remainder of the journey.

When they eventually succeeded in contacting him he agreed, if somewhat reluctantly, to try and find them and take Debbie on to her destination. "Mind you it will be two hours or so before I'm there," he warned before they rang off. His prediction was accurate, and those in the car had a long, cold, anxious wait.

Everyone was relieved when Debbie's dad turned up at last, and his daughter climbed into the back seat of his car, where she hoped to curl up and go to sleep. The others were then free to concentrate on their problem, which was how to get back to Wolverhampton.

It was late when Debbie and her dad arrived at Hope House.

When Audrey came out to meet them, Debbie's father, who had not been exactly thrilled to be contacted on a mid-winter evening to transport his drug-addicted daughter to a rehab centre, greeted her with, "I'm glad we've made it." Then, turning to point to the hunched up figure following him up from the car park, went on, "I have been driving for nearly a hundred miles with something out of 'The Exorcist' in the back seat of my car!"

When father had left Debbie in Audrey's care he stamped off, back to his car to return home. The manager of Hope House was shocked at the state of the young woman before her. She had lost weight from their summer time encounter. Debbie, though, had lost more than weight. Her fire had been extinguished too. The haggard, five-stone figure with the thin, wrinkled face and deep-sunk eyes looked ten years older than the bubbly person who had so impressed her five months before.

"Debbie, is that you?" Audrey asked, finding it hard to keep back the tears.

"Yes, it's me," came Debbie's embarrassed confession. "I'm ever so sorry."

There followed a painful, stressful five days during which Debbie was confined to bed going through yet another period of withdrawal. The symptoms were awful, the sickness was terrible and Debbie was always distressed.

When she had returned to some measure of normality the Hope House staff were pleased that Debbie had begun to eat again, and was showing evidence of spiritual restoration. She seemed to be always consulting her Bible and they took this as a positive sign.

What they did not realise was that although Debbie's physical appearance had begun to improve and she had actually started to put on weight, her mind set was still not right.

She had the feeling that all these committed Christian people, with their insistence that the Bible was the fundamental handbook of their spiritual teaching, were somehow trying to indoctrinate her. That was why she was checking everything out. It was not that her earlier fervour for the Word of God had returned, but rather that she was afraid of being brainwashed into the bizarre beliefs of some curious cult.

Debbie was suspicious, not only of all that was being taught, but also all that was being done for, and around her, in the first few weeks in Hope House. Coming into it from a criminal subculture where nobody trusted anybody, and where everything had its price, she believed that there was something sinister about the whole set up. Audrey and her team weren't putting up with all the hassles she and the other residents were subjecting them to, just because, as they claimed, they 'loved them for Jesus' sake.'

There had to be more to it, she reckoned. Were they keeping them under surveillance to pick out potential candidates for further training in the propagation of their quirky ideology? Or were they employed by the government to spy on them to learn about the drugs trade across the country?

With all these misgivings racing around in her mind, Debbie was never completely at ease. She became convinced that her every movement was being monitored, twenty-four hours a day. This was a crazy place, she reckoned, in which all her mail was being opened, all her phone calls tapped, all her activities recorded on hidden CCTV cameras and her room was bugged with minute listening devices.

To make matters worse Jim kept phoning up to speak to her and ask for permission to visit her. Both requests were refused with Audrey or another member of the senior staff simply telling him that 'Debbie wasn't available.' They would then inform her that her boyfriend had phoned, but it wasn't their policy to allow residents to take 'calls from outside for at least a month after coming in'.

This began to infuriate Debbie. Was it not just another proof that there was something weird about this repressive establishment?

Matters came to a head one weekend in March, when Debbie had been in Hope House for just over ten weeks. Jim phoned late on Friday night, insisting that he be allowed to speak to Debbie. Recognising that she could not put him off forever, and hoping that Debbie was now sufficiently settled in her new environment not to be swayed by whatever proposals he would come up with, Audrey consented to allow Debbie to come to the phone.

On hearing that she was going to be allowed to take 'a call from her boyfriend,' Debbie arrived in Audrey's office not knowing what to expect. How would she react to hearing Jim's voice again after all this time?

After he had gone through a number of preliminary greetings, Jim asked aggressively, "Debbie, have you any idea where you are? You are in prison! In fact I have been in a prison or two in my time and a lot of the guys in there on long sentences have more freedom than you have!"

This outburst only served to increase Debbie's doubts about Hope House and the advisability of staying there. While she was listening to Jim's opinion of the institution in which she was, according to him, being incarcerated, Audrey was mounting a silent counter attack.

She placed two photographs right in front of Debbie. The first of these had been taken the day after she came into Hope House, and the other nine weeks later. There was an unbelievable difference in the two images. Despite her continued mental reservations, Debbie had now begun to look like an attractive bright-eyed woman once more. But would this indisputable photographic evidence prove sufficient to counteract her drug-dealing boyfriend's emphatic arguments?

Jim's last words before ending the call presented Debbie with an ultimatum. "I am going down to Llanelli tomorrow and will be near that place where you are being held," he began.

"You can make a choice. I will come and collect you if you want me to, but if you want to stay there, stay there. All I have to say is that if you decide to stay, that will be it. You will never see me again! I will phone tomorrow at noon to see what you have decided. Bye." With that the line went dead.

Both Debbie and Audrey spent an anguished night after that. Debbie was in agony, wondering what she should do, and Audrey spent the night in an agony of prayer, wondering what she would do.

By Saturday at lunchtime Debbie had made up her mind and when Jim phoned Hope House she told him, "Just come and collect me."

When Audrey heard this she was angry and disappointed. She was angry with Jim for having inveigled Debbie away, and disappointed at Debbie for having succumbed to the lure of her former life and the wiles of the devil, both of which were represented in the intervention of her boyfriend.

"He will not be coming here," she told Debbie, emphatically. "If you must leave, I will take you out to the car park at Mc Donald's to meet him." Debbie passed on that arrangement and the conversation closed.

The founder manager of Hope House took a dim view of starting, but failing to finish the programme, and in Debbie's case she chose to express her disapproval in a very practical way. She left her office, returning in what seemed like a few seconds and tossing Debbie two black bin liners.

"You have fifteen minutes to get all your stuff into those bags and out into the boot of my car," she ordered, and left Debbie standing holding them.

When she had gathered all her bits and pieces together Debbie appeared out through the door with a bag in each hand, labouring along. Fiona, a senior counsellor, and someone whom Debbie had really come to respect, stepped forward and offered to carry one of the bags. She was just about to reach for it when Audrey's voice cut in, "Don't you dare help her with those bags. She's leaving! Let her carry her own bags!"

Audrey and Fiona drove their disappointing dropout to Mc Donald's car park in nearby Cross Hands, and when they found that Jim had already arrived, waited until she had collected her two bags from the boot. Each of them then gave her a hug and said, "Goodbye."

Debbie walked across to Jim's car with her 'luggage, and Audrey and Fiona drove away. As they made their way back to Hope House, Fiona was in tears.

Audrey still had a spiritually-inspired intuitive notion about the promising young woman, whom they had just been forced to return to the temptations of her former lifestyle, however, and declared, fondly but firmly, "Don't worry about Debbie, Fiona. God has His hand on her life. She'll be back!"

Having waited an extra minute until the two ladies from Hope House had disappeared down the road, Debbie opened the door of Jim's car to get into it. She threw her bags into the back and then stepped into the front passenger seat.

The old familiar smells, the fetid, clinging stench of drink, drugs and cigarettes, which were the odours of an almost forgotten existence, bombarded her nostrils. Her stomach turned over. She looked across at Jim, whom she had so much looked forward to meeting again, in the fantastic free world outside Hope House, and he was like a skeleton. His hair was untidy and his face pale, thin and drawn. Just like she had been before 'going into prison.' He looked dreadful.

"Great to see you again, Debbie " he said, with a smile that contained just the remotest hint of a satisfied smirk. "Let's go!"

As they joined the M4 to head eastwards, back to Wolverhampton, Jim lit up a cigarette, slipped a tape of gangster rap music into the player and turned the volume up full blast before looking over at Debbie and smiling again. This smile was intended to be reassuring. It was meant to say, 'Welcome back to our old ways, Debbie. Nothing has changed...'

It was early afternoon on Saturday, March 13, 1999. Debbie Forrest had been in Hope House for more than ten weeks and now she was free. She was away from chapel morning and evening. She had escaped from what she perceived to be a rigid regime of observation and indoctrination.

Debbie had thought she would feel wonderful when this moment came. But she didn't. She felt wretched.

Debbie thought it would be super to be free. But it wasn't. Instead she felt sick.

The mind that had been so unreasonable in Hope House had been afforded a sudden shot of sanity.

Looking across at Jim, who was tapping his hand on the top of the steering wheel to the beat of the blaring music, and smelling the cigarette smoke drifting all around her Debbie was gripped with a sudden sense of despair.

She bowed her head in her hands in the front of the car, and half-cried, half confessed, "O God, what have I done? What have I done? I have made a big mistake. One awful big mistake!"

18

AWESOME

They were only forty miles further on when Jim's mobile phone rang.

He answered it and Debbie heard him say, "Yes, she's here," and then he handed the phone across to her.

"It's your mother," he informed her, casually.

"Oh hello, mum, and how are you?" Debbie began, trying to sound all friendly and free.

The lady at the other end of the line was in no mood for plastic pleasantries. "What do you think you are doing?" were her first words, spoken with a lot more aggression than affection. It was clear that she was in no mood for a cosy mother-to-daughter confab.

"I'm coming home. Is that not good? Tomorrow is Mother's Day and I'll be home for that," Debbie replied, trying to appeal to her mum's maternal nature. "I thought you would be pleased."

"No! It's not good, and I'm not pleased!" Eileen stormed on. "You haven't finished the programme!"

She was livid.

"How did you know?" Debbie enquired softly, recognising the futility of pursuing the 'I thought you would be glad to see me' angle of approach.

"Audrey phoned to tell me you had left!" was the answer to that one. "I'm just mad at you!"

Debbie had already gathered that and so, unwilling to engage in a quarrel with her mother, and equally unwilling to admit that she was also already mad at herself, brought the conversation to an abrupt end. "O.K. mum, O.K. I'm out now and there's nothing any of us can do about it," she declared. "I'll see you sometime after I get back there. Bye in the meantime."

When they arrived back in Wolverhampton their first stop was at Jim's new flat. He was extremely proud of it, and had made some preparations for Debbie's return, although not quite sure if that would actually happen, or when it would be.

Jim had a modern telephone system installed in this new place, one that worked. Their previous phone had been cut off for non-payment of bills. There were two new tracksuits and a couple of pairs of trainers for Debbie. All the furniture appeared as though it had only just been delivered.

Having taken Debbie on a conducted tour of his new operational HQ he turned to her and asked, with a glow of self-satisfaction, "Well, what do you think of it?"

"It's all lovely. Great," Debbie could only admit. "Such a change from when I went away."

"Yes," Jim replied, with a sly twinkle in his eye. "Business has been brisk this last month or two."

Another indicator of the upturn in Jim's trading fortunes was the quantity of his 'merchandise' around the flat. In the earlier days Debbie and he could never afford to accumulate large stocks of 'gear.' Now, though, any drugs squad officer would just have loved to have been smashing in the door of this place. Sniffer dogs would have ended up dizzy, having run around in circles, wondering where to bark first.

Jim was holding large supplies of heroin and there was more crack cocaine in that flat that evening than Debbie had ever seen in one place in her drug-using drug-dealing life.

It would have been an 'Aladdin's cave' for an addict. Debbie, though, was not an addict, or so she thought. She had been 'clean' for nearly eleven weeks.

Something else had changed during Debbie's stay in Hope House. Jim had acquired a new circle of friends to match his more upbeat image in his more upmarket flat. As these people began to arrive at his latest abode to meet Debbie, and help celebrate her 'release from bondage,' she realised that these might be new, but they certainly weren't any better, friends. They were merely a better class of crook.

When all those whom Jim had expected to call that evening had arrived they sat around a table chatting, getting to know Debbie. Then, as was customary in such a situation, the crack-pipe came around.

Debbie was in a dilemma. The smell of drugs, when she had stepped into the car beside Jim in the early afternoon, had turned her off. Now, though, she had become used to the sight and smells of the set up once again. As those ahead of her used the pipe her body began crying out for crack.

What should she do?

When it came her turn everyone gazed across at her. The silence was intense.

What would she do?

Struggling desperately with this decision she looked across at Jim, and raised her eyes as though to ask, 'what do you think? What should I do?'

Her boyfriend just looked back at her and shrugged his shoulders. It was clear that he wasn't going to be of any help.

Debbie then looked around all the other faces at the table. She had never come across such an expressionless crowd before. It was clear that they weren't going to offer any advice one way or another, either.

After a momentary pause Debbie reached out for some crack, set up the pipe, and smoked it. She had barely taken the first long draw before the conversation, which had earlier been sliced off into sudden silence, started up again, as though somebody had just switched on the TV in the middle of a clamorous crowd scene.

The exchanges around the table could now continue in a more relaxed fashion. Debbie had returned to Jim, and had graduated to being accepted by his friends by proving that she could still smoke crack.

That was the beginning of yet another rapid downward slide.

In less than a week Debbie was back 'chasing' heroin, and not long after that she was injecting once more. In two month's time she looked just as she had done the previous autumn.

Debbie wasn't eating. She wasn't sleeping. She was using drugs day and night. The weight started to drop off her again. The healthy-looking woman who had escaped from that 'crazy-cookie' establishment, Hope House, into the big, free world, now looked exactly as she had done the day her dad had introduced her to Audrey as being 'something out of 'The Exorcist.'

Two further complications, one to do with her spiritual mentality, the other with a gradual breakdown of a long-standing relationship, served to render that spring and early summer increasingly distressing for Debbie, following her return to Wolverhampton and almost immediate relapse into drug-use.

Her spiritual life had hit rock bottom. In Hope House she had been reading the Bible, for whatever reason, and joining in prayer and Christian worship. Having been wrenched suddenly from that encompassing atmosphere of Christian care and transported, in the space of about six hours, into the haunts and habits of her former existence, Debbie's love for the Lord iced over. She seldom read the scriptures and found it hard to pray, on the rare occasions when she tried to. She felt too embarrassed to go back to church.

This spiritual decline annoyed her in the brief periods of rationality between the time the effects of one heroin 'hit' wore off and the next one kicked in. 'I can't do anything right,' she often fumed at herself. 'I couldn't keep my good job, I couldn't look after my lovely little child, I couldn't live a clean Christian life, and now the worst thing of all. I couldn't even complete the course at Hope House. Oh, yes, dozens of others could, but I couldn't. Not me. Not Debbie Forrest.

Failure, failure, failure, that's me. I always have been and always will be, a total and abject dead loss. At anything and everything I try to do.'

As the days dragged by it became evident to both Debbie and Jim that the relationship between them was not as close as it once had been. When Jim saw the rapid deterioration of Debbie, from an improving and positive person back into the depths of despair, he hated himself for having insisted that she come out of Hope House. He had told her, less than a year before, that she would 'have to go' there. Now he had been the one to bring her out of it again after only ten weeks.

When Debbie realised the mistake she had made in listening to his harangue, which at the time only served to fuel her own misgivings, she resented him. She was also, however, angry with herself at having given in to his blatant blackmail.

The arguments that had always been an integral element in their stormy relationship intensified. She soon began to accept that she was living in the same flat as Jim, not because she terribly wanted to, but because it provided her with somewhere to sleep and an endless supply of heroin and crack, which she could use to eradicate reality.

'If only I could get back into Hope House,' she began to reflect in her more measured moments, 'then I would make another attempt to sort myself out. Maybe it wasn't such a bad place after all.'

How could she ever break the bands that had tightened around her, and were again threatening to strangle the life out of her, though?

Her already mounting problems were even further exacerbated by the arrival, in mid-June, of a police warrant for the non-payment of fines. In the world where Debbie had operated for so many years, she and her accomplices had been to court often and had been fined often. However, if they couldn't afford to buy food, they certainly couldn't be bothered paying fines. Every pound they got their hands on, whether by fair means or foul, went on fuelling their obsessive and excessive addictions.

The warrant stated that Debbie owed the court £650 in unpaid fines and she called at the local police station in response to it. There she was told that her case had been referred to Wolverhampton Magistrates' Court and would be heard during the afternoon of Friday, July 2, 1999.

Debbie's mum, Eileen, accompanied her to the Magistrates' Court that day and they arrived in good time and waited for Debbie's case to be called. How was it going to go? they both wondered. Some of Debbie's comrades in crime had been given prison sentences for not paying their fines. Was she going to end up, not in Hope House prison, but in real prison? It was a distinct possibility.

The two women, sitting reflecting on Debbie's fate, were totally unaware of the arrangements that were being made by the court officials, to have her case heard. Their problem was that the court that had been scheduled to hear the case was running late and it had begun to look as though they would not be able to fit it into their programme for the day.

Back in Court 9, however, judge George Clarke and his colleague had finished their day's list just before three o'clock and sent a message to the administrators asking if there was anything more to be done before they prepared to leave for home. This offer came as a godsend to the organisers who said, "We have a young lady who has been called to answer a warrant for unpaid fines. Could you deal with that one?"

"Of course we could," George replied. 'It shouldn't take long. Send her in.'

It was 3.15 p.m. when Debbie was shown into Court 9 to appear before judge Clarke for the non-payment of fines. Debbie's mum slipped silently into a back seat to observe proceedings, and to pray.

When George Clarke looked down at what would probably be the last defendant to appear before him that day he was shocked. He had presided over hundreds of trials but had seldom seen anyone as woebegone as this young woman, who looked more like an old woman. She reminded him of pictures he had seen of the gaunt, emaciated prisoners discovered in concentration camps by liberating forces, at the end of the Second World War. There was something strangely appealing and authoritative about her pathetic presence, however, something he couldn't quite explain.

From the moment Debbie had entered that courtroom the atmosphere had become suddenly electric. It was as though some invisible supernatural power had accompanied her into the room, and would only leave when she left.

"You have outstanding fines of £650," judge Clarke began, looking down at her from the bench. "How do you intend to pay these to the court?"

"I can pay you two pounds a week for as long as it takes," Debbie volunteered.

"Two pounds a week! That's an insult to this court!" George Clarke retorted, trying to appear as insulted as he sounded. "Do you realise that it would take you more than six years to pay off what you owe at that rate? You are on Income Support. You can afford more than two pounds a week."

"Let me explain," Debbie went on, taking up an excuse she hadn't planned to use. She felt that the words had been placed in her mouth without ever having been processed by her brain. "I am going to Hope House a Teen Challenge rehab centre in Wales. I will get five pounds a week pocket money there. I will need two pounds fifty for a phone card and fifty pence for stamps. That will leave me two pounds. You can have that. I will send it to you and I promise it will never be late."

The judge was intrigued. He had never come across anything like this before. There, standing before him, was what had obviously once been an attractive young woman, and what sounded like an intelligent young woman, talking about living on five pounds a week!

"So you are a drug addict," he said, clearly deep in thought.

"Yes. I am," Debbie answered with an open honesty.

"And this Hope House, what is it?" George Clarke was interested to find out.

"It is a Christian rehabilitation centre and when I go there Jesus Christ is going to set me free from all my addictions," Debbie told him with convincing confidence.

This was most unusual. "And who is sending you there?" came the next question from the bench.

"The pastor of my church," Debbie replied. This was stretching the truth to breaking point. The pastor of Debbie's church had sent her on her first pilgrimage to Hope House, and would no doubt send her again as many times as she wanted or needed to go. But she hadn't been near his church for more than six months!

"Have you used drugs today?" the judge went on to enquire.

"Not yet, but who knows, before the end of the day I will probably have to," came another forthright response.

"Thank you for being so honest," George, the judge, said slowly, as though bringing the questioning to an end. "Just wait a moment. I want to consult my colleague."

With that George and the other man, who had been listening intently to all the goings-on, retired to the rear of the court and began whispering to one another.

Neither Debbie, who had been mysteriously guided into what to say, nor her mum, who had been mysteriously guided into what to pray, could hear what they were saying, but it was fascinating.

"You may think it peculiar," George was telling his colleague, " but I feel inclined, for some reason that I can't quite explain, to remit all this young woman's fines."

"That's exactly how I feel too," the colleague replied, a little to George's surprise. "There is something about her that convinces me it is what we should do."

With that immediate consensus of opinion their deliberations didn't last long, and when judge Clarke returned to announce their verdict to Debbie, neither she, nor her mum nor anybody else in the court could quite take it in.

"I am remitting all your fines," he declared. "Go to Teen Challenge and sort yourself out. Clean up your life and then hopefully you will be able to return as a sensible member of society."

This was incredible. Unbelievable. Unheard of!

Debbie was walking free from court yet again!

On the way home she began to sing. It was a worship song that she had learnt in church at least two years before, but which sprang back into her mind at that moment. It was,

'You are awesome in this place, Mighty God,
You are awesome in this place, Abba Father,
You are worthy of our praise,
To you our lives we raise,
You are awesome in this place, Mighty God."

In a pause for breath before starting to sing that verse all over again, Debbie looked across at her mum. She was crying. "Awesome. That's the word Debbie. Awesome, that's the word for what happened there this afternoon," she croaked through her tears.

And their 'Mighty God' hadn't finished demonstrating His awesomeness to them yet either.

The two women had just returned to granddad's house, where Eileen lived, when the phone rang. It was Jean Stead, a senior counsellor from Hope House, asking to speak to Debbie.

When Debbie took the phone Jean had a simple message for her. It was, "We have a place for you. We are all praying for you, Debbie. We want you to come in on Monday."

This was truly awesome! Two hours earlier Debbie had told a judge in Wolverhampton Magistrate's Court that she was going to Hope House, without having a clue when, or if, she would ever go. Now Jean was on the phone to tell her to come in on Monday!

"Thank you Jean," Debbie replied. "Thank you for your prayers and your offer. I will probably see you on Monday."

Eileen was thrilled at the prospect of her daughter returning to Wales. Surely this time she would stay until she was sorted out, once and for all.

Emily was also delighted to hear that her mum was going back to Hope House. It opened the door to the prospect that perhaps she could, even yet, have a real, loving caring mother to come home to, like most of the other girls in her class.

What nobody, except Mighty God, was to know, however, was that as the weekend wore on Debbie had begun to question whether she could face what she knew would be another distressing session of 'cold turkey.'

God's intervention, both in His overruling power and perfect timing had been 'awesome.'

Her response had been nothing more than a pathetic 'probably.'

What should she do?

Debbie had until Monday morning to make up her mind.

19

JUST STAY UNTIL YOU'RE BETTER, MUM

On Sunday afternoon Debbie surmounted the first obstacle that stood in the way of a return to Hope House. She had to devise a plan to move out of the flat, with as many of her possessions as she could carry, without arousing Jim's suspicions. If he thought that she was contemplating going back he would have been furious, and he had cultivated a nasty habit of expressing his fury with his fists.

Her first move was to hide all Jim's dirty clothes in every nook and cranny she was sure he wouldn't be liable to look in for the next day or two, and then pack as many of her own clothes as she could into a suitcase.

When she had finished her packing she went into the living room where Jim was watching TV and said, as casually as she could, "I'm going down to my mum's to do some washing."

Totally unaware of her plan, and glad that Debbie was showing an interest in doing something other that sitting around like a fearsome phantom using heroin and crack, he spared a moment to glance up at her and reply, "That's good. Will you be late back?"

"Yes. I probably will," Debbie told him. "I intend to spend an hour or two with mum and granddad, when I'm there."

That was her cue to leave, and when she arrived at her mum's house she washed all her clothes. Her plan to spend the remainder of the evening with her mum and granddad had to be sacrificed to the pull of her addiction later on, though.

Debbie hadn't long finished her washing until she began to feel claustrophobic in the house. The world was closing in on her. Mum and granddad were beginning to annoy her as they chattered on and on about what were, to her, complete trivialities.

She had escaped from Jim's flat. Now she would have to escape from her mum's house. But she couldn't go back to Jim!

It was nearly nine o'clock when she rose during a gap in the gossip and announced, "I'm going out for a while, mum. If Jim phones just tell him I'm out."

As soon as she was clear of her mum's house Debbie went straight to the nearest telephone kiosk and phoned a dealer to order £80 worth of heroin and £80 worth of crack cocaine. She had brought all the paraphernalia she needed to make up a massive 'hit,' out with her. All she required now was an adequate supply of hard drugs. What she had ordered should be enough to give her final relief from a frustrating, futile, failure-ridden existence.

The dealer told Debbie that he would meet her 'up at the Parkfield Tavern in half-an-hour's time,' and that he would 'have the gear with him.'

He was there as arranged and when the packages he had brought were exchanged for the money Debbie had produced, the woman who was preparing to self-destruct went out into the seedy toilet at the back.

There was only one way, she had decided back in granddad's, to put an end to this whole meaningless muddle of crack and Christianity, heroin and hopelessness. She would kill herself. She had tried it before, and failed. But she was determined not to fail this time.

Debbie, in her despair, reckoned that she had let her daughter down, her mum down, her entire family circle for that matter, down, and worst of all she had let God down. She had once been so praising and so positive in her Christian life. Now, though, she had gone as far as she could possibly go in the opposite direction. She was at such a low ebb physically and so utterly messed up mentally that she couldn't be bothered reading her Bible, praying, or even thinking happy God-thoughts any more.

If she could end it all now it would save her having to make up her mind whether or not to start all over again in Hope House.

The toilet out at the back of the Parkfield Tavern was a grotty place. It had stone walls with beards of white fungus growing out of damp black cracks at floor and ceiling level. The floor was covered with small but smelly puddles and sodden cigarette-butts.

The sole source of light was a bare, begrimed and smoke-blackened bulb.

This was the environment in which Debbie had aimed to have her last huge 'fix.' Using the slime-covered cistern as a table she prepared a lethal cocktail of heroin and crack and poured it carefully into a syringe out of the pack she had brought with her.

She then stood up on the dirty toilet seat, and with the greasy light bulb at her left ear, injected the concoction into her groin. This was stage one of a carefully contrived plan to cause minimum distress to those left to deal with the dead body she would be leaving them. Stage two was to jump down immediately after making the 'hit,' sit on the toilet seat until she slumped lifeless either to the side against the damp wall or forward against the back of the door. If she could manage to jump down before she fell down that would save her smashing her face and head in. It would be bad enough, she reckoned, for her mum to have to identify her corpse on a mortuary slab but if her body were all bashed up it would be even more disturbing. This would be her last act of consideration although nobody would even know about it to thank her for it.

Part one of stage two was performed according to plan. After injecting herself with enough of a potion to kill her in minutes Debbie dropped the needle and scrambled down to sit on the toilet seat and await stage two, part two. That was the slumping down dead bit.

But nothing happened. Debbie sat, bent forward with her head in her hands so that her body would roll rather than fall when life left it, for ten minutes, and then her hearing went. She rapped the back of the door with her knuckle, but couldn't hear the noise. It was like being under water. Her head felt pressurised from outside and silent and insensate inside. Perhaps this was the way she was going to die. Her brain would just shut down its functions one by one, with hearing the first to go...

No. That wasn't to be it either. She remained there, pulling her clothes more tightly around her as the chill of the oncoming night began to cause her arms and legs to tremble, but nothing else happened.

Having been there for nearly an hour, and having come to realise, after the second concentrated attempt, that she was incapable of taking her own life by overdosing on drugs, Debbie gave up. Her tapping test revealed that her hearing was returning and if closing time came in the pub she would not be able to make it out on to the street.

She had chosen that isolated toilet in the back yard so that she could have lain there dead until the morning without being discovered. It did not, however, rank amongst her list of first choices of places in which to spend the night alive.

It was after midnight when she started back towards her granddad's house, and nearly one o'clock in the morning when she reached it, having had to make frequent stops because she felt either sick or dizzy or both.

When she arrived into the house Debbie found her mother in an agitated state. She was anxious about her daughter, and was also angry at her daughter at having made her anxious. Deep down, though, she was pleased to see her back alive. Little did she know at that moment that if Debbie's plan for her death had worked, and God's plan for her life hadn't overruled, she would never have seen her daughter alive again.

"Where have you been? I have been worried sick about you! Jim has been on the phone three or four times to see if you were here, as you haven't returned to the flat!" she began as soon as Debbie struggled in through the door. The cork had been removed from the bottle of her built-up concerns and the contents came spilling out in a stream.

"I was up at the Parkfield Tavern," Debbie confessed truthfully, but refrained from going into any details of what she had been doing there.

"Oh, Debbie, I'm so glad you're back safely," mother went on a few minutes later, her relief taking the edge off her edginess. "I have had such a problem knowing what to tell Jim. Sure he doesn't know that you are going to Hope House in the morning?"

"No, he doesn't," Debbie replied before going on more slowly, "and to tell you the truth I don't know whether I am going myself."

"Of course you are going!" Eileen retorted. This was the first time she had ever suspected that there was any doubt about the matter. "I am going over to collect Emily at ten o'clock and then we are both going to take you down to Wales."

"Oh are you now? That's very kind of you." Debbie countered, finding it difficult, even in her confused condition, to resist a mild sarcasm. "Remember it's me you are talking about after all, and I will tell you in the morning whether you are taking me down to Wales or not!"

After her mother had retired to bed Debbie sat up the remainder of the night smoking crack and thinking, wondering, deciding.

By the time the light of another summer day had begun to brighten the room around her, she had made up her mind. She wasn't staying here with her mum and granddad, and she wasn't going back to Jim. She would return to Hope House, and stay there until she was clean, however hard it would be, or how long it would take.

It was a brave, God-guided decision.

Eileen went round to Kevin's house early that Monday morning, July 5, and collected Emily as they had previously arranged. Having left the lifting of Debbie to the last minute they returned to granddad's house to pick her up. When Debbie was just about to walk out of the house, carrying her suitcase of newly-washed clothes, her mum said to her granddad who was sitting in sullen silence in the living-room, "Are you not coming to the door to say 'goodbye' to Debbie?"

"No, indeed I am not," came the ill-tempered reply. "I am glad to see the back of her."

Debbie was taken aback that her once-upon-a-time loyal supporter should have adopted this attitude, and replied, her tone of voice echoing her surprise, "Oh no, granddad. Are you, really?"

The old man had seen Debbie through some difficult times, but increasing age had effected decreasing tolerance, and his granddaughter's antics over the past few years hadn't helped. The grief she had caused both her mum and him the previous evening had been the last straw.

"Yes, I most definitely am! " he snapped back angrily. "Get out of my house! You're no good! You've never been any good, and no good will ever come out of you! Clear off! Get out of my sight! And don't ever come back!"

Although Debbie had already come to the conclusion that she was 'no good, and that no good would ever come out of her,' many times herself, she didn't take kindly to having her granddad, whom she had loved so dearly for so long, express it in so many words. It was a startling wake-up call and produced a positive result. It caused Debbie to stiffen her resolve, and mutter to herself as she left the house to which she had been told in no uncertain terms that she 'wasn't ever to come back,' "I'll show him!"

With that emphatic 'vote of no confidence' and her own counter resolution uppermost in her mind, Debbie joined her mother and daughter out in the car. Then the three generations of women who had gone to church together, and had become Christians the same evening, set out for Wales together. One of them had a floundering faith, a match-stick body and a fickle mind. The other two would have taken her anywhere to see her restored to the fiery faith, the healthy body and the sound mind they had both once known and loved.

They were to spend far longer on the journey than was really necessary. Debbie kept insisting that her mum pull into every service area on the motorway, so that she could go into the toilets. She felt so sick, and yet all she wanted to do was use some more of her dwindling supply of drugs.

When they reached Ross-on-Wye, a town on the English – Welsh border, Eileen turned into a roadside café, declaring, "I think it is time we had something to eat."

"You and Emily go in and have something," Debbie was quick to respond. "But the last thing in the world I want is food."

When her mother and daughter had disappeared into the café Debbie produced her needles and 'gear' from a plastic bag she carried in her handbag. She had just enough heroin left for one final 'hit' and so while Eileen and Emily were in having a meal she had what she had come to depend upon for daily sustenance. That was an injection of heroin while hunched over in the back seat of the car.

Having decided to return to Hope House, and having had her resolve pumped up by granddad's final abusive remarks, Debbie then took another purposeful step towards making a significant and lasting clean up of her life. With her mum and daughter still in the café she struggled out of the car carrying a plastic bag containing all the paraphernalia she had accumulated to help satisfy her drug-smoking drug-shooting dependency. The only item of equipment not in the bag was the dessert spoon she had used to measure out and prepare so many 'hits.' It was in her other hand.

She crossed to a flower-bed at the corner of a car park in which a number of straggling roses, which were adorned by a selection of wind-blown crisp bags and ice-lollipop papers, were struggling into bloom. Debbie looked a forlorn waif as she began to dig in the soil in one of the less-tramped spots of the flower bed with her spoon.

It was a summer afternoon and there were a few other people around, but the determined drug addict didn't care. She had a job to do, and only a short while to do it. The two in the café would definitely soon be out.

When she had scooped out a hole big enough to hold all the accoutrements which had for so long accompanied her addiction, and deep enough to avoid them being unearthed by some inquisitive child or scraping animal, she rolled up the plastic bag and placed it in it. Then carefully, almost ceremoniously, she placed the spoon on top of the bag, and began pulling the soil back into the hole with her bare hands. To complete the burial process she stepped over onto the soil to firm it down tightly, and then bent forward to ruffle the surface of it slightly. These actions would, she hoped, render the hastily-dug makeshift 'grave' as inconspicuous as possible.

The ultimate commitment came as she turned her back on the flower-bed and began shaking the soil off her hands. "That's it," she declared aloud to an audience of only two, God and herself, "I don't ever want to use drugs again."

With all the enforced stops and starts it was late on in the afternoon when the tired trio arrived at their destination. The reception they received cheered all three of them up, however.

Audrey was waiting for them, and when she saw Debbie, who was in just as bad a state as she had been six months before, on her first trip into Hope House, she threw her arms around her. "We are so glad to see you again, Debbie," she said with genuine feeling. "We have been praying for you and always believed that God would bring you back to us."

Debbie's mum and Emily didn't want to start straight back for Wolverhampton and so they stayed and had a meal. It was a lovely summer evening and they sat around in the sun outside for more than an hour after they had eaten, talking to Debbie. Both mum and daughter could see that although she still looked ghastly, her attitude had already become less tense. It was as though she had recognised, possibly even subconsciously, that she had finally arrived where she needed to be, and where God wanted her to be.

Emily's last words to her mum, before nanny and she set off on the three-hour journey home, summed up everybody's desire for Debbie. The eleven-year old clung around her mum's neck and whispered over and over again, "Just stay until you're better, mum. Please stay until you're better!"

20

A MATTER OF LIFE AND DEATH

Debbie was shown straight to her room as soon as her mother and daughter had left. Audrey knew that there were difficult times ahead and the sooner the returned resident began the painful withdrawal process, the sooner it would be over. There was little point in wasting time.

The next few days were horrendous. Debbie's body was overtaken by agony and her mind by anguish. She seemed to be vomiting continually and had frequent bouts of diahorrea. The perspiration poured from her. There were times when the abdominal pain was so excruciating that she squirmed around in the bed like an eel on a hook.

Day and night merged into one continuous blur of wretchedness and the girl in the room next door became accustomed to hearing an occasional, repetitive, thump, thump, thump that made the pencils and pens on her table bounce about, at all hours. That was Debbie banging her legs and feet against the wall in desperation.

The physical symptoms of the 'cold turkey' experience that Debbie was passing through were accompanied by an instability of mind that rendered her incapable of logical thought. Her brain began throwing up a series of horrific images from her horrific past. It was like a non-stop nightmare. She had barely begun to focus on one shocking picture before it was replaced by another, equally awful.

Debbie became gripped with a sense of fear and panic. As the physical pain became virtually unbearable she became convinced that she was going to die. She had never, in all her attempts to clear the drugs out of her body and out of her life, experienced anything like this.

'These are your last hours on this earth,' her manic mind kept yelling at her.

'You are going to die. No human being ever endured pain like this and lived...'

That was what the devil sneered at her non-stop. 'You are going to die... You will never see your lovely little daughter again...You are going to die... You should never have come here... You are going to die!'

That was only one half of the battle for the life and loyalty of Debbie Forrest, however.

What the woman writhing in the bed in physical, mental and spiritual torment didn't realise was that on the other side of the door the staff of Hope House were taking it in turns to walk up and down the corridor outside, interceding with God for her. They were beseeching Him, in the Name and for the sake of His Son, Jesus, who had conquered sin and death by His death and resurrection, to grant Debbie physical, mental and spiritual release and recovery.

It was a titanic struggle and it lasted for days.

The staff kept a constant watch on her, calling in frequently to sit with her, offer her drinks, which she usually refused since she felt so terribly sick, or to change her bed. On a number of occasions the clothes they removed from Debbie's bed were taken outside and burnt, they smelt so foul.

On Wednesday morning, Fiona Fallon, the counsellor who had been so sorry to see Debbie leave in March, and who had been equally thrilled to welcome her back in July, called into the room. Debbie was in agony as usual, but she found Fiona quietly inspiring, and she trusted her. She felt she could ask her anything and be given an honest answer.

In an effort to encourage detoxing residents to persist with the punishing effects of physical withdrawal, the Hope House leaders had left a copy of the book, 'Tough Love', by John Macey, National Director of Teen Challenge UK, in each bedroom. The book recounted the stories of a number of lives that had been changed by the power of God through the work of Teen Challenge. Debbie was not in any fit state to read a book, but she was drawn to the 'before and after' photographs of a young man on the cover, any time she was well enough to even look at it.

Reaching out of bed, Debbie lifted the book and held it up to Fiona.

"Is that the same man in both those photographs?" she asked. It seemed impossible. One was the image of a grey-faced, frightened-looking youth whereas the photo beside it had a contented-looking healthy young man smiling out of it.

"Yes, that's the same man," her counsellor assured her without hesitation.

"How can you be so sure?" Debbie was interested to find out. "Do you know him or what?"

"I can be so sure because, yes, I know him. In fact, I live with him! The man in those pictures is my husband Jay, before and after God entered, and changed his life," Fiona went on to explain.

Now Debbie could understand why she had been so sure of her facts. "That's amazing!" she gasped.

"Yes, I know it is," Fiona was happy to concede. "But the God who transformed Jay's life can pull you through too, Debbie. Just stick with it. Look at the pictures on the cover of the book every now and again. They will show you what God is going to do for you."

It was good advice, and Debbie started to glance at the contrasting pictures and draw occasional consolation from them, in her less tormented moments. If God could do that for Jay Fallon He could surely do it for her.

Next morning Audrey, the centre manager, who had been monitoring Debbie's progress with intense and prayerful interest, came into the bedroom. She had a damp face flannel and a comb in one hand and a towel hanging loosely over her wrist.

"Don't come near me with those!" was Debbie's instant reaction when she saw the comb and facecloth. "I can't be bothered washing!"

"I'm sure you can't, " Audrey replied sympathetically, "but Pastor Macey was wondering if he could come in and take a video of you. He has a very good reason for wanting to make a 'before and after' video, but he will probably explain that to you himself, if you are agreeable. He thinks it would have the same, possibly even a stronger, impact, as the pictures of Jay on the cover of his book."

She then broke off her conversation to nod across to where 'Tough Love' was sitting on the table in the bedroom, before going on to ask, "How would you feel about it?"

"I couldn't care less what you do," Debbie replied, phlegmatically. She was still trying to fight her way out of the 'before' stage. All her energies were being used up just keeping her alive and sane. The prospect of an 'after' still seemed little more than a distant dream.

"Will you let me give your face a quick wipe before Pastor Macey comes in with the camera?" Audrey then enquired, gently.

"O.K." the listless figure in the bed agreed reluctantly.

Audrey was as quick as she had promised with her 'wipe,' but trying to comb Debbie's hair was another matter. It had been soaked with perspiration so many times that it was totally unmanageable. Audrey gave it a few strokes with the comb, but when she saw this was upsetting Debbie, gave up.

Having satisfied herself that she had done what she could to make Debbie feel comfortable with the idea of a video camera in her bedroom, in her state, Audrey went off and brought the National Director of Teen Challenge UK back with her.

All three of them talked for a few minutes about the proposed content of the video and then Pastor Macey interviewed Debbie about her life on drugs and recorded it. Debbie found this difficult because her mind was still so disturbed by the effects of her earlier life style that recalling her descent into depravity proved not a particularly pleasant experience.

When the interview was complete Pastor Macey expressed himself pleased with the recording and proceeded to share the vision he had for having it made. "Teen Challenge is badly in need of a properly equipped and medically supervised detox centre," he explained. "If we had one it would mean that people wouldn't have to go through the agonies you are experiencing this week. We would have more to rely on than our two famous 'P's', prayer and paracetamol. I intend to take another series of footage in a few weeks time when you are well again, and then we can use the video to create an awareness of our work."

Here was somebody whose mind had advanced far beyond Debbie's. She couldn't imagine life in a 'few weeks time.' She was firmly entrenched in 'the here and now,' and she could see no way out. It was like sinking hopelessly, and struggling fiercely, in a quicksand, with the tide coming in.

"Are you happy enough with that?" Pastor Macey felt duty bound to enquire of the leading character in his half-made promotional movie.

"Yes. I'm happy enough with that," Debbie replied, and then for the first time in that wearisome week, and guided by God rather than her own dismal thought pattern, she made reference to life beyond 'cold turkey.'

"That is, on one condition," she went on to add.

"And what is that?" he enquired, fascinated. This was an encouraging sign. Debbie was recovering the capacity to reason, and bargain!

"It is simply that you give me a job here in Hope House when I am through all of this," she said.

The two most senior members of Teen Challenge involved in the Christian rehab centre for women looked across at one another and smiled, knowingly. It was as though the idea had already crossed their minds some time before.

"All right, I will," Pastor Macey promised, without apparently even giving it a second thought.

Early on Friday afternoon Jo-Anna Russon came into Debbie's room with a carton of orange juice. She offered it to Debbie, who declined as usual, and then enquired, as all the leaders did before leaving the room, "Is there anything more I can do for you, Debbie, before I go?"

"Yes," Debbie replied, "I wonder could you read me something out of the Bible?"

"Certainly," Jo-Anna said, slightly surprised but extremely pleased. "Where would you like me to read?" This was another positive sign. Debbie was actually asking to hear the Word of God.

Still unable to recall any of the portions that had proved so meaningful to her in her early days as a Christian, Debbie told her, "It doesn't matter. Pick something you like, or that would maybe be helpful to me."

Jo-Anna lifted Debbie's Bible from the table and began to read from Deuteronomy chapter thirty. Debbie had invited her to pick something that might be 'helpful' to her and she had done just that.

As the words drifted across to Debbie in the bed, she found them more challenging than helpful, initially. Jo-Anna was reading,

'…See, I have set before you today life and good, death and evil…'

These words stung Debbie's errant mind to attention, and she was even more awakened to her condition and position as the reading continued,

'… I call heaven and earth as witnesses today against you, that I have set before you life and death, blessing and cursing:

therefore choose life, that both you and your descendants may live: that you may love the Lord your God, and that you may obey His voice, and that you may cling to Him, for He is your life and the length of your days…'

When Jo-Anna had finished reading the chapter, Debbie requested that she read the last few verses again. There was one phrase in there that she thought she had heard and wanted to make sure that she wasn't imagining it. Jo-Anna was only too happy to do as she had asked, and no, she hadn't imagined it.

The phrase, 'therefore choose life,' was in there, as God's recommendation to His people. Life was to be preferred to death, blessing to cursing.

Later that evening, Debbie lay and thought, 'the choice is mine. I can choose life or death, the devil and drugs or God and the Christian life.'

Just before nine o'clock Debbie prayed aloud. It was a short but passionate commitment, "Lord, I have made my choice and I have chosen life. I want to live. And I want to live for You!"

It was after eleven o'clock when one of the Hope House team appeared beside her bed and whispered softly, "We were praying for you this evening, Debbie. This was Teen Challenge graduation night down in Swansea City Temple. I have never been in a prayer meeting quite like it in my life! Pastor Macey told everybody about you and then asked us to stand and pray for you in his or her heart. There were 350 people standing in that church praying for Debbie Forrest!"

"Thank you," Debbie replied gratefully. What she didn't tell her, however, was that when they had been praying, she had been choosing! And she had chosen life.

That Friday night seemed to drag past very slowly, but it was only on Saturday morning that Debbie discovered why. It was a wonderful discovery to make, too.

She had begun to think, and feel, and appreciate her surroundings, normally again. Time had actually begun to register with her once more. She found that she could drink a carton of juice slowly, without feeling sick. It was like waking up a totally different person, in a totally different room.

Perhaps the most wonderful discovery of all was to find that the darkness and smothering smog of gloom that had been oppressing her mind for days, had gone, and light had begun to flood back into her life. Gone too were both the fear of death, and the possibility of death.

God had 'set before her life and death,' and she had chosen life, so He had dispatched death.

Debbie felt somewhat stronger by Sunday morning, but still too weak and shaky to contemplate joining the others at church, although they had invited her to. Just after the residents had finished their lunch one of the staff brought Debbie up a roast beef sandwich. It had been made from a slice of the dinner roast, and someone had cut it into little squares.

'That's the way I used to cut up the sandwiches for Emily to try to make her eat them when she was four,' she mused, allowing herself her first real smile for ages. Then she picked up the tiny squares one by one and ate them! Having nibbled at them like a nervous mouse at the start she gradually realised that she could swallow the bread and meat without feeling she wanted to bring it straight back.

This was yet another marvellous milestone reached on the road to recovery!

When Debbie had finished her 'lunch' she stood up and looked at herself in the mirror. She was still a pitifully thin and very sick-looking lady, but she no longer looked like a corpse. A sparkle had already begun to return to her eye, and she felt positive about the future. She was going to live. And what was more she was determined to keep a promise she had made nearly two years before. She was going to live for God and serve Him with whatever remained of her life.

Debbie's condition continued to improve, slowly but surely, for another week and on the following Sunday morning Jean Stead arrived up in her bedroom. She had come with a specific question and it wasn't long before she asked it.

"Would you like to be baptised, Debbie?" she enquired.

Debbie was rather shocked at the idea of it, at first. Baptism wasn't something that she had ever seriously contemplated in her unstable spiritual state, and she certainly didn't think she was ready for it yet. She was just creeping up out of the 'Slough of Despond' and was still in the process of checking that none of the slime and grime of her former life were still sticking to her.

"It's too soon," Debbie countered. "And anyway I can hardly stand. And as well as that…"

"Have you repented of your sins?" Jean interrupted Debbie's clumsy attempt to concoct excuses.

"Yes. I sure have!" came the emphatic reply.

"Is Jesus Christ your Lord and Saviour?" was Jean's next question.

Yes. Indeed He is," was Debbie's equally definite response.

"Then what is stopping you from being baptised?" Jean went on. She was not to be deterred. "You need to make this public confession of your faith, Debbie. You have died to your old life, and are now alive in Christ. Baptism is a very practical way of demonstrating that to the world."

"I agree with you," Debbie told her, "But I …"

"Good," the lady on the mission continued. "There's a baptismal service tonight in the City Temple. You will need some white clothes and a swimming costume, but don't worry about that. We will sort something out. If you could be ready to leave about half-past five, it would be good."

"All right," Debbie replied, submissively. "I'll be ready."

When Jean left the room Debbie thought over what seemed to have been a rather hasty, and possibly even pressurised, decision. As she lay, deep in thought, on the top of the bed, in which she had spent so many hours of anguish in the previous week, she began to realise that everything Jean had said had been perfectly true.

Reviewing the events of the previous thirteen days in some detail she thought, 'I have buried all my drugs stuff… I have chosen life… I have vowed to serve the Lord for the rest of my days… and as if all that weren't enough I have even asked the National Director of Teen Challenge for a job in Hope House!

Come to think of it, why should I not be baptised?'

21

AS WHITE AS SNOW

"This is Debbie Forrest," the pastor announced to the amazed congregation in Swansea City Temple. "You will remember, we were praying for her on Teen Challenge graduation night."

As Debbie walked forward to be baptised there was a collective gasp of astonishment and appreciation. Although she looked washed-out after the experience she had just lived through, there was a light of joy on her pale face and a sense of purpose in her step that broadcast her belief in what she was about to do.

When she stepped down into the water, to be baptised by immersion, Debbie recognised the man who was waiting for her. He was the man who had been asked to perform her baptism.

It was the man whose photograph had inspired her during some of her most dreadful hours in the previous harrowing week. She had picked up the book 'Tough Love,' stared at the cover pictures and vowed to herself, 'If he could make it, so can I.'

It was Jay Fallon.

Fiona had told Debbie about Jay. He had been a gang member and drug addict from Glasgow before his conversion. She had been a drug addict and prostitute from Wolverhampton before hers. Now they were side-by-side in a baptismal tank, and then the one baptised the other.

Although Debbie still felt weak and shaky after her illness, her baptism afforded her a tremendous sense of satisfaction on two counts. Firstly she had obeyed what she considered to be a scriptural ordinance, and she had also witnessed to a captivated congregation and to the world at large that the former Debbie was dead, and that the newly-created Debbie was very much alive, and just itching to get going for God.

As she regained her appetite for wholesome food in the days that followed Debbie began to return, slowly but surely, to better physical health. Flesh began to cover her bones, colour came back to her cheeks and her body assumed the contours of the feminine form once more.

The only lingering problem was in her mind. She would still occasionally be haunted by graphic images of the past. It seemed that the devil always chose to bring them before her when she was in a church service or settling down to read her Bible.

'You're a hypocrite,' the voices would accuse. 'You will never be clean. Although you have become a Christian, and even though you have been baptised, it makes no difference. Your body will be tainted forever by what was done to you, and how you have abused it in so many different ways.'

It was Jay whom God used to see Debbie through this particular crisis. For more than two weeks after her baptism Debbie had endured frequent satanic sieges on her spiritual stability. These left her depressed, for she was so keen to keep all the vows and promises she had made to God, both in private commitment and public confession, but she always felt restrained, hampered, held back.

She felt like a goat on a tether. No matter how long the rope the goat always came to the outer limit of its ability to go any further. There always appeared to be tasty green grass to munch into or luscious soft sprigs of hedge to climb up to, out beyond its boundaries. It couldn't sample these succulent delights, however. All because of the constraints of the tether.

That was like Debbie. She yearned more than anything to reach out into fresh pastures for God. The problem was that despite her most earnest efforts she was unable to extend beyond the perimeter of a confining circle that had been marked out in her mind by recurring disturbing images of her earlier life.

Jay's contribution to her complete mental and spiritual conquest of her oppressive thought patterns came one morning when he had been invited to speak at 'chapel' in Hope House. He had taken for his text on that occasion the words of Isaiah 1; 18,

'"Come now and let us reason together," says the Lord,
"Though your sins be as scarlet,
They shall be as white as snow;
Though they be red like crimson,
They shall be as wool."'

Having read this verse over twice he asked, "What exactly is God telling us here? He is inviting us to come and sit down and talk this matter over reasonably and rationally." Jay then proceeded to preach powerfully, using examples from his own experience, and that of others, to illustrate how God could make the cleansed sinner as white as snow and as pure as wool.

"God doesn't care where you've been, or what has happened in your life. If you have trusted in Christ as your Saviour He has cleansed you from all your sin," he declared at one stage.

Debbie felt that God had led Jay to present that message specifically for her.

When the service was over it was quite some time before any of the girls moved. Obviously Debbie wasn't the only one to feel the impact of the preaching in her heart that morning. Many sat with their heads bowed, praying.

Recognising that Debbie had been moved by the Spirit of God, Jay came across, and pulled a chair up beside where she was kneeling, weeping. He put his hand on her head and said, "God has forgiven you, Debbie. When God looks at you, He doesn't see your past. He doesn't see all the bad things that have happened to you, and all the bad things you've done. He sees you clothed with the righteousness of Christ, a pure and spotless virgin in His sight."

Those words struck a chord with Debbie. She looked up suddenly through her tears and begged, "Could you say that again, Jay, that last bit?"

"What I said was that God now sees you as a pure and spotless virgin in His sight, Debbie," Jay repeated, before going on, "You are clean. Believe me Debbie, you are clean. God says you are as white as snow!"

"Thank you, Jay. Thank you," Debbie wheezed, drying her tears. "Now I see it. It is only now that I can bring myself to really believe it. And it's absolutely wonderful!"

Having come to recognise that her past was all behind her forever, Debbie began to bury herself in the Bible. It was summer and daylight came early. This was a blessing to her, for as soon as the first shafts of light started to slant into her bedroom, Debbie was up at the window with her precious Book. It was just like being saved all over again. The appetite for her daily food, that was gradually building up her once-weakened body, was more than matched by her renewed appetite for spiritual sustenance from the Word of God to revitalise her long-starved soul.

Jean Stead's husband, Jim, had advised her once, "Start by reading the red, Debbie. If you have a Bible with all the words of Jesus highlighted in red, I suggest that you begin by reading every word that the Saviour spoke while here on earth. Just read all of them. Read the red and pray for the power!"

It was excellent advice and Debbie acted upon it with unbridled enthusiasm. As she did so she was often arrested in her reading by the promises given by the Son of God to His children, who were ordinary people like herself. Her heart overflowed with joy and praise when she came across personal assurances of the Saviour such as;

'Daughter, be of good cheer, your faith has made you well. Go in peace.' (Luke 8 ; 48)
    or
'Neither do I condemn you; go and sin no more.' (John 8 ; 11)
    or
'These things I have spoken to you, that in Me you may have peace. In the world you will have tribulation; but be of good cheer, I have overcome the world.' (John 16 ; 33)

Having read the red in about three days Debbie then started into the black. She just wanted to read as much of the Bible as she could. She found strength and succour for her soul every time she sat down with it, for if she wasn't 'blown away' with the first few verses, or even chapters that she read, she simply sat there until she was.

One morning she was reading in the first chapter of Revelation and came upon John's description of 'one like the Son of Man.' As she read down it she was overcome, much as the writer had been, with a sense of the awesome might and majesty of God.

'His head and hair were white like wool, as white as snow, and His eyes like a flame of fire:
    His feet were like fine brass, as if refined in the furnace, and His voice as the sound of many waters;
    He had in His right hand seven stars, out of his mouth went a sharp two-edged sword, and His countenance was like the sun shining in its strength…'

Debbie read this description of her Lord over and over again. She felt numb before it.

'Eyes like a flame of fire... a voice like the sound of many waters... a face like the sun shining in its strength...'

This wasn't the Jesus of the images in the churches of her childhood. This had nothing to do with the statues of Mary holding the limp body of a dead man. This was the all-powerful, ever-living, altogether lovely, resurrected Christ!

On her way out of chapel that morning she said to the student who had been sitting beside her, "Have you ever read Revelation chapter one? There is a fantastic description of the Lord Jesus in there."

"Oh no, Debbie, I have never read that," came back the shocked student's immediate reply. "You shouldn't be reading in Revelation you know. That will scramble your brain, that will!"

"If twenty years of smoking cannabis didn't scramble my brain, and neither did four years hooked on heroin and crack cocaine," Debbie laughed in response, " I don't think reading the Word of God will!"

On her journey through the Bible Debbie was also thrilled to unearth the beauties of the Song of Solomon and learnt some of what she considered to be the most beautiful passages, off by heart. The other girls thought she had gone all sentimental and soft when she began to say to them, "Wait to you hear this, isn't this beautiful? 'He brought me to the banqueting house, and his banner over me was love.' And there's more. Later on he goes on to say, 'Many waters cannot quench love, nor can the floods drown it.'"

Before the end of the summer Debbie had discovered not only some of the marvellous beauties of the Bible, but also that there had been hundreds of books written about the Bible. They were called commentaries. She started to read books by Matthew Henry, Dr. Martyn Lloyd-Jones and Charles Spurgeon about the teachings of scripture. When her mum or dad came to take her for a day out of Hope House the only place she wanted to go was to the CLC bookshop in Swansea. There she would be quite happy to spend all the money she had saved out of her allowance to buy either another commentary on the Bible or another translation of the Bible!

Such was Debbie's passion for the Scriptures and desire to share them with her fellow-students that some of the other girls often quipped good-naturedly, "We don't need a concordance in this place. All we have to do is ask 'Scripture Sue' Forrest! She knows the Bible off by heart!"

It wasn't quite true, but Debbie gradually began to feel the positive effects of the process described in another verse she had found in one of her many readings of the Bible one day. It was in Romans chapter twelve and urged Christians to become, 'transformed by the renewing of your mind.' Debbie found that the constant concentration on the Word of God had led to a more positive attitude of mind. She could now think straight again, and was beginning to realise the truth of the experience outlined in the second half of Romans 12 ; 2. She had started, she thought, to 'prove what is that good and acceptable and perfect will of God,' for her life.

For three months everything went well. Debbie was making remarkable physical, mental and spiritual progress. She did not look, sound or feel anything like the bewildered, broken woman whom her daughter had told, with tears in her eyes, 'Just stay until you're better, mum.'

Then, quite unexpectedly, came her biggest test of all.

Debbie came out of her last class one evening in early October and was met by a staff member who said, "I wasn't able to disturb you in class so I have booked you a telephone call for tomorrow morning. It's Derek."

"Oh no!" Debbie burst out in spontaneous despair. Suddenly the horizon of her life had all turned black. "That's Jim."

"No," the girl who had taken the call insisted. "He said his name was Derek."

"He may have told you that he was called Derek," Debbie went on to inform her, " but it's definitely Jim. That was his way of getting past you. He knew you wouldn't recognise the name, but I would. You see last year we ran a credit card scam. He was Derek at that time, and I was Lynn."

A cold shiver ran down Debbie's spine when she was forced to dip into her unsavoury memory bank. Anxious not to dwell on the past, or be upset in the present, Debbie told the staff member, much to the girl's surprise, "I'll not be taking the call."

That was what she had resolved, but it didn't work out.

Halfway through the next morning Audrey sent Fiona to call Debbie out of class. On the way back to the office Fiona explained, "Jim is on the phone. He is claiming very strongly that we are holding you here against your will. Audrey wants you to speak to him and let him know that we are not. We will both stay with you as you speak to him."

When Debbie entered the office Audrey smiled at her and nodded across to the telephone. She picked up the receiver and said. "Hi, Jim. How are you doing?"

"Well thanks, Debbie. It's great to hear your voice," Jim replied, and it was clear that he meant it. "And how are you?"

"I'm just fine," his former girlfriend continued, "and I want you to know that I'm not being held against my will. I like it here. This is my life now."

She paused, and looked at Audrey and then Fiona. They both smiled reassuringly back and Debbie took a deep breath and launched into what she had decided she would have to tell Jim if she ever heard from him again.

"I have something to tell you, Jim. You probably won't like it, but it's true," she began, nervously, wondering how he would react. "I'm walking one path and you are walking another and those paths will never meet. I'm sorry, Jim, but it's all over. I never want you to phone me, or try to make contact with me in any other way ever again. Sorry, but it's finished."

There was silence on the line for what seemed like at least twenty seconds before Jim's voice came on again, unusually submissively, to say, "That's all right. I will try and understand. But remember, Debbie, I love you. And I always will."

It was Debbie's turn to let the meaning of what Jim had said enter her mind and affect her heart, before replying, quietly but firmly, "I love you too, Jim. But sorry, it still has to be goodbye."

With that she put the phone down and immediately burst into tears.

Not wanting Audrey and Fiona to see how deeply the ending of the relationship with Jim had affected her, Debbie jumped up from the chair at the centre manager's desk and made for the door.

"Are you all right, Debbie?" Audrey and Fiona asked simultaneously.

"Yes, I'm all right," Debbie assured them, "but I want to be left on my own for a bit." She then closed the door behind her and walked across to the laundry, which she knew would be empty when all the other girls were in class.

Having shut herself off in the laundry Debbie sank down on to the floor, buried her head in her hands, and sobbed uncontrollably. After all she had been through with Jim, all the shouting and the thumping, the few happy days and the many heroin days, the discussions about the Bible and the arguments about drug-dealing, after it all, she was forced to recognise that she had loved him dearly. Sitting there on the laundry floor the parting appeared like a living death. It were as though someone had cut open her chest and torn out her heart.

'Many waters cannot quench love,' Solomon had written in his lovely song, centuries ago, and Debbie had quoted to her friends, just weeks ago. They thought she had gone all sloppy and starry-eyed at the time.

Now she was beginning to really appreciate, through bitter experience, that Solomon had been dead right in his decree.

22

A BRAND NEW BRIDGE

After Debbie had made her clean break from Jim she began to pray more earnestly, study more intensely and work more diligently. She abandoned herself completely to God and His will for her life. And He was preparing to reveal that will to her in miraculous ways.

One morning in November, during a break in classes, Debbie was sitting with some of the other girls, having a cup of coffee in the dining room. They didn't often have visitors in Hope House, especially in the winter months, and so the resident students were interested to discover that they had a well-dressed couple as guests that morning. Debbie was particularly fascinated to notice that the gentleman, who was sitting at an adjacent table speaking to Audrey and a lady whom she presumed to be his wife, had a strong Birmingham accent.

Debbie hadn't heard that accent since leaving the West Midlands, and so, when she saw Audrey excusing herself from the table, she went across to speak to them. She welcomed them to Hope House and found out that they 'had heard about this place from a couple of different people' and since they 'had come down to south Wales for a short break,' had decided 'to call and see it for themselves.'

When she had completed all the preliminary small talk, Debbie began to tell the stranger and his wife her life story. It was frustrating, however, for although they were both trying to appear to be listening to her ever so politely, it was obvious that the man in particular was looking for someone. Every time the door opened and another girl came in, or someone rose from a table at the other side of the room, he turned his head to see who it was. At one stage he actually whispered to his wife, "She's certainly not in here, Trish."

The lady, Trish, seemed to be taking marginally more interest in Debbie and her story than her husband, so the undeterred testimony-teller asked her, "Would you like to see what I was like before I came in here? I have a photograph up in my room."

"Yes, that would be interesting," the lady replied.

With that Debbie hared off up to her bedroom and brought down two photographs. The first of these had been taken a few days after she had come in, and the other three months later, as part of Pastor Macey's 'before and after;' record. She handed these to Trish, who studied them carefully, and muttered, "That's amazing."

Having looked at them for what she considered a respectful period the visiting lady passed them across to her husband, remarking nonchalantly as she did so, "You ought to take a look at those, George."

Straining to focus on the situation unfolding before him, the gentleman glanced down at the photographs in his hand. Suddenly his casual glance was transformed into an intent gaze. It looked as though he had just been struck by lightning.

He stared at the 'before' photograph, and then across at Debbie.

Then he repeated the process, staring longer and harder, second time around.

Turning to his wife he said, in a tone of total disbelief, "This is who I'm looking for. This is the woman I've been telling you about!"

Although Debbie had recognised the stranger's accent he hadn't given her his name, nor had she told the two guests who she was, so there had been no formal introduction between them. How then could he possibly have recognised her from a photograph? she wondered. And why was he looking for her?

"Do you not remember me?" the gentleman went on to enquire, the dawn of recognition lighting up his face. "Let me remind you. Wolverhampton Magistrate's Court... A Friday in early July... Over £600 in unpaid fines... My name is George Clarke, and I was your judge that day."

Debbie was speechless. She had stood before so many judges that she would never have known one from the other. This was the man who had remitted all her fines, when she had told him that she was going to Hope House.

"Oh thank you!" Debbie exploded, in gratitude. "But how did you find me here?"

George Clarke continued to stare incredulously at Debbie before going on, "There was something inexplicable about you in court that day that intrigued me, and when I went home from work I told Trish here about you, and about you saying you were going to Hope House. She had heard of it before from some of her friends. They were able to fill her in with a few details and so we decided to come and look you up."

Having finished that explanation of how he and his wife had come to be there, George asked, "Now that we have found you, how are you doing? I didn't even recognise you! You are all cleaned up! You don't look like the same person!"

"That's because I'm not the same person! I'm a new person!" Debbie told him in reply. "The old Debbie Forrest is dead. This is the new one you are looking at!"

George and Trish stayed and had a meal with Debbie and then she took them on a conducted tour of Hope House. She had planned her route so that her bedroom would be towards the end of their walkabout, and when they reached it Debbie invited them in.

As her two visitors sat in her room, still marvelling at the change in her life, Debbie took the opportunity to tell them how it had come about. She told them the story of how she had come to faith in Christ, how she had struggled with her addictions, and how she had eventually overcome them in Hope House.

Both of her guests listened with rapt attention to every word she was saying, and within minutes all three of them were in tears. It was such a powerful story.

"You have done well," George broke in to remark at one stage. "You ought to give yourself a pat on the back!"

Debbie thought he had missed the point. "No, George, I have done nothing," she countered. "That is what I am trying to tell you. All I have done is stay here. I told you in court that Jesus Christ was going to set me free from all my addictions, and He has. There is no doubt in my mind about that. You can see the evidence of it."

It was true. Back in July Debbie had been standing before him, a broken, scrawny, sickly drug-addict, claiming that Jesus Christ was going to set her free in Hope House. He had been mysteriously mesmerised by her then.

Now here they were, five months on, and he was sitting before her in Hope House. She had become transformed into an attractive, fluent, effervescent young woman, bearing incontrovertible testimony to the fact that Jesus Christ had set her free in all the ways she had maintained He would. He was mysteriously moved by her now.

George Clarke, the judge who had felt constrained to remit all charges against her, just sat and wept in her presence. "This is totally unbelievable... most amazing...absolutely incredible..." he kept saying, obviously struggling for superlatives. "I have never seen anything quite like this, or indeed like this place, anywhere before."

When it came time for George and Trish to leave, there were hugs and kisses all around. Debbie had never been hugged by a judge before, and found it rather unnerving at first, but recognised it to be yet another token of the grace of God, working in her life.

During those emotional goodbyes George said something that Debbie was to find tremendously encouraging. "You know, this visit to Hope House, and your story, has changed my life, Debbie," he affirmed. "I will never be the same man again. We will keep in touch. We will have a lot to talk about in the future."

Debbie waved after the car as it drove down to the gate and wondered if he really meant it. Would posh people like them ever want to 'keep in touch with' a single mother from the back streets of Wolverhampton? Would George Clarke, West Midlands magistrate, ever want to contact Debbie Forrest, delivered drug-addict, again? That remained to be seen.

Meanwhile there was plenty to do. Debbie was soon to be allowed home for the weekend for the first time, and she had to make plans for that. Now that she had been 'transformed by the renewing of her mind' she realised that it was time to make amends for all the hurt she had caused, to so many different people, in so many different ways, in her rebellious heroin-addicted days.

She began by writing to her Aunt Maureen. It would be difficult to go home, and possibly meet her mum's sister again, without first having apologised to her. Less than a year before, Debbie and her aunt had been engaged in a very acrimonious disagreement about their different lifestyles. This bitter bickering had caused a severe rift in family relations.

In her letter Debbie explained that her life had been changed by the power of God, she was now off drugs completely, and was extremely sorry for all the hurt she had caused. She went on to admit that many of the accusations she had made had been complete fabrications, without a shred of truth in them, and asked humbly to be forgiven.

Aunt Maureen replied within a week, in a warm and friendly fashion, assuring the returning prodigal that all was forgiven. Debbie smiled wryly as she read her gracious aunt's last sentence. She had concluded her letter by saying, 'I can't wait to see the old Debbie back.' Although appreciating exactly what she meant, Debbie thought, 'Just wait until you see me, Aunt Maureen. It's not the old Debbie, but the new Debbie, that's coming back!'

Having prepared the way by letter for a possible meeting with Aunt Maureen, Debbie had another burden on her mind. She had to go back to the house to which she had been warned never to return, her granddad's.

On her first weekend away from Hope House, however, it had to be her first stop. It was where her mum lived, and where she was expecting to stay.

Debbie had no idea what kind of reception she would receive from her disgruntled granddad, but she had hoped to break down at least some of the barriers he had erected by bringing him a present. His eyesight was very poor so she had bought him a large-print edition of the Amplified Bible.

When Debbie walked into the house he was sitting at the table, looking out the window. She gave him a hug and a kiss and said, "I'm home, granddad. I'm back. It's Debbie!"

The old man was completely taken aback.

"I just can't believe it! Are you sure it's you, Debbie? You're not the same person as the woman that went away," he exclaimed hoarsely, struggling to come to terms with the miraculous change in his 'useless' granddaughter.

"You're right, granddad," Debbie told him, laughing through her tears. "I'm not the same person as the woman that went away. I have been completely changed. Would you like me to tell you about it?"

Without waiting for an answer, she pulled out a chair from below the table and took hold of the hand that was lying loosely on it. She looked into the ageing face and both of them began laughing and crying time about.

They sat together like that for some time, and then Debbie began to tell her granddad of the love of God and the provision of salvation. She had been praying for him every day in Hope House, and now that the opportunity had presented itself, she felt she ought to witness to him.

When she had told him of God's love for him, and Jesus' death on the cross to take away his sin, and His power to heal the broken-hearted and provide new life for all, she said, "You need to give your life to Jesus, granddad. You need to be saved."

"Yes, I know," granddad responded, the tears streaming down his face.

"Would you like me to pray with you, and as I do you can ask Jesus into your life?" Debbie volunteered.

"Yes, please do," her granddad whispered, barely audibly.

Debbie then began to pray for the man who had earlier told her he never wanted to see her again, still holding his hand, and when she had said 'Amen' softly there was a momentary pause and he said, 'Thank you,' softly.

In the midst of this warm response Debbie detected that her grandad's appreciative 'Thank you' to her was also an appreciative 'Thank You,' to his Saviour.

Sliding the Bible she had brought him out from below his hand she went on to suggest, "Would you like me to read you something from the Bible I brought you?" It was little more than a rhetorical question for by the time he had replied, "Yes, please," she had turned to Psalm 23. It was one of the passages of scripture she was sure he would recognise, and began to read,

'The Lord is my Shepherd, to feed, guide and shield me, I shall not lack,
He makes me to lie down in fresh, tender, green pastures:
He leads me beside the still and restful waters
He refreshes and restores my life, my self,
He leads me in the paths of righteous, uprightness, and right standing with Him,
Not for my earning it, but for His name's sake...'

Granddad sat listening with evident interest and appreciation while Debbie read, and when she had finished he asked, "Could you read that again, Debbie?"

That weekend at home proved to be an unforgettable emotional and spiritual experience for Debbie, made particularly special by having re-established a warm relationship with granddad and hearing his frequent request, "Debbie, could you read me my Psalm again?" One of the last things Debbie did before leaving to return to Hope House was to mark 'his' psalm for him in his new Bible, so that he could find it easily and read it as often as he liked.

It was a long journey back, but Debbie made it with a light heart.

She had made an effort to repair a broken bridge, but God, in His grace and power, had allowed her to build a brand new bridge.

Debbie and her granddad were now united, not only by human ties, but also in their love for Him.

23

HE BROUGHT ME INTO HIS BANQUETING HOUSE

During the autumn months, when Debbie was taking a lively interest in all that was going on in Hope House, the senior staff discovered that she had a pleasing singing voice, and one of her next trips out was on a musical assignment. The lead singer with the Teen Challenge girls' group, 'Living Hope', had recently moved back to her native Scotland, and as the group had a number of outstanding bookings to fulfil, the other members asked Debbie if she would consider taking her place. Debbie was delighted to accept their invitation for it opened up another avenue of opportunity through which to honour her commitment to serve the Lord with the rest of her life.

Her delight was increased tenfold when she discovered that her first singing engagement with Living Hope was to be on a Saturday night in January 2000, and had been organised by Oldswinford Christian Fellowship, a Brethren assembly in the West Midlands, close to Wolverhampton.

Debbie cried all the way up in the minibus. She couldn't believe that she was going out on her first major singing engagement, after just six months on the rehabilitation programme, and that she was going to see Emily again. Debbie's mum had brought her down to Hope House to visit a number of times already during her stay there, and they had spent many blissful hours together in the course of that first thrilling weekend at home. This though, would be special. Not only was she going to see Emily, but Emily was also going to see her mum in a way she had never seen her before, as lead singer in a Christian praise group.

This promised to be some night!

Living Hope's new lead singer was overwhelmed at the thought of it! And she didn't even know the half of it!

When the group arrived at the Primary School in which the meeting was to be held, they all went into a small room for a short period of prayer. They then moved across into the main assembly hall to set up and check their equipment.

Although it was still at least a quarter-of-an-hour until the scheduled starting time, their audience for the evening was already gathering, and Debbie had only just appeared out on the stage with the others to do their sound checks when she heard a voice she recognised calling out, "Debbie."

It was her mum, and sitting beside her, beaming broadly, was Emily.

Sound checks were forgotten. Debbie leapt down from the platform and clasped her daughter in her arms and hugged her tightly. After a few moments of hearty hugging, Emily's ecstatic mum decided that it was time to allow her beautiful young daughter a chance to regain her breath, so she turned her attention to her mum and threw her arms around her. What Debbie hadn't realised when she had jumped down from the platform was that her mum and daughter had brought someone else with them, and she was standing patiently waiting her turn to be hugged.

It was Aunt Maureen, standing quietly, her face a picture of adoration and admiration, waiting for Debbie's attention. When her niece turned to her she exclaimed, "Oh Aunt Maureen! It's you!"

Her aunt, who had already expressed her forgiveness by letter, put her arm around her and replied, "It's great to see you again Debbie. You look brilliant!"

Debbie was so pleased to see her, too, and to witness the smile that translated forgiveness in words into forgiveness in action, and hugged her as well.

When she had finished talking to her mum, her daughter and her aunt, Debbie was about to rejoin the others on the platform when she saw a hand wave from the other side of the room. It was a man's voice that called out, "Hello there, Debbie," in greeting this time.

Debbie stopped short for she knew the voice, but couldn't quite put a face to it. Her eyes shot open, and her mouth fell open, in astonishment. It was George, her fine-remitting magistrate, with his wife Trish beside him. "It's lovely to see you!" Debbie exclaimed, in a spontaneous expression of warmth and gratitude. "How did you know I was going to be here?"

"I didn't know you were going to be here!" George Clarke replied, genuinely surprised. "Trish had heard that Living Hope, a group from Hope House, was singing here tonight and at the services tomorrow, so we decided to come along."

Having given them both an appreciative, welcoming kiss, Debbie said, "I hope you are not in a hurry away afterwards. I would love to have longer to speak to you."

"Don't worry, we'll not be rushing away," it was Trish who spoke up before George could say anything. "There will be plenty of time to talk later on." Neither Debbie nor George was, at the time, in a position to interpret her genial, accompanying smile as anything more than an indication of the depth of their friendship.

As she was turning to make a second attempt to return to the stage Debbie saw another man, four rows back from George and Trish, lift his hand and wiggle his fingers in a friendly gesture. This sign with his hand was accompanied by a broad grin on his face. It took Debbie a minute to figure out who he was, and then she remembered.

Yes. Of course. It was Derrick Cole, the man who had spoken to her one dismally depressing day in Bilston town square. It was the man who had told her that God had a plan for her life and had prayed with her and for her, standing in the street! Now he was there to hear her sing the praises of God, as a Christian. He was present to see Debbie step up onto another rung of the ladder of God's plan for her life. And he hadn't even known that she was going to be there!

This was unbelievable! She called down to Derrick, "See you afterwards!" and glanced down towards the door before turning to go back to the platform. There was a woman she knew coming up the aisle, scanning across the rows of chairs, probably deciding where to sit. This was someone, who, like Derrick, she hadn't seen for a long time. It was Lynne, the West Indian lady from Emily's 'tambourine church,' the lady who had given her the Bible she had so much treasured in her early, unspoilt weeks as a Christian.

It was uncanny. Debbie was so excited. It seemed that so many of the people who had been used by God to bring her to Himself, and guide her in His ways, had all congregated in the same place to hear her make her first public appearance in His service. Debbie skipped down to her, and greeted her with, "Hello, Lynne. It's wonderful to meet you again after all this time. Thank you for all your prayers. Don't go away after the meeting. I want to have a chat with you!"

Lynne was startled. She barely recognised Debbie, she had changed so much. " Oh. It's you, Debbie," she responded, after a moment's delay.

"See you later," Debbie went on, hastily. She was prompted into the sudden 'see you later' reaction, for one of the other girls had come down and whispered, "Can you come up now? We are nearly ready to start!"

As the programme began Debbie was carried along on the crest of a wave of spiritual delight. Her emotional euphoria was fuelled by a motivating mixture of anticipation and apprehension. This was her big moment, her debut for God. How would it go?

She needn't have worried. Ever since learning that she would be travelling to sing at the Oldswinford weekend, Debbie had been praying fervently that God would help her. And He did. When she took the microphone in her hand to start singing His praise she felt immediately at ease. It was exhilarating.

Those who had arranged the evening had asked Debbie if she would tell something of what God had done in her life, at some point in the programme. She was happy to do this, and although she had thought about it at some length many times before the event, when the time came to speak her testimony only lasted a couple of minutes.

The length of time it took to recount her story was of little importance to the audience, however. It was what she said, and the power and conviction with which she said it, that charmed the hankies from the handbags.

She began by telling everyone, "I don't need to introduce myself to some in this audience, really. I have already met a few people in the hall this evening who know what I was like, and indeed I am very thankful for the part they played in helping me in various ways and at different stages."

After pausing to scan down over the pack-out crowd, Debbie went on, "There are probably quite a number here tonight, though, who don't know my background, the mess I was in and the wreck I had made of my life, before God intervened and cleaned me up, and if there are let me tell you just a little bit about it... I was brought up in Wolverhampton. I began smoking cannabis in my teenage, and later on, when I was caught growing it, I lost my job, my car, my home, everything. I then became a heroin and crack cocaine addict. Things reached a very low ebb. I was as skinny as a rake, constantly sick, and sometimes suicidal. I tried more than once to end it all by taking an overdose, but it didn't work. I used to be mad at myself for I was such an abject failure at everything that I couldn't even kill myself. Life was, I thought, both hopeless and pointless.

Then Emily, my daughter, who is here tonight, my little daughter as she was then, asked me to go to church with her and I said, 'What! Church? Me go to church? I can't go to church like this, darling.' Emily wasn't to be put off, though, and at last I gave in and we went. And it was there, in the warmth of that church, surrounded by lovely Christian people, the like of whom I had never met before, that God broke me down and I accepted Jesus as my Saviour.

I was delighted to be saved, have my sins forgiven, and be a child of God. It was great, but I was soon to find that the devil didn't like it. You see I had a cleansed spirit in a drug-addicted body and there was a big battle that I haven't time to tell you about, but I just want to say that last July I entered Hope House. There with the help of God and the staff I have come through and am here this evening as a living witness to prove what the Lord Jesus can do in the life of anyone who is willing to trust Him…"

People were sitting on the edges of their seats, agog. Debbie, and her story had held the audience spellbound. When she had finished this riveting first public presentation of her testimony Debbie announced the next item that Living Hope were going to perform.

As the group prepared to present their next piece there was a shifting and a shuffling in the body of the hall. The ever so brief interval had afforded the audience a few seconds for hankie-finding, eye-wiping and nose-blowing before settling down to listen to the next carefully chosen, and heartily sung, song. There could be no doubt that Debbie's earnest, honest contribution had made a deep impact on all present.

This was to become very obvious at the end of the meeting. People that Debbie had never met in her life before were lining up to tell her how they had been 'blessed' by her 'ministry both in word and song.'

What though of all the others whom Debbie had told not to be 'rushing away' or had promised to 'speak to later?'

They would just have to wait. And they did, gladly.

Debbie wanted to speak to them one by one. It was marvellous to see them all again, as each of them had played a significant part in her earlier life. The first to come across to her was Derrick, and they recalled the morning he had challenged her in Bilston. Debbie reminded him of what he had said that morning. It was, 'I believe God has a plan for your life.' Considering what she had told an entranced audience an hour or so before, his prophecy seemed to have come true.

When Derrick had gone, Lynne came over to join the group around Debbie and they hugged one another yet again. "I will never forget how kind you were to me, and how patient you were with me, in those early days," Debbie told her gratefully.

Lynne was just about to take her leave also when Trish arrived back amongst the dwindling number of people still with Debbie. "Please don't go," she said. "George and I would like you to come round to our house for a cup of tea with Debbie's mum and aunt and Emily."

Debbie looked across at her quizzically. She knew nothing of this. Sensing her slight bewilderment, Trish stepped forward and explained, "I have a surprise for you, Debbie. You are coming to stay at our house tonight. George and I volunteered to keep two of the girls from Living Hope and when I learnt that you were coming I asked if you could come to us. Dionne is coming too."

Before Debbie could compose herself sufficiently to make any coherent reply, George spoke up. "It's a surprise for me, too, Debbie, I might add! When Trish suggested that we keep two of the girls overnight I agreed that it would be a good idea. But what she didn't tell me was that one of them was going to be you! I didn't even know that you were going to be here!"

Half-an-hour later Debbie found herself sitting in George and Trish's beautiful bungalow outside Wolverhampton. She wasn't alone with them either. Gathered in the same room were her daughter, her mum, her aunt Maureen, Lynne from the Apostolic Church and Dionne from Living Hope.

As the tea and cakes were passed around George said to Debbie, "You must be tired. Would you like a little stool to put your feet up on?" Debbie shook her head to decline his offer. She was afraid to speak in case she burst out crying.

When the guests who had to go home began leaving for home, some time later, the gracious host and hostess had an idea to put to the by-now dumbfounded Debbie. "Perhaps Emily would like to join us for lunch tomorrow," they proposed.

This was arranged. Nanny was to bring Emily to the morning service and then George and Trish would bring her back for lunch with her mum.

It was incredible.

Later that evening when Trish showed her two guests to their bedroom, Debbie was overwhelmed. The room was warm and a bedside lamp cast a welcoming glow all around. On the pillow of each of the two single beds lay a teddy bear and a little net of chocolates, tastily tied in a bow with ribbon.

Debbie didn't know whether to laugh or cry, so, not for the first time in the past few months, she did both, in turn. It was so amazing and so affecting. Sleep was not a priority with Debbie that night. Dionne and she kept switching on and off the light just to check that this was real. Surely they couldn't be dreaming!

"Can you imagine it, Dionne?" Debbie kept asking, her voice bathed in wonder. "I was once a junkie in the dock before this magistrate. Now I am lying in a bed in his house being treated like the Queen! Only God could work a miracle like that!"

When Dionne had eventually dropped off to sleep, Debbie was still wide-awake. She lay staring up into the cosy darkness thinking that this was like something out of a fairy story. Then her Christian consciousness assumed control and she began to equate it to a number of Bible stories. But which one? This experience felt as though someone had taken The Prodigal Son, The Good Samaritan and The Sinful Woman of Luke Seven and rolled them all together! Debbie lay marvelling at it for a long time until sleep overcame her at last also.

Living Hope took part in the service in Oldswinford Christian Fellowship the next morning and afterwards Emily joined her mum at George and Trish's home for lunch. This was yet another unforgettable event. Debbie sat beside her little daughter and was served by the magistrate and his wife. After the first course Debbie's Hope House training began to show and she jumped up to help clear the table. She was immediately told that this was her day off. "You just sit there with Emily," George told her. "You are our honoured guest today. We will serve you."

There was little for Debbie to do but sit down again. She took Emily's hand and struggled to fight back the tears once more. She didn't want to appear too emotional in the presence of these exceptionally kind people.

When the main course was served Debbie looked at the beautiful food on the table and the silver cutlery she was using and another of her 'love' verses from the Song of Solomon flashed across her mind. It was, 'He brought me to the banqueting house, and his banner over me was love.' Debbie could think of no better way to describe how she felt at that very moment. Those words captured it exactly.

With lunch over, Trish had another suggestion to make to Debbie and her delighted daughter. "Would you pair like to go along to the park to feed the ducks? I will come with you if you like," she said.

It was a wonderful offer, and within ten minutes all three were setting out for the park, dressed in winter coats to keep them warm in the chill of a January afternoon. As the trio approached the duck-pond Trish volunteered, "I will wait here at this little bridge. You two go on and feed the ducks."

That was a sublime half-hour. It was the first time for many months that Debbie had been able to spend time alone with her daughter. Emily broke chunks off the slices of loaf that Trish had given her and tossed them to the band of noisily impatient ducks in the water. Debbie stood with her arm around her. They talked and laughed as though they were the only two people left on the planet.

This was the crowning glory, the icing on the cake.

The grateful mother could let the tears flow freely now, as she thanked God for this marvellous climax to such an extraordinary weekend.

Debbie had cried all the way up in the minibus the previous afternoon.

She sang all the way home in it that night.

Many of the choruses she had learnt in the Apostolic Church in Wolverhampton, as many of the worship songs from Hope House as she could remember, and all the pieces she had presented with Living Hope that weekend were given a hearty rendition. The girls in the minibus joined in, but when their throats dried up or their enthusiasm flagged Debbie carried on alone, singing a solo.

She just couldn't stop praising the Lord!

24

OH NO! NOT ANOTHER ONE!

"You have kept your promise and finished your course so I am now about to keep the promise I made to you," Debbie's dad told her on the telephone. His daughter had progressed positively through the residential programme at Hope House and was by then in her final week.

The call had come quite out of the blue so Debbie felt that she had to enquire, "And what was that, dad?" Whatever his promise was, she obviously hadn't been sufficiently focused in her mind when he had made it, to remember it.

"I told you that if you cleaned up your life I would buy you a car to start you out on the road to normality once again," her dad reminded her. "And I have one for you. I will come down and pick you up and bring you back here to my house where the car is waiting. It is ready for you to drive away."

"That's great, dad! Thank you ever so much! I will be ready and waiting for you when you come," Debbie replied, making no effort to conceal her excitement at the wonder of it all. Here was her dad, who had once described her as 'something out of 'The Exorcist,' buying her a car!

Her dad was pleased that his fulfilled promise had received such an appreciative response, and went on, "I have your uncle Keith here staying with me, and I am planning to bring him along for the ride. It will pass an hour or two of the afternoon for him. We will be with you later."

When they did arrive as expected, in mid-afternoon, Debbie cried when she saw her uncle Keith again. And he cried when he saw her.

Debbie was touched when she saw the physical state of her uncle. He had been involved in an industrial accident about six months earlier and had almost lost his life. A turbine had exploded at the power station where he had been working, and he had suffered extensive steam burns to his body.

Uncle Keith's tears at the sight of his niece were not caused by distress or compassion, however. They were, instead, tears of pure joy and delight. He was thrilled to see Debbie looking so healthy and vibrant. "The last time I saw you looking as well as this you were thirteen!" he declared at an early stage in their emotional reunion.

It was an hour's drive back to Fishguard where Debbie's dad lived and worked. He had a restaurant there and as they were approaching the town of Carmarthen on their return journey he said, "I hope you two don't mind but I need to stop off in Tesco's here and stock up on some supplies."

Debbie and Keith had no objections to a short break and when the restaurateur had disappeared into the depths of the grocery store they settled on a bench outside. It was a sunny June afternoon and as they sat there together Debbie's uncle couldn't help remarking repeatedly, and incredulously, on the change in his niece since the last time they had met.

He sat gazing at her in awe-struck admiration. "I just can't believe it is the same person," he said over and over again. "You look so attractive... so alert... so alive..."

When he had run short of words to express his amazement at the transformation that had taken place in

Debbie's life, uncle Keith continued looking across at her in fond silence. It was at this point that she began to enquire after his condition.

"Yes, God has done marvellous things in my life, it's true," she began. "I am doing fine now, but what about you?"

A dark cloud of despair crossed her uncle's face. Debbie had heard from some other members of the family that he had been left severely traumatised after his accident. He was clearly depressed and she detected a sense of almost panic in his voice as he burst out, "I'm not very well, to be honest. I have had lots of skin grafts, and I still have to go for more. I am almost afraid to go to sleep at night for I keep having these horrendous nightmares. I don't know how I am ever going to get over this. I just don't know what I am going to do…"

His voice tailed away into hopelessness and his head turned away in embarrassment. He was in both physical pain and mental turmoil, but the person to whom he had just opened his heart had been in that position often before. She knew exactly how he felt, and exactly what to say.

Reaching over to lay a sympathetic hand on his shoulder, Debbie said softly, "I have felt just like that so many times. I know what it's like, but I can assure you that there is hope. It took the power of God to change me from what I once was to what I am now, and that same power is available to you."

Sensing that the transformation in her life was a very potent and practical witness to her uncle, and that he was listening attentively to her every word, Debbie continued, "Jesus is the only one who can put all the broken pieces of your life back together again. He wants to reach down and change you from the inside. He can heal your emotions, calm your confusion and make you a new person. Jesus wants to come into your life, uncle Keith. He alone can help you."

Debbie paused for a moment. Tears were running down her uncle's cheeks. She allowed him a few seconds to come to terms with the truth she had just told him before enquiring gently, "Do you want to receive Jesus into your life? You can do that here, and now, you know."

"Yes, I do," uncle Keith replied. He nodded his head to add visual emphasis to his croaky vocal response.

Busy shoppers continued to hurry past with their plastic bags and piled high trolleys while Debbie progressed to the next phase of her compassionate personal outreach campaign with her heartbroken uncle. She began by telling him, in language that he could understand, about the sin that causes unrest, and even distress, in peoples' lives, and about God's plan of salvation, designed to restore such hurting people to Himself. Having kept her explanation as simple as possible, Debbie went on to spell out the need for a personal response. Jesus had made many appeals, in the Bible, for burdened people to come to Him, she said, quoting a few examples. He invited them to open their hearts to Him, and if they did, He in turn would reward them with peace, rest and satisfaction, the like of which they had never known before. All that remained for the anguished soul to do was to respond to Jesus' invitation, and open his or heart and let the Saviour in.

Having had the power of God to change his life, and the desire of Jesus to enter his life, explained to him so clearly, Debbie's uncle whispered, "I want to accept Jesus into my heart right now. But what do I do?"

"Do just that," Debbie told him, with a beaming smile on her face and mounting tears in her eyes. "Accept Jesus into your heart. I will pray with you and as I pray outwardly, you pray inwardly, confessing your need of Christ, and asking Him to come into your life and make you His child."

Totally oblivious to any of the steady stream of shoppers who may have been watching, Debbie then bowed her head and began to pray for the broken man beside her. While she was praying, her disconsolate uncle did as she had instructed, and invited Jesus into his heart and life.

When Debbie opened her eyes it was to witness uncle Keith sitting with his head slightly bowed, and to hear him say simply, "I've done it." The overjoyed Debbie threw her arms around him and planted a loving kiss on his tear-streaked cheek.

That was a beautiful moment.

That was the moment when Debbie led the uncle, who had taught her how to make wine, to the only One with the power to turn water into wine.

The Lord had promised to give oppressed individuals 'beauty for ashes, the oil of joy for mourning and the garment of praise for the spirit of heaviness.' Uncle Keith had that experience on a bench outside Tesco's supermarket in Carmarthen that sunny summer afternoon. Since God had imparted new life to him in that very minute when he had opened his heart to Jesus, Debbie's uncle felt an amazing metamorphosis take place in his mind. The old sense of pessimism and pointlessness had gradually evaporated to be replaced by a warmth of security and satisfaction.

Debbie and her uncle had only been children in the family of God together for about ten blissful minutes when Debbie's dad came along pushing a trolley stacked with his 'stock up.' He looked across at the two who had made no move to rise from their seat in the sun, and was just about to tell them to follow him to the car, when he noticed that his brother appeared to have been crying.

"What's up with you, Keith?" he asked, gruffly.

"I've just become a Christian," his brother told him, smiling sheepishly, not quite sure how his 'good news' would be received. His diffidence was understandable, given Debbie's dad's instinctive reaction.

"Oh no! Not another one!" he exclaimed, with a mild but manifest sarcasm. "That's all we need! Another one! Another Christian around the place!"

Outburst over he gave his trolley one almighty shove, and having propelled it a few more steps turned around and called over his shoulder, "Come on, you pair. Are you coming or not?"

On the remaining leg of the journey to Fishguard Debbie found her mind alternating between praising God for her uncle Keith's salvation and wondering about whatever it was that lay ahead. What kind of car had her dad chosen for her? He had stubbornly refused to tell her, insisting that he wanted it to be 'a surprise.' And surprise it certainly was!

For some reason Debbie imagined that her dad would have chosen a small car for her, so when he drew up beside a big dark blue Volvo Estate outside his house, she was rendered totally speechless.

"There you are, Debbie," her dad said, trying to sound matter-of-fact. "That's your car. I chose it especially because it seems to be in good condition."

Debbie was thrilled. Her dad was so kind. Before leaving for her return journey she was to discover that not only had be bought her the car but he had also taxed it, insured it and put it through M.O.T. The final phase of his fulfilled promise in appreciation of Debbie's transformation was to hand her an envelope with money in it.

"That will put petrol in it for you once or twice," he told his dumbfounded daughter.

When she had thanked her dad profusely, and promised to 'keep in touch' with uncle Keith, Debbie drove her latest acquisition proudly back to Hope House, where she was just about to finish phase three of her programme.

Having reached that point, all that was left for her to do before graduating was to complete her fourth and final phase. Hope House usually arranged for women who had reached that stage to become engaged in activity within a church or become involved in some aspect of community service. This assignment was seen as a bridge out into 'normal life' and was monitored by Hope House staff. It remained to be seen where Debbie would be sent for her 'placement.'

The rapidly maturing Christian was rather disappointed initially to learn that she was 'being kept on' at Hope House. Pastor Macey and Audrey, the centre manager, told her that they were offering her 'an internship.' Debbie thought that they had just made this term up. 'Internship' sounded, she reckoned, like a fancy-sounding, face-saving American word, which being loosely translated meant 'we don't really know what to do with you now.'

She couldn't have been more mistaken, however. The truth was that the leadership had identified her as a future leader and were planning to use her phase four 'placement' to train her as a staff member!

Debbie enjoyed her months on 'phase four.' As a trainee staff member she had occasional days off and these were to prove particularly precious. She would plan to set off early in the morning, drive up to Wolverhampton in her big, powerful Volvo, and pick Emily up from Kevin's house. They would then go across to stay with Debbie's mum and granddad and spend a wonderful time of sharing together. Next morning Debbie would leave Emily off at school and motor back to southwest Wales in time to commence her afternoon shift at Hope House.

It was during those days of 'internship' that Debbie became more fervent about the commitment that she had once made at a crisis point in her career. She had vowed loosely to serve the Lord with the rest of her life, but Debbie had now become passionate in her desire to make every moment of the remainder of her days count for God. She wanted to be as extreme in the service of God as she had been in the service of sin.

Debbie had once thought that she would like to go and serve God in Africa. She had read about stalwarts of the faith, people who had been willing to dedicate their lives to the spread of the Gospel, whatever the cost. During her stay in Hope House she had either bought or borrowed books about people like David Livingstone, Jim Elliott, Brother Andrew, Gladys Aylward and Hudson Taylor. On reading these stirring biographies Debbie had often wondered if she would have the grace to endure the hardships, and power to achieve the results, in a manner, and to the extent, that such outstanding Christian trailblazers had done.

It was a big question. In her more impassioned moments Debbie would pray, "Lord help me to be a mighty influence for You. I don't want to end up as a back pew Christian... a Sundays-only Christian... a rocking-chair Christian. I want my life to count for You. Now, today, tomorrow, and every day in the future…"

When she learnt that Rheinhart Bonke was coming to hold a meeting in the National Indoor Arena in Birmingham, Debbie decided to take her mum and Emily along. There were thousands at that Saturday evening rally but amongst the very few people whom Debbie saw that she recognised were George and Trish and even then they were some distance away in the huge auditorium.

As the meeting proceeded the speaker proclaimed that it was possible for the Christian to know the power of God in a very real way, in his or her life. By that he meant 'power to witness, power to overcome temptation and the power to stand up and be an influence for God in a world that hates Him…'

That was what Debbie had been craving and when an appeal was made at the end of the meeting for 'anyone who wanted to be prayed for' to come forward, she was amongst the first to move. In the highly-charged prayer session that followed, Rheinhart Bonke prayed for Debbie, mentioning particularly the two specific needs that Debbie had identified. One of these was personal and immediate but the other would produce, if granted, a rich spiritual harvest in the future.

He prayed that Debbie would be given the power to overcome the problems she was having with her thought life and be granted purity and clarity of mind. Debbie's second sincere request was that she would be given a compelling freshness every time she was called upon to share her testimony. What she longed for was that when she stood up to recount the multitude of mighty things that God had done in her life she would be enabled to present it in such an articulate and powerful manner that people would be irresistibly drawn to her Saviour.

After the rally Debbie stayed overnight with her mum and granddad and as she was setting off to return to Hope House on Sunday afternoon she felt 'on fire' for God. She was convinced that God had answered prayer in relation to her struggles with her thought life. Since the previous evening she hadn't been bombarded with any of the inappropriate thoughts that had often caused her such concern in the past. This of course could have been partly due to the fact that it was still only the 'day after the night before' and her mind had remained on a permanent spiritual 'high' since that occasion.

What though of her desire to sound verbally fluent and prove spiritually fruitful in the presentation of her testimony?

What would happen when she was afforded the opportunity, probably sooner rather than later, to find out if her prayer in that regard had also been answered?

25

CLEANED UP

Working as an 'intern' in Hope House gave Debbie an insight into the ups and downs, the rewards and the difficulties, of working with women with severe addiction problems. It helped her to appreciate, in a very real way, the care and consideration that had been shown to her when she had come in as a resident, more than a year before.

One of the responsibilities, which seemed to grow up around her as a matter of course, rather than having been allocated to her initially in any official capacity, was to become lead singer and team manager of the singing group, 'Living Hope.' Since her debut, back in January, the management of Hope House recognised that Debbie possessed not only a natural ability to sing in public, but also an infectious enthusiasm for sharing the Gospel, whether in word or song, that brought the best out of those around her. Thus, as part of her phase four training programme they were happy to allow her to lead Living Hope out into churches across England and Wales, when invited.

In this role Debbie learnt much about the practicalities of working with people, and about the protection and blessing of God. Tom Stables, who held a senior position with Teen Challenge, and his wife Lorraine, accompanied the group to nearly all of their engagements. Tom did most of the preaching, leaving Debbie and her group of 'girls' to sing a number of pieces and arrange for a few of them to tell of the mighty change God had wrought in their lives. As it would be impractical for them all to travel together, Tom and Lorraine usually made their way to the different venues by car, bringing the 'sound man' with them.

This left Debbie with the job of driving the minibus, full of usually quite excited young women, to wherever it was that they were going. The group of girls, which could vary in number from six to eight, and in composition as individuals moved through the different phases of their programme, looked upon a trip out with Living Hope as a special privilege. It was, on many occasions, the first trip out of Hope House for them with anyone other than members of their own families, since coming in. If anything unusual, either physical or spiritual, happened on their outing into the outside world, it was set to prove a talking point for days and weeks to come.

One such unplanned-for interlude occurred early on a Saturday morning. Living Hope had been booked to take a youth service at a distant English location that evening and Debbie and her group had set off from Hope House at six-thirty. It would be a long, tiresome journey and the girls would need time to unwind before taking the platform, hence the dawn start.

They had just driven down the slip road on to the M4 and Debbie was thinking of the long trip and then the evening meeting ahead, when a voice from the back of the bus piped up, "There's smoke in here, Debbie, in the back of the bus."

The girls were in high spirits, despite the early start, and Debbie thought that they had decided to play a joke on her, as others had done before, just to raise a laugh.

"Will you for goodness sake keep quiet in there, you lot," she replied good-naturedly, without troubling to turn around. "We haven't even left Swansea yet and we still have a long, long way to go. Settle down. I need to concentrate on getting you there."

These girls had been specially chosen. They were selected, not only for their singing ability, but also for their willingness to adhere to the rules of Hope House and their perceived capacity to behave acceptably when 'outside.' One of the principles that had been taught very forcibly was that they were to obey their leaders at all times, and they were to be particularly respectful to Debbie when out with Living Hope.

So they did as they had been told. They settled down, and kept quiet.

It was hard, though, for they were choking.

Eventually one girl began to cough uncontrollably, and another, sensing that those around her were beginning to panic, decided to voice all of their fears.

"Debbie, it's getting worse. It is really very smoky in here now!" she exclaimed. The effort of speaking caused her to start coughing too.

Realising, from the urgency of this latest bulletin from behind her, that perhaps this wasn't just a prank after all, Debbie spared a second to glance back over her shoulder.

She was instantly horrified.

It was true. The seating area in the rear of the bus was filled with smoke. The suffocating occupants were barely distinguishable through the gloom. Her response was immediate.

Calling out, "Sorry girls!" she swerved over on to the hard shoulder of the motorway and slewed to a stop. She then jumped out and raced around to open the back doors. A cloud of smoke streamed out and curled away up over the roof. The spluttering members of Living Hope were next to emerge hastily, one by one, clutching at dry throats and wiping smarting eyes.

When she was sure that everyone was safely out, Debbie called the emergency services and the police and a fire engine were soon at the scene. The girls loved the high drama of it all, now that they were out of any danger. They had been thrilled to be going away for the weekend to sing, but they couldn't have imagined that their adventure would begin with a rescue from a smoke-filled minibus!

A second phone call, this time to Hope House, saw emergency transport arranged and after a delay of nearly two hours Living Hope carried on to fulfil their engagement. As they resumed their journey the group members were still chattering about their experience, telling of the feeling of fear that gripped them when the bus filled up with smoke, and the sense of relief that followed when they were safely back out in the fresh air.

Debbie saw a sermon in it, however. She encouraged them to draw parallels between their recent experience and their life experience. Had they not been choking, suffocating, gradually perishing in sin but now they had been rescued into the exhilarating fresh air of new life in Christ? They should, she counselled, be thanking God, not only for His preserving grace in their lives, but also for making them His children in the first place.

By the time they reached their youth service engagement that evening they had a lot to tell, and a lot to sing about!

On another weekend the group had been booked, or so they thought, to take two meetings, one on the Saturday night in the Wirral, just south of Liverpool, and the other on the Sunday night somewhere in Cheshire.

The group had been warmly received in the Wirral and there had been a very positive response to their presentation of the Word of God, in song, in testimony and when Tom had preached. Having been greatly heartened by that meeting, and after a night spent in overnight accommodation, which had been kindly arranged by the Wirral church, the group set off southwards the next afternoon. The girls had been told that the church they were going to was 'even bigger' than the one they had been to on the Saturday night, so they were approaching this final engagement of the weekend with an element of anticipation.

When they found the church it appeared to be, as had been predicted, very much larger than that of the night before. It was still almost an hour before the service was due to commence but Tom, Debbie and the team always liked to arrive in good time for their bookings in order to have all their equipment set up and tested before it was time to start.

There appeared to be very little life about this church, though.

Debbie and the girls climbed down out of the minibus and Tom and Lorraine joined them as they walked up to the church door. The 'sound man' was left to sort out his gear in the car.

They pushed open the heavy door and filed into the empty, echoing porch. All was still. Eventually Tom walked out and through another door and met a well-dressed lady coming to meet him.

Her welcome, which she tried to make warm, also sounded wary. "Oh hello," she began. "It is lovely to see you, but dare I ask, who are you? "

"We are from Teen Challenge, and we are here to take your evening service," Tom volunteered.

"Oh yes. Of course," the lady replied, trying now to sound convincing. "We hadn't been expecting you quite so soon. Just excuse me while I go out to the car and make a phone call. I will be back in to see you again in a few minutes." With that she hurried off, out through a side door.

"Not expecting us so soon!" Tom repeated with an amused glint in his eye. "They weren't expecting us at all if you ask me!"

It was probably true, but no one ever admitted it. The lady was back as she promised, 'in a few minutes,' and a short time later others began to arrive. The Living Hope team were in the middle of setting up, to take whatever part they could be afforded in the evidently already arranged evening service, when a man appeared with food for them all. The lady with the phone had obviously arranged for someone to visit the local Mc

Donald's and bring in a selection of food and enough soft drinks for the visiting party. They were shown into a kitchen at the back of the church, and when they had finished their meal they were ready to begin the meeting.

The opening worship was conduct by members of the church but then Living Hope were introduced and invited to sing. When they had performed a few pieces Debbie gave her testimony, and it was then that she became acutely aware that God had answered the second of her prayers on that Saturday night in The National Exhibition Centre.

The words came tumbling out, guided by God, and it was clear by the receptive attitude of the congregation that they were penetrating deep into many hearts and minds. When Debbie had finished recounting her struggles with sin and her satisfaction in salvation the group sang again, and then Tom preached.

When he had finished speaking he made an appeal. Seven people came forward in response, and following counselling they all accepted Jesus as their Saviour.

Even though the church leaders may not have been expecting the team from Teen Challenge to arrive there that evening, God had been. He demonstrated this by pouring out His blessing in salvation, in a manner that the church hadn't seen for years!

One of the highlights of Debbie's period of ministry with Living Hope was when Tom, Lorraine and she took a group of eight from Hope House on a ten-day tour of Denmark. It was Debbie's job, as usual, to see the team transported safely from place to place, and her M4 escapade paled into insignificance when compared to her Danish ordeal. The Welsh incident, although scary, was short-lived, and bore no comparison to driving eight animated young women around a foreign country, with the steering wheel on the other side of the bus and the traffic on the other side of the road!

The logistics of always having to turn up in the right place at the right time were far outweighed by the social benefits and spiritual blessings of the trip, however. Living Hope toured with a Danish Teen Challenge group, visiting large churches that had made every effort to ensure that they had capacity crowds assembled to hear them. These audiences were made up of people who were heavily addicted to drugs or alcohol, or both, plus prostitutes, single parents and many others who, although apparently well off, had found life empty and meaningless and were desperately craving a sense of fulfilment.

At each venue Living Hope sang in English, and the Danish group followed them in their native language. Debbie and the other girls from Hope House took turns, at the rate of two per night, to tell how they had come to Jesus, and the change He had made in their lives. The local group then adapted a similar pattern during their contribution to the programme. Following a successful format, worked out back at home in Britain, Tom then brought a closing message, speaking with the aid of an interpreter.

After each meeting Tom, Lorraine and Debbie were usually called upon to counsel, again through interpretation, people who had been stirred by the truth of what they had heard, and wanted to become Christians.

This trip proved a tremendous inspiration to Debbie in a number of ways. Firstly, and on a very practical level, she was able to witness the work, and organisational structure, of Teen Challenge in another country. The spiritual bonus was that she was able to meet other committed leaders like herself, single-minded Christians whose declared goal in life was to see lives cleaned up, indeed created anew, through the mighty power of the Gospel.

It was also interesting to note that although the young people with whom Teen Challenge Denmark was working came from a different cultural background they had exactly the same problems as the women who presented themselves at Hope House. The thrill came for Debbie in recognising that if the problems were the same, so was the solution.

These young people were undergoing an identical programme to that being run at Hope House and other centres operated by Teen Challenge U.K. The supreme delight lay in appreciating that they were also being pointed to the same Saviour, who alone had the power to change lives. Had He not instructed His disciples to 'Go into all the world and preach the Gospel?'

The lesson for Debbie was that the message of salvation and the resulting marvel of transformation were not confined to southwest Wales. They had been carefully crafted, by their Chief Designer, to make a global impact.

When they returned from Denmark, and with requests for appearances continuing to come in from all over the country, Pastor Macey approached Debbie one day. He had a proposal to make.

"I think it is time that Living Hope considered producing a CD," he suggested. "That would serve a dual purpose. It could be used, most importantly, as a tool for evangelism, by preserving your music and its message, and making them readily available to the public. Any funds raised from the sale of it could be used to help further our work."

Debbie agreed with him in his vision for a CD, but was somewhat apprehensive about the prospect of appearing in a recording session. That would be yet another 'first' for her. When she had dedicated her life to the service of God she had never dreamt that singing on a CD would constitute part of her ministry. But if that was how her Heavenly Father had planned it, she would go along with it!

Tom Stables, who helped organise many musical items and events for Teen Challenge, and Andrew Griffiths, who had often travelled with the group as 'sound man,' undertook to arrange a recording session. They converted the lounge at Hope House into a makeshift studio, and after a few practice sessions, Living Hope, with Debbie as lead singer, recorded their first album.

Tom and Andrew had sourced backing tracks for most of the songs in Living Hope's repertoire, and recording them was reasonably simple. There were others, however, for which the backing was not so easily found. This presented only a minor obstacle, for Tom suggested a way in which it could be overcome.

"Could you not just sing using a metronome to keep time, Debbie?" he ventured.

"I'll give it a try," Living Hope's only hope replied.

As she sang one of the pieces, the deep gratitude in Debbie's heart as she thought of the incredible concept expressed in the words, helped carry her through. The extra emotion more than compensated for the missing music. She sang the chorus of 'When He Was On The Cross' with such obvious feeling, that all those present were virtually moved to tears. With only the tick, tick, tick of the metronome as accompaniment, her clear voice rang out with,

'He knew me, yet He loved me,
He whose glory makes the heavens shine,
I'm so unworthy of such mercy,
Yet when He was on the cross
I was on His mind.'

When the recording session was complete and the final touches were being put to their CD, Living Hope were asked to choose an appropriate name for it. It might be an idea, someone thought, to use one of the song titles as the album title.

The members of Living Hope had no problem with that. There was one piece that they all loved singing for it so aptly described their experience of life, before and after conversion. It was called, 'Cleaned Up When I Messed Up.'

This was shortened to 'Cleaned Up,' and a colourful sleeve was produced with a cameo of the lead singer incorporated into it. That singer included a touching spoken two-minute testimony as one of the tracks, explaining how her life had been marvellously and miraculously 'cleaned up.'

Her name, she said, was Debbie Forrest.

26

SISTER DEBBIE

With her enthusiasm for spreading the liberating news of the Gospel worldwide having been intensified by her experiences in Denmark, Debbie began to consider the possibility of becoming involved in missionary outreach. She found herself contemplating this option more seriously when serving missionaries, or Teen Challenge representatives from other lands, visited Hope House and reported on what God was doing through them in the regions where they were working.

As she pondered the prospect of serving God in some foreign country her mind automatically turned to the continent of Africa. If she were to become engaged in Christian work abroad it would most definitely have to be in Africa. Nowhere else even entered the reckoning.

The reason for this had its roots far back in her childhood. Debbie's passion for Africa was a fire which had been kindled when she was a carefree little girl in Primary School. Although the idealistic exuberance of a childhood commitment had been largely extinguished by a tortured teenage and drug-addicted early adult life, it had now been fanned into flame by the irrepressible exuberance of a Christian commitment.

It happened at least once a year back then. Sisters of Mercy came into Debbie's school and addressed all the girls, who were seated cross-legged on the floor, at the morning assembly. They showed the pupils short films of little black boys and girls, who had few clothes and less to eat than they had. Many of the images from these films touched Debbie's heart, for although the children pictured were patently less well off than her, their smiles revealed rows of gleaming white teeth. The deep faraway look in their big, pathetic, water-glinting eyes was instantly appealing.

The sisters, who had been to Africa, had helped these boys and girls to regain some kind of quality of life and hope for the future, through both their spiritual teaching and practical ministry, the pupils were told. The only problem was that they needed money to help carry on this valuable work. They were asking the girls if they would like to contribute to it. If they would, they could bring a little gift of money, however small, into school and give it to their teacher. Some little African child would no doubt thank God for their kindness.

When Debbie was seven, and eight, and nine she always responded to this appeal, and as she grew older her contribution increased, to reflect an increase in her pocket money. It wasn't just her donation that increased, however. Her determination increased, too.

Sitting on the floor of the school assembly hall, when nine years of age, what had been for the past year or two an emotional stirring in her heart, hardened into a single-minded, but perhaps somewhat starry-eyed, plan of action. When I grow up I am going to go out to Africa and help those poor little boys and girls and their mothers, she resolved.

Now her time had come.

She would love to go to Africa and tell not only the little children, but also their mothers and everyone she met, about

Jesus, and His love, and the blessings of the new life that He alone could give.

How did she go about it though? Where did she begin?

Recognising that if she were ever to travel abroad she would require a passport Debbie applied for one in May 2000. With this in her possession and a longing to do something for the women and children of Africa in her heart, she was eager to set out as soon as possible.

It was a huge continent, however, comprising many contrasting countries. How would she ever decide which one of these to visit? Each country had its own particular social and economic needs, but they all needed the Saviour. Who could give her advice? It would be great, especially when making her first visit, if she could possibly accompany a group going out. The problem was where did she go to find one of these?

Debbie prayed for guidance and proceeded to make her interest in Africa widely known. Every time a visiting pastor called at Hope House to speak at 'chapel' she made a point of asking him before he left, "Have you heard of any teams going out to Africa, even for a short time? I would love to go there."

It seemed that the answer to such queries was always a polite, but definite 'No.' The pastor on the spot was usually filled with a mixture of admiration and regret when approached by the determined Debbie. He admired her spirit but was sorry that he couldn't help her realise her dream.

The only ray of hope to glint off the steady stream of negative responses invariably came as a closing comment to each of them. "Sorry, I don't know of any teams going out at the present, but if I hear of anything suitable in the future, I will let you know," most of the pastors promised.

They must have either forgotten about her, or else nothing 'suitable' had come up, however, for the summer months passed and nobody contacted Debbie.

She began to question her aspiration to go to Africa. Was it nothing more than a mere romantic childish notion revived? Perhaps it wasn't God's will for her at all. Perhaps she would be better to continue concentrating on life in Hope House and forget all these fairy-tale fancies about black babies under blue skies...

Then, one morning in early September, when thoughts of Africa were not uppermost in Debbie's mind, Audrey called her into the office. The centre manager was well aware of Debbie's longing to visit what had once been known as 'the dark continent,' and so she began with the cheering remark, "I have good news for you."

With Debbie's curiosity immediately aroused she went on, " I have just had a phone call from Cardiff Elim City Temple. They said that someone had told them we had a girl here who was interested in going to Africa. They have a team going out to Uganda in November and were wondering if they could interview her."

Audrey could see the look of amazement tinged with excitement on Debbie's face at this declaration, so she continued with a twinkle in her eye, "Well can they? I have to let them know. Would you like to go Cardiff for an interview, and then possibly go to Uganda with a team, Debbie?"

"You know the answer to that, Audrey," Debbie replied immediately with a laugh. "Of course I want to go for an interview in Cardiff, for I would dearly love to go to Uganda."

When the two women had discussed the possible dates and times supplied by Cardiff Elim City Temple for Debbie's interview, and decided upon a suitable one, Audrey agreed to set it up. Debbie left the office with her heart pounding, her mind in a whirl and her entire spiritual being praising God.

On the day of the interview Debbie travelled from Swansea to Cardiff by train. One minute she felt confident, the next nervous. Her confidence stemmed, at least in part, from the fact that she was carrying in her handbag a reference from Pastor Macey, the National Director of Teen Challenge. Surely that would be enough to take her anywhere. She was slightly worried, though, about her lack of experience in both foreign travel and Christian work. What if these people were expecting someone who had been a Christian for years and had a profound knowledge of the scriptures?

The train journey seemed to pass quickly, for in an effort to boost her self-confidence, or calm her lurking fears, Debbie peppered heaven with some brief but passionate prayers. She asked God to help her answer whatever questions she would be asked, and then proceeded to imagine what these questions might be, and formulate appropriate responses.

On arriving at the Elim City Temple in Cardiff Debbie was met by Rev. Stephen Ball, the senior pastor who had undertaken to interview her. After some preliminary discussion Rev. Ball asked Debbie why she wanted to go to Africa. That was an easy question, and one the prospective team member had been anticipating during her trip across on the train.

She told of her childhood ambitions, originating from the visits of missionary nuns to her Primary School, and her recently revived desire, fuelled by the visits of missionaries to Hope House.

Rev. Ball appeared impressed with that response and then went on to make a number of enquiries, designed to assess Debbie's perceived usefulness as a team member on a Christian mission to an African country.

"Excuse me asking," he began, "but do you preach?"

"No, not really," Debbie told him. "I wouldn't see myself as a preacher."

"Well do you sing?" the interviewer went on.

"Yes, I suppose you could say that I sing," Debbie replied, rather modestly. "We have a group in Hope House called Living Hope, and I go out and sing with them."

The interviewing pastor was encouraged by this positive response, and it led him on to ask, "So you sing. That's good. Do you lead worship?"

"No. I'm afraid I don't," the applicant for Africa confessed. "I've never had a chance to lead the worship in a church situation."

Rev. Ball sat back and thought for a few seconds before continuing, "You can sing, and that could be useful, but what else can you do?"

This time he wasn't so much asking for details about specifics, as opening the door to possibilities. He would dearly love to take this spirited, and obviously spiritual, young woman to Uganda, but it would be helpful if she could contribute more to the team than just a pleasant singing voice.

"I can give my testimony," Debbie volunteered hesitantly. She wasn't sure whether 'giving your testimony' appeared on the 'ultimate checklist of Christian credentials for team members in Uganda.'

It must have, if even farther down the list, for it seemed to strike a chord with her interviewer. "That sounds interesting," he said. "Could you let me hear your testimony?"

Debbie slipped her hand into her bag and pulled out her 'before' photograph and handed it to him. "That's what I was like before I was saved," she explained, and then began telling him her fascinating life story. Conscious that she was in an interview, and not a meeting, Debbie summarised her testimony, picking out the points she had found to make an obvious impression in a larger-group scenario.

As she was talking, Debbie noticed that Rev. Ball took occasional glances down at the photograph, followed by longer, incredulous stares at her. He seemed to be unsure if the person he was hearing speaking was actually the same person he was seeing in the photograph.

When she had finished her testimony, the pastor smiled, and said immediately, "We would like you to come with us to Uganda, Debbie."

They were both pleased that Debbie was going to join the team travelling to Africa and began discussing more detailed arrangements. Just as Debbie was preparing to leave Rev. Ball broached the subject that she had been avoiding in relation to her trip of a lifetime. It was the matter of money. How much was it all going to cost?

"The total cost of the visit will be £850, Debbie," he told her. "And if you wouldn't mind we will require a deposit of £150 as soon as possible. Will that be a problem?"

After a short, sharp, and hopefully not too noticeable, intake of breath Debbie replied reassuringly, "Oh no. Not at all. No problem. That will be fine!"

Ten minutes later, as she was walking back to the station, for she didn't want to spend the money taking a taxi, Debbie was in a daze. She was delighted to be going to Uganda, but had no idea how she was ever going to meet the cost. 'What have I done?' she kept asking herself. 'I have just told that man, '£850, no, that's not a problem.' And I don't have a bean! What am I going to do now?'

By the time she arrived back at Hope House she had decided on at least her first move. She went straight to the office of her friend and confidante, Audrey Rankin, seeking advice.

Audrey listened sympathetically as her young 'intern' recounted the day's events. She was mildly amused to witness Debbie, who was so enthusiastic about everything she did, having worked herself into such a quandary of anticipation and agitation.

"What should I do, Audrey?" was Debbie's immediate concern.

"How much money do you have?" the centre manager enquired.

"I have seventy pounds saved up," the anxious applicant volunteered. "But that's all I have in the world!"

"Well then, post if off to them," Audrey advised. "Tell them that you will send the rest when you get it."

"When I get it," Debbie echoed, dubiously. "But where is it going to come from?"

"We will pray about it, and the Lord will provide it," was her spiritual mentor's confident response. "Trust Him."

They prayed together about it there and then, and continued to do so, both together, and individually, for weeks. When Debbie had posted off all her savings, as the first instalment on her deposit, she was amazed at what began to happen.

Money started to come in. Debbie received cheques through the post, and gifts of cash into her hand, and in some cases these were from people she had never met before. They just confessed to having heard her 'story' and felt 'for some reason' that they ought to have fellowship with her.

Before she was due to set off with the others Debbie was overwhelmed by the power of God to provide for her need. She had also learnt two lessons, one about specific prayer, and the other about implicit faith, from Audrey. Although neither of the two women ever told anyone of her need, Debbie, who 'hadn't a bean,' was able to pay her £850 in full, before the departure date!

It was early November when the party of eight, led by Pastor Ray Smith of Cardiff Elim City Temple, arrived in Africa. This was a tremendous thrill for Debbie. Not only had God implanted the desire in her heart to go there, but He had also, in a most miraculous way, provided the funds to help her realise this lifelong ambition.

Debbie hadn't been long in Uganda, either, until He was to reveal that He had a special purpose for sending her there. This was particularly evident in a women's meeting Debbie was called upon to address one evening.

There were more than eight hundred women, many of whom were accompanied by tiny children, assembled in a large arena for the evening meeting. The building did not have any walls, just an extensive tin roof to shade the audience, who were sitting closely crammed together on the dirt floor, from the searing rays of the sun. The 'platform' was a raised concrete structure at one end.

As she sat waiting to be introduced, Debbie's mind flashed back to her childhood. A school assembly hall, films of African children, a desire to help them, and their mothers. The voice of the chairman catapulted her back into reality. "And now I would like to introduce to you Sister Debbie," he was saying. "She has come to Uganda with a special ministry to women and children, and we welcome her tonight."

'Sister Debbie.' The words rang in her ears. She had heard the nuns who had come to speak to the girls in school being called 'sisters.' Now she was 'Sister Debbie'. With, what was more, 'a special ministry to women and children.' And she was in Africa.

When she stepped up on to the platform and looked down, all Debbie could see was a sea of faces, looking up at her, waiting for her to speak. She read from 2 Kings chapter 4, about the Shunamite woman and her son. With her ministry to 'women and children' in mind she told the story of this woman's vision for a son and how God granted her this desire, through the man of God, Elisha, and how, when he died unexpectedly, God had restored him to life, again through the ministry of Elisha.

This led her to tell of her childhood vision for the women and children of Africa, and how God had made it possible for her to be there that day. He had, Debbie went on to inform the spellbound crowd, a vision for her life, and to illustrate this point proceeded to recount the story of her conversion.

Just before she began telling her testimony Debbie handed a copy of her 'before' photograph to one of the women in the front row and told everyone, "I am passing around a photograph of what I was like before I came to know Jesus. I would like you all to have a look at it. It will show you better than anything I can say, what God has done in my life."

As she carried on speaking Debbie could see the photo being greeted with astonishment as it passed around from one wondering woman to another.

When she had finished recounting her compelling life story, Debbie made an appeal. "You have seen and heard what God has done for me, and He can do the same for you, if you will only repent of your sins and come to Christ. Or perhaps you are a believer, and you are conscious that you are not living for God as you should, and would like to dedicate your life to His service. If you would like someone to speak to you about these things, please come out to the front," was her earnest invitation.

Debbie thought she had learnt by then to expect great things from God, but she was totally taken aback at what happened in response to her appeal. Almost one hundred women came forward for counselling. One of the church leaders ended up having to make his appeal from the platform, but it was for some more church members to come forward to assist the counselling team.

Many women were saved that evening, and many more were restored to a more meaningful, and ultimately more effective, relationship with their Heavenly Father.

As she moved from person to person, with all the other team members, busily counselling seeking souls, Debbie made no effort to wipe away the tears of joy.

God had allowed her to fulfil what had once appeared little more than a childish fantasy. As 'Sister Debbie' she had been used to make an eternal difference for Him.

Amongst the women and children of Africa.

27

IS THIS IT, MUMMY?

Debbie came back from Uganda in late November 2000,with a thankful, but humble heart. She felt so privileged to have seen God work in the lives of others in such a significant way, through her testimony, but somewhat mystified that this should happen. Who am I, she kept asking herself, that I should be used to see so many people commit themselves to Christ? I'm nothing but a converted heroin-addict from a very ordinary background in an industrial city. Why should God, in His grace and mercy, choose to use me to see hundreds of people brought to the Saviour?

After having reported on her visit to Uganda to all in Hope House, Debbie settled down into the routine of work there once again. As she continued to rejoice in the power and blessing of the Divine presence in her life she became increasingly conscious that she was losing out as a person, because of a human absence.

There was a vital piece of the jigsaw missing, and Debbie could never feel that the whole picture of her life was complete until it was in place.

The missing piece was a missing person.

Her name was Emily.

Soon after embarking upon phase four of her programme Debbie had become aware of life in the world outside Hope House once again. She would probably soon be leaving the relatively protected environment in which she had been living for well over a year. How could she do that, though, without the daughter whom she loved so dearly and missed so much, sharing her new station in society?

Debbie began to pray that God would allow her to be reunited with Emily at some stage in the future. It was a burden of prayer that was always on her mind. The decision as to when, if ever, that would take place, however, rested entirely with Kevin. He and his wife had raised her lovingly for the past five years, while Debbie had been messing up, and then God had been cleaning up, her life.

What the fond mother didn't realise was that Kevin had been carefully noting, and consistently marvelling at, the change that had taken place in her life. She was no longer the Debbie of the desperate drug-addicted days. The person who came to his house to collect their daughter was now a composed and competent woman.

Recalling the promise he had made to her, on the day he took Emily into his care, Kevin phoned Debbie at Hope House one afternoon at the beginning of December. Debbie was not surprised to hear him on the phone, for Kevin would always consult her when major decisions had to be made in relation to Emily's welfare.

She was, however, completely astounded when he asked, not long into the conversation, "Would you like to have Emily back soon, Debbie? I gave you my word that we would reconsider her position when you had sorted yourself out. You have certainly done that. In fact I have to say that Emily, Helen and I are extremely proud of you. Would you like to have her back with you?"

It was barely believable. Debbie was struck dumb for the most of half-a-minute. "Of course! I would love to have Emily back with me, Kevin. I have been praying that one day you would permit her to return. This is an answer to my prayers," she replied excitedly, when her power of speech returned.

There followed a significant silence on the line. Suddenly recognising the reason for this Debbie repressed her emotions, dropped her voice, and said softly, "Thank you, Kevin. I know this can't be easy for you. Helen and you have been so good to her, and must love her like I do."

This declaration of consideration and appreciation sparked off a dreadful element of doubt in Debbie's mind. "Perhaps she may not want to leave you and come to me," she continued.

"It isn't easy for me. You are right, Debbie. I don't want to see her go. Helen and I would very much love to be keeping her with us, but I made you a promise and I want to honour it. And anyway, it is probably better for her to be with her mum. Don't worry, either, about her not wanting to go to you. We have talked about it and she says she wants to go and live in Wales with you now."

Debbie found it hard to contain her elation. Up until five minutes ago it had been business as usual at Hope House. Now she was discussing when she would go to collect Emily to bring her down to Wales to live with her once more.

Kevin and she agreed that it would be best for their daughter if she were to remain at school in Wolverhampton until the end of term. She could then spend Christmas with Kevin, Helen and her little half-sister Harriet. Debbie would collect her on New Year's Day, 2001, allowing them to commence life together as mother and daughter for a second time. They considered this the most satisfactory arrangement, as it would allow Emily about a week to settle into her new surroundings, before the beginning of the spring term at school.

That was a fantastic way for both mother and daughter to begin 2001. No one appreciated better than them the words that seemed to be on everyone's lips. 'Happy New Year!'

Debbie had driven up to Wolverhampton and found Emily in the final stages of preparing for her next life adventure. She had most of her belongings, including every letter, every card, and every tiny memento that her mum had either given her or sent her over the five years they had been apart, plus her clothes, packed carefully into her bags, ready to depart. Her mum transferred all the bits and pieces Emily had considered important enough to take to her new home in Wales, to her spacious estate car. Then they were ready to leave.

After a rather emotional parting with Kevin, Helen and two-year-old Harriet, they were off. As they drove down the motorway, en route to recommencing life together, Debbie and Emily were both overcome by the excitement of it all.

The mum, who had to try hard to concentrate on her driving, kept taking quick glances across at her daughter, just to remind herself that this was real, and with every glimpse she felt like exploding into praise to God.

The daughter, on the other hand, wasn't interested in the road, or the journey, or the distance or the speed. She just sat gazing across at her mum, in doting admiration.

This was the mum for whom she had prayed with such childish simplicity and sincerity, 'Please don't let my mummy die.'

This was the mum who had taken her to church

This was the mum whose life God had transformed.

This was the mum who had begun to build a future for herself, serving God.

This was the mum who had prayed that she would be allowed to become an integral part of that future.

Now here they were, in a car, just the two of them, heading out into the future, together. There was just one question on Emily's mind, and although she thought she knew the answer to it, decided to ask it, nonetheless. An affirmative response would bring ultimate reassurance.

"When nanny and I we were going down to Wales to see you all those times last year, I used to love the journey down, but I hated leaving you and having to come all the way back," she admitted, with a broad smile. Having introduced the topic she then leaned forward, so that she could see both her mum's eyes past the shock of golden hair at the side of her head, and went on, "When I complained about this nanny always said, 'Don't worry, Emily, one day you will be going down and not coming back.' I think this must be the day she was talking about. Is this it, mummy?"

Moved by the genuine love and virtual disbelief underlying this earnest enquiry, Debbie sniffed to help hold back the tears, released her left hand from the steering wheel for a brief interlude, and reached across to grab Emily's right hand.

"Yes, love, this is it," she replied, giving the hand in hers a mighty squeeze.

Pastor Macey, pleased that Debbie was to be reunited with her daughter, and conscious of the positive effect that this could have, both on her development as a Christian and performance as a prospective employee of Teen Challenge, arranged for the pair to move into a house owned by the organisation, in the village of Gorslas. This accommodation came complete with in-house child-minders, for Debbie and Emily would be sharing it with Nicol and Veronique. This couple from the Seychelles, who were already working for Teen Challenge, were delighted to consider caring for the charming twelve-year old when her mum was on duty at Hope House, as part of their ministry.

Monday, January 8, 2001, was to prove a big day for both Debbie and her daughter.

That was the day when Emily was enrolled in her new school. Although absolutely delighted to be with her mum once more, Emily hadn't been looking forward to that occasion This was because it would involve an extra element, on top of the normal difficulties attached to switching schools in the middle of an academic year.

In addition to the worry of settling into an unfamiliar system and hoping to make new friends, Emily knew that she would have to attend classes in the Welsh language. This was a deep source of concern to her at first, but the joy of being with her mum far outweighed any difficulty she might be called upon to encounter. Her fears were to be all dispelled anyway, as the weeks wore on, for with the company of Debbie, the encouragement to Nicol and Veronique, and the consideration of her teachers she was soon coping quite well in her new environment.

After leaving Emily off for her first day at her new school, Debbie drove on over to Hope House to commence her day's work. During the morning someone contacted her to say that Audrey wanted to see her in the office. On presenting herself there Debbie was to discover that Pastor Macey had joined Audrey and they both appeared to be waiting for her.

The two most senior administrators of Hope House, the very people who had interviewed her about her turbulent past during her first traumatic week there, were sitting side by side, and each smiled a welcome as Debbie entered. They had seen this woman develop by leaps and bounds, both as a person and as a Christian over the intervening year and a half. Now they were about to nudge her development up another notch.

When they had spoken for a few minutes about Emily and how she had fared on her way to school Pastor Macey introduced the purpose of the meeting. "We have been very pleased with how you have performed during your phase four, Debbie," he began, "and so from today we will be putting you on the payroll. We are proposing to employ you as a staff member, if you would be willing to join us."

Debbie flushed with pleasure and embarrassment, and blinked before croaking virtually involuntarily, "Oh yes. Certainly. Thank you."

Witnessing the initial look of confusion on her friend's face give place to one of growing contentment, Audrey chipped in to add the practical aspect to the package. "You will be getting your first pay packet this week. We will be classing you as a staff member from now on," she went on, with a broad grin.

It was almost too much to take in.

Debbie's life, which had earlier been nothing more than a succession of distressing dives, deeper into dark despair, had now turned around completely. It seemed that everything that had happened in the past three or four months had been a further advancement into the realm of shining hope. God was revealing 'the plan' Derrick Cole had prophesied He had for her life, all at once!

The only dark cloud in the sky of this inspiring new sphere, which Debbie appeared to have entered, was the fact that Fiona, who had taken a personal interest in every aspect of her life since she had come on the programme, had left. Jay, Fiona's husband, had been called to the pastorate of a large church in Birmingham, and the couple had moved to the midlands of England, to allow him to take up this post.

Debbie missed Fiona. She had always trusted her and often confided in her. It felt as though a vital, if invisible, prop had gone from her life.

This gap was soon plugged, however, when Audrey asked Debbie if she would undertake what had been Fiona's teaching role in Hope House. Although she missed the listening ear, wise counsel and gentle encouragement of her close associate, her absence forced Debbie into strengthening her own spiritual standing.

She prepared for her new role every bit as thoroughly as she had done when setting up a seminar to promote asthma inhalers across England, and every bit as prayerfully as she did before giving her testimony, whether in Kidderminster or Kampala. Debbie held her students enthralled, right from the very first time she stood up to teach the studies. Her enthusiasm for her subject was infectious. The girls had no option but to be carried along on the current of her commitment, and to marvel at the breadth and depth of her knowledge.

When it came to teaching Biblical truth, Debbie's earlier passion for reading and studying the Word of God, stood her in good stead, but it was when touching on matters to do with addiction that she came particularly into her own. Since her classes were made up entirely of a mixture of either delivered or detoxing addicts, her teaching came across with unquestionable authority. Debbie had 'been there, done that,' on a level with the worst of them.

She had lived their life. She spoke their language. She had felt like they felt, however they felt.

Debbie loved it. As she stood expounding the scriptures, and watching the eager faces light up before her, she often thought it was like dropping pennies, clunk, clunk, clunk into a piggy-bank. She felt unbelievably privileged to be adding precious gems to their growing fund of spiritual enrichment.

One morning, shortly after she had begun teaching in Hope House, Debbie remained seated at the desk at the front of the classroom, as the girls were filing out for their mid-morning break. Her eyes followed them as they converged on the doorway over to her left. All of them had once been addicted to either drugs or alcohol. Now many of them were saved and rejoicing in their newly-found freedom in Christ. Every single one of them had been giving Debbie her undivided attention when she had been leading the Bible study.

It was the impact of one of the scripture passages she had been referring to, that had left her pinned to her chair. She had been telling the girls, many of whom had lost jobs, friends and even contact with their families, as a result of their addictions, about God's plans for the remainder of their lives. In the course of the lesson she had pointed them to Joel chapter 2. There the prophet states God's purpose for His wayward people, with the promise, 'I will restore to you the years that the locust has eaten.'

Debbie sat in a trance in the by-now empty room, looking at, but not seeing, the rows of vacant desks each with an open Bible and a notebook on it. She was in a daydream of delight, applying the verse to herself.

God has restored my daughter to me, she thought, on reflection.

God has brought me into the most harmonious relationship with my family that I have ever known.

And as if restoring me into the warmth of my own family circle weren't enough God has gone a step further by supplying me with a second family at Hope House. Here I have Pastor Macey who cares for me like a spiritual father, Audrey who watches over me like my spiritual mother, and all the rest of the staff whom I have come to regard as my brothers and sisters.

To crown it all God has provided me with a job too. And what a job! Can there be a better occupation in the whole world, she mused, than teaching God's Word to students whose minds and souls are like sponges, and then watching them endeavour to apply it in their lives.

She smiled as she recalled Emily's question on the drive down the motorway. 'Is this it, mummy?' she had enquired.

That had been 'it' for that moment.

What Debbie didn't realise at the time, however, was that although the return of Emily to her life had been a thrilling and vital part of 'it,' that was really only the start of 'it.'

This must surely be God's complete 'it,' now.

28

I WANT MY LIFE TO COUNT

Debbie's distressing week in detox proved invaluable in re-emphasising to Audrey and Pastor Macey something of which they were already becoming increasingly aware. They had always recognised that it would be good to have their own professionally staffed and properly equipped detox unit at Hope House. Having witnessed Debbie in the throes of 'cold turkey,' the need for such a facility was stepped up a category in their forward planning programme, from 'useful addition' to 'absolute necessity.'

One of their most ardent supporters in the pursuit of this aim was Debbie. Her appreciation of the need of a detox centre at Hope House stemmed not only from her own personal experience but also from helping counsel a succession of addicts who had followed her onto the programme.

As part of her commitment to this cause Debbie had given her testimony at the opening of a new detox centre for boys at the Teen Challenge Centre in Keighley, Yorkshire. In the course of her remarks she recounted her many unsuccessful and frustrating attempts to rid herself of her addiction before her agonising week of 'prayer and paracetamol.' Debbie's graphic account of her horrendous experience, plus the testimony of other residents of Hope House on different occasions, helped highlight the urgent need for the detox unit for girls that was already being planned.

In the months that followed sufficient funds became available, through the kindness of many, often anonymous, donors, to procure a large property near Hope House, with this purpose in view.

This was a wonderful answer to prayer, and opened the way for the creation of a much needed and long awaited facility for the girls entering the programme. The management were anxious to see this in operation as soon as possible but as they pushed forward with their plans they came upon an unforeseen, but not insurmountable, snag.

As there was a difficulty in obtaining the support of the local GPs, who would expect to be called upon occasionally to attend at the new detox unit, this was sited in the main Hope House complex, and not, as Pastor Macey and his team had envisaged, out in the recently acquired property which was to be named Hope Acres.

This presented them with a second challenge. They had already been prayerfully anticipating the job of finding a qualified Christian nurse who could establish, and run, a detox centre to the highest of medical standards. Now they would also have to find a means of using Hope Acres to its best advantage in the advancement of their work.

They need not have worried about the appointment of a nurse to manage the detox centre, however. God had been preparing His person for the position long before they ever knew that they would even need her.

In the autumn of 1997 Julie Murray left her home in Bangor, Northern Ireland, to enrol as a student nurse in Chester University. Over the following Easter weekend she attended a meeting, at which a group called 'The Evidence' was to sing, in a church in Wallasey, across the River Mersey from Liverpool. The Evidence was the male counterpart of the group with which Debbie was later to become lead singer, 'Living Hope.'

Julie was impressed by The Evidence, who were a group of former drug-addicts who sang and praised God for their deliverance from addiction. She then found her heart strangely moved as Pastor Macey gave an outline of the work of Teen Challenge, focusing on specific examples of young men who had been transformed both physically and spiritually through its ministry. It was as though a gentle conviction was stirring within her saying, 'you ought to be doing something about this.'

What, though, could she do? Her answer was to do all she could at that moment, which was to buy Pastor Macey's book, 'Tough Love,' and sign up to sponsor a student. In his address the Pastor had said that his book would give the reader a deeper appreciation of the lasting value of the work of Teen Challenge, and it was certainly to do that for Julie. Having bought the book, Julie remained around in the church for some time speaking to some of the Teen Challenge staff members present, for she was anxious to learn as much as she could about the various aspects of the work.

During the remainder of her years as a student nurse Julie continued to receive frequent newsletters and updates from Teen Challenge. As her interest increased she began making occasional trips south to the centre in Wales where she was to meet Audrey Rankin, who managed Hope House, and make further contact with Pastor John Macey, National Director of Teen Challenge U.K. Her belief in both the spiritual and social significance of the organisation intensified with every visit, and having become aware of the global nature of their ministry, volunteered to go out to work with Teen Challenge in Bombay, India, for a few weeks. She had just graduated as a nurse in August 2000, and decided to fit in this mission trip to Bombay before taking up a full-time nursing post.

Julie hadn't been any more than three days in India until God began to speak to her very forcibly about the present impact and ultimate purpose of her life. Surrounded by so many women, caught up in drugs and alcohol addictions, and prostitution, with many of them suffering from aids, her whole being, body, soul and spirit was affected.

On the night before she left Bombay, Julie was in a TB hospital ward where Mya, a young woman was dying. Pus oozed from the abscesses on her head. Her body was wasted to such an extent that all her bones were visible through her skin. She was so weak and sick that she could barely speak.

As Julie helped nurse that young woman her heart was touched. Looking at her, with tears in her eyes, and the compassion of Christ in her soul, she prayed, "Lord, lead me to make a difference in the lives of people like this. I want my life to count for You, and for them."

When she returned from that momentous trip Julie took up a position as a nurse in Liverpool Women's Hospital. She enjoyed the work, but as she saw how her patients were cared for, her mind kept reverting to a ward in Bombay, and Mya, dying in much less favourable circumstances. She couldn't seem to get away from that image. It haunted her through all her reflective moments.

Not long after she returned from India Julie had a phone call from Pastor Macey. He had recognised in her an admirable combination of sincere spirituality and sound common sense, the night he had first met her briefly in the church in Wallasey. His initial impression had been backed up during her visits to the Teen Challenge centre in Wales from time to time, when he had noted her intelligent appreciation to the purpose and value of the work. Extremely favourable reports of her competence as a nurse and commitment as a Christian on the Bombay team had led him to recognise that Julie would be an ideal person, perhaps even God's person, for the soon-to-be-created post in the work amongst the women.

He had a proposal to make. "Would you consider working permanently with Teen Challenge?" he enquired of the recently qualified nurse, who had just begun to establish herself in her chosen profession. "We are in the process of planning a detox centre for women in Hope Acres, a property which we have just been enabled to purchase. What we need now is a qualified nurse to head up this project, and were wondering if you would be interested?"

Julie felt honoured to have been asked, but again her mind flashed back to Mya. "Thank you so much for thinking of me," she replied, "but my immediate reaction is to say, 'No.' If I go to work with Teen Challenge at all it will be in India. My heart is in Bombay."

"Will you at least consider it?" Pastor Macey went on. "And I will give you another call in a few weeks time."

"Yes, I will think about it and pray about it," Julie promised, before adding, "but I can't honestly see it."

During the autumn months of 2000 there was a struggle in the soul of Julie Murray. This was not a Debbie-type struggle, a trying to cast off the constraints of an addicted body from a Christian soul type struggle. Julie's struggle was that she wanted to make a difference for God. She wanted her life to count for Him, and to the blessing of others. Her problem was, how best could she do that? Or where?

Every time Pastor Macey phoned her, she told him that she was still thinking about India. He was giving her updates on the progress in Wales.

It seemed that in her personal devotions, virtually every day, Julie was being challenged about her level of personal commitment to the ministry of helping the hurting and lifting the fallen, while introducing them to the love, light and life that are only to be found through trusting in Jesus. Her line managers in the hospital where she was working were convinced that she had a bright future in nursing. There was no doubt that within a matter of a few years she would be promoted to a senior position within the profession. That prospect sounded very attractive, and would probably prove quite rewarding, from a human standpoint. If it happened, though, would it make any difference for God? was how Julie reasoned.

One morning she read Isaiah chapter 58 and was particularly struck by the contrast of challenges, and the resulting promises to those bold enough to take action in relation to these challenges.

'If you extend your soul to the hungry
And satisfy the afflicted soul,' she learnt from verse ten,
'Then your light shall dawn in the darkness,
And your darkness shall be as the noonday.
The Lord will guide you continually,
And satisfy your soul in drought,
And strengthen your bones;
You shall be like a watered garden,
And like a spring of water, whose waters do not fail...'

That was it. That was what Julie was after. That was making a difference for God.

Gradually God was inclining her mind towards the concept that perhaps she was the person He had chosen to establish a detox centre in Hope House. Who could be more 'hungry' for freedom from sin, and peace and joy in their lives, than the girls who came there? Could there be any more 'afflicted soul' than the heroin, crack or alcohol addict?

After a period of prolonged heart-searching over the Christmas holidays Julie phoned Pastor Macey in January 2001 from her home in the Wirral.

"I have made up my mind," Julie told him. "I am prepared to come and help set up the new detox centre at Hope House, if you still want me. I have thought and prayed about it a lot, and now believe that it is what God would have me do."

The Pastor was pleased. "Of course we still want you, Julie. We have been praying for more than a year now that God would send us the right person to set this vision in motion, and we believe that you are that person," he assured her.

They discussed possible dates for Julie to start and as she had to give adequate notice to her current employers it was agreed to aim at May 1 as a target date for opening the new facility. There would, however, have to be a lot of careful planning before that date, and extensive ordering of new equipment and medical supplies.

As part of this preparation Julie travelled down to Wales in mid-March to meet the management team and talk through the final arrangements for her employment, and the ordering of the necessary equipment. It was when Audrey was showing her around the various buildings belonging to Hope House Teen Challenge, and they were considering how to make best use of them in this exciting and long-prayed-for new development, that Julie was first introduced to Debbie.

The two young women looked at each other and smiled. They recognised each other at once, for although they had never spoken before, it was to transpire that they had been in the same meeting on at least two occasions in the past.

"Nice to meet you, Debbie. I know you to see, and I've heard you give your testimony. Excellent it was, too," Julie was first to disclose her recollections.

"So that's where I have seen you," Debbie responded, a light ray of recall spreading across her face. "You were at a meeting where I was singing with Living Hope, some time ago. Remind me, where was that?"

"At my church in the Wirral, one Saturday night last year," Julie told her. "Do you remember it?"

"Yes, I remember it well," came the reply. Debbie could hardly forget it, for it had been the warm and welcoming night in the Wirral before the quandary and questioning night in Chester.

"But I saw you before that, too," Julie volunteered. "I was sitting three rows behind you at the Reinhart Bonnke rally in the NEC in Birmingham. Then I recognised you when you got up to sing that Saturday night."

"Were you there as well?" Debbie enquired, fascinated. "I have met hundreds of people who were at that meeting."

An immediate aura of understanding was established between the two women during that first, and what was little more than introductory, encounter. Each seemed to instantly and instinctively appreciate the other's deep sense of purpose in the service of God. And in just over a month's time each of them was to find herself challenged in the new role which she was called upon to fill for Him.

With the detox centre having to be set up in the main complex, Debbie was asked to base her practical ministry in Hope Acres, which was in the process of being refurbished. It was decided that this large house with its spacious grounds could be used most profitably as an outdoor work and activity centre during the afternoon sessions and a residence for the girls who had progressed to phase three of the programme, at night. Debbie's duty was to organise the work rosters in this valuable, recently procured building, in addition to her already timetabled morning teaching.

Julie took up her post as had been agreed, on May 1, 2001 and the first girl was admitted to the six-bedded detox centre which she had helped plan, a few days later. She learnt rapidly about how to nurse these girls, many of whom arrived with a terrible, and often tormenting, mix of physical, emotional, mental and spiritual problems. Within months, when she had been put in charge of admissions, and became the first person contacted by the often desperate young women applying for a place in Hope House Julie was happy.

She felt fulfilled. She knew she was where God wanted her to be.

It was quite clear that she could make a difference in the lives of hurting, hopeless people here.

Her life had started to count.

Every girl in a detox bed, under her supervision, was another life touched, and another number chalked up, for God.

Pastor Macey and Audrey, who had prayed for a suitable person to set up the detox centre they had envisaged, and who had employed Julie, were happy too. They had thought that if they could find a godly woman with the capacity to witness to and discipline the addicts entering Hope House, with at least the minimum required standard of nursing qualification, rather than someone who was a brilliant nurse but with a wishy-washy Christian commitment, they would be satisfied.

Their most recent appointee hadn't been long in her post until they recognised that God had given them far beyond all that they had asked or even imagined. Julie Murray was proving to be both a godly woman and a brilliant nurse.

The arrival of Julie on to the staff at Hope House was to prove a tremendous blessing to Debbie also. Her coming helped fill the void created by the departure of Fiona, some six months before.

As Debbie saw the results of Julie's work in the detox centre, she immediately recognised, from past experience, her competence as a nurse.

As she witnessed her on occasions counsel the girls under her care she appreciated that she had a genuine heart of compassion.

As she listened to her present the Word of God in morning or evening chapel, she recognised that she had a tremendous spiritual passion.

As she began to have more frequent personal conversations with Julie, however, Debbie discovered something else. This nurse from Northern Ireland had a warm, appealing and totally trustworthy personality.

Julie was someone who rated on a par with Audrey and Fiona, both of whom she had often approached for help and advice.

She was a woman Debbie would have no hesitation in treating as a confidante.

A colleague she could look upon as a true friend.

29

UNDER AFRICAN SKIES

Not long after the opening of the new detox centre, with Julie in charge, the work at Hope House was to be struck a stunning blow. Audrey Rankin, the centre manager, and hub around which the women's work at Teen Challenge had been revolving for years, became seriously ill and required urgent hospital treatment.

Since Audrey was very much involved in a wide variety of activities, her illness meant that an urgent reorganisation of many schedules was required, with other members of staff gladly volunteering to fulfil her list of engagements. One of the most pressing of her commitments to be covered was a planned, and not too distant, trip to Africa. Audrey, who was to be accompanied by her husband Mike, their son Paul and daughter Naomi, was due to take a team of girls to South Africa and Swaziland in less than six weeks time.

With a series of engagements having already been booked the tour could not be cancelled, so Pastor Macey turned to someone he was sure could cope in the situation. Debbie.

"As we all know, Audrey will not now be leading the group out to Africa," he told her. "My wife Ann and I are going instead and we would like you to come with us and bring Emily along as well, Debbie."

It was a kind offer and a thrilling prospect but there was much to be done. With only a little over five weeks to go, Debbie would have to procure a passport for Emily, arrange for her to have all the necessary injections, and groom a group of girls for the trip. When there the team from Hope House would be expected to take meetings in schools, prisons and Teen Challenge centres. One of their most important engagements was to be the annual graduation ceremony at the centre in Swaziland.

Debbie worked hard with the team in the intervening weeks, blending them into a pleasing singing group and advising individuals about giving their testimonies. Well aware from past experience of the significance of dancing in the culture of Africa, Debbie asked Julie to help her choreograph simple dances to some of the pieces they were planning to sing.

After all the last minute preparations had been completed the party arrived into Johannesburg at the end of July, and their first meeting was in the township of Soweto. It was a wonderful experience for the girls, some of whom had never been out of Britain before, to see so many black and white people coming together, united in the praise of God and the presentation of the Gospel. Apartheid was not an issue with this congregation.

As two of the young women from Hope House told of the marvellous change that God had made in their lives, the large audience were deeply impressed. It was an exhilarating experience for the team leaders too, for they knew these young women well. Six months earlier they had been peddling and using drugs on the streets of the UK. Now they were standing up in Africa, witnessing to their faith in Christ.

One of the highlights of the evening was the graceful dance routine. The group from Hope House asked Emily to join them as they glided smoothly around the stage. They were moving to the music of 'Jesus My Saviour' and 'Thank You For The Cross.' With the use of such themes as their background music the dance routines they performed could not afford to be in any way showy or sensuous. And they weren't. They came across rather as a visible psalm of praise from the grateful hearts of girls who knew more than most what it meant to rejoice in release from the bondage of a life of sin.

With Debbie and her singing and testimony team having created a spiritually charged atmosphere, Pastor Macey brought a closing message and a number of people came forward and committed their lives to Christ. It was a promising start to their two-week African trip.

Travelling from South Africa into Swaziland was like taking a step back in time. The party had left a rich and prosperous country to enter a poor one, struggling along in a time warp, at least fifty years behind.

Their destination was the Lighthouse, which was the Teen Challenge centre in Swaziland. On arriving there the group was met by Kevin Ward, the Director of the work in Africa, and introduced to all the staff. It was an inspiring and instructive experience for Debbie to witness the work of Teen Challenge in another continent, having been already well aware of the impact of the work in Europe. And if it was a trip further on around the Teen Challenge learning curve for Debbie, it was an absolutely thrilling time for the girls on the team. Not only did it give them an insight into the wider work of Teen Challenge, but it also afforded them the opportunity to relax and enjoy themselves under spiritual supervision. They made the most of it, too!

One of the projects the girls were asked to undertake when in Swaziland was to paint a series of striking African designs, which had been stencilled on the wall. One afternoon Debbie went across to check how the work was progressing and heard the girls laughing as she approached.

When she entered the room where they had been working, the laughing ceased all of a sudden, and a deathly hush descended. The girls stopped as though playing 'statues,' paint-laden brushes poised in paint-plastered hands. They had been caught literally red-handed, not to mention green-handed and blue-handed and yellow-handed. Having tired of painting African designs on the walls of Hope House in Swaziland the girls had decided that it would be much more fun to paint patterns on each other. One had her face streaked with red paint, another was green with blotches of blue, while the third face was predominantly yellow with dots and spots of red. The designs were of necessity totally abstract in nature, the controlling factor in their composition being who could get closest with her colour of loaded brush to make first strike.

The painters looked at each other sheepishly, and then across at Debbie with pitiful hangdog expressions. They were expecting a rollicking for engaging in such infantile behaviour. It didn't come, though.

Much to their surprise Debbie burst out laughing. They looked so pathetic. A group of women in their early twenties had been taken on a foreign trip and trusted to undertake a simple painting project. Now, having been discovered messing about on the job they looked just like a group of nursery-school children caught with their hands in the jellybean jar.

"What have you lot been up to?" Debbie enquired, finding it totally impossible to appear angry at her 'naughty schoolgirls.' "Go and get yourselves cleaned up as best you can and as soon as you can. We can't go out and take a meeting this evening with you looking like warriors covered in warpaint!"

The girls were amazed, their leader was amused, and the bond between them had given a valuable shot of 'lock-tight' adhesive.

One of the most memorable meetings conducted by the team during that trip was held one afternoon in a women's prison. This was the first visit by the girls from Hope House in Wales to a prison in Africa, but not, for most of them, their first time in a prison. They knew what prisons were like. Some of them had served prison sentences of a year or more.

When the team had taken their seats at the front of the large, covered compound where the meeting was to be held, the prisoners were marched in. They were all dressed in washed-out-blue tunics and pale blue headscarves. They appeared so disconsolate, an identical and resigned ribbon of guilt, as they filed up in orderly fashion to take their places then sit down in silent rows.

Two of the girls started to tell about their former lives and the prisoners identified with them straightaway. There could be no doubt about it, that although there was a vast difference both in continent and culture, the experience of one set of women very closely resembled that of the other. One of the speakers recalled the prison sentence she had served for 'possessing a 'class A' drug with intent to supply.'

By the time it came Debbie's turn to address the large audience every woman in it had been arrested all over again. This time, though, it wasn't by some police authority arriving with a warrant, but by the convincing witness, both in word and song, of a small group of women like themselves. These people hadn't come into their prison to propound some airy-fairy theory that bore no relation whatsoever to their lives. Every woman in the pale blue lines, drawn across the compound dust, could empathise with these speakers. They were broadcasting on their wavelength.

There was an air of silent expectation as Debbie began to read from Luke chapter seven in the Bible. She commenced to read at verse 36, about the 'woman in the city who was a sinner,' and who had brought the alabaster box of ointment to anoint the feet of Jesus, when he was sitting at a meal in the house of Simon the Pharisee.

In the course of her message Debbie gave her testimony, telling how that she had once been a sinner, a woman of the streets, like the woman in Luke seven, but God had changed her life completely. Now all she wanted to do was kneel at the feet of Jesus and praise Him for the mighty transformation in her life. This was the underlying theme of all Debbie's messages, that God can change lives, no matter how deeply-dyed in sin they happened to be. The photograph that she had sent out to be passed along row after row of spellbound prisoners established her as a walking, talking, singing, and totally compelling visual aid to back up her every word.

Debbie was little more than halfway through what she had planned to say when a woman rose from where she was sitting, crossed carefully into the clear passageway that had been left up the middle of the crowd, and bowed down with her face almost touching the ground. She remained there as Debbie continued to speak. Her soul had been touched and her spirit broken as she saw her own sinfulness in the light and beauty and sinlessness of the Saviour.

"Oh God, please forgive me. Please save me," she begged softly, as Debbie continued to speak.

That woman was but the first of many to come to faith in Christ that afternoon. When Debbie had finished her message she made an appeal, inviting anyone interested in hearing more about how they could have their lives changed by trusting in Jesus, who had died to make salvation possible, to come forward. The woman in the aisle was first to her feet, only to move forward and bow her head in contrition at the front, and many others followed her example. Debbie and her team counselled all those who came forward, and many committed their lives to the Lord.

It was so wonderful to witness the joy on the faces of these women. They were people who had been bound by the powerful chains of sin and many of them had still lengthy prison sentences to serve. Now, though, their whole outlook on life had changed for they had been released into spiritual freedom by the Great Emancipator who had proclaimed that one vital purpose of His mission to earth had been 'to set at liberty those who are oppressed.'

When they had completed their programme of meetings the party were taken up into the mountains for a few days break before they were due to return to Britain on August 12. They were staying in a complex of huts, especially designed for visitors.

It was cooler in the mountains, and a pleasant relief from the heat of the plains. The girls were delighted to arrive up into the cooler air. They hadn't been long there, however, until Pastor Macey said to Debbie, "It would be a good idea to organise the girls into work-parties to collect wood before the sun sets. We will need it for the fire."

Debbie thought he was joking. Does he imagine that this is the jungle or something? she mused. Do we have to light a fire to scare off the wild beasts?

Spotting the look of bemused incredulity on her face, Pastor Macey went on to explain, "It can become quite cold up here in the evenings, and besides, we will need a fire to cook our food."

It was fun collecting the wood. Young women, some of whom had grown up in Britain's inner cities, had never collected wood for a fire before and didn't realise that there was a knack to it. Not just any old piece of wood would do. Some brought handfuls of tiny twigs, which really weren't much use. They weren't thick enough. Others came trailing sturdy branches, which weren't much use either. They were too thick and would take too long to cut.

The groups of girls, running free through the loose brushwood, calling to and laughing with each other, enjoyed the simple activity of collecting firewood. It was such a novel experience for all of them and they worked with a will.

Soon they had built up a pile of 'acceptable' wood in an open space and Pastor Macey lit a fire and began cooking the food.

Later on, after they had finished their meal, they sat in a circle around the fire as night closed in about them. The firelight flickered on the faces of the girls as they leaned forward, some of them with arms outstretched to make the most of the heat. The stars twinkled overhead in the rounded canopy of the blue-black African sky, and the throb of a drumbeat from a distant village reached their ears.

The drumbeat was not the only sound to drift out across the plains that night though. The girls were singing, and as they sang Debbie was struck by the wonder of it all. Here were a group of girls, who had been heroin addicts in the UK less than a year before, sitting singing under the night sky in Africa. What they were singing about tugged at Debbie's heartstrings too. As she let her eyes rove around the circle she saw a light in their faces that had its origin, not in the outward flickering of firelight, but in an inward serenity of soul.

They were singing about the Father's deep love for them. About the love 'that made a wretch His treasure.'

They were singing, '…I'm so unworthy of such mercy, yet when He was on the cross, I was on his mind.'

They were singing,' And there'll be joy in the morning, joy in the evening, joy all day long.'

Debbie was overwhelmed at the marvel and magnitude of the situation. She stopped singing, drew her finger up to one eye then the other, to flick away the tears, before saying inwardly, in a question that was nothing other than a heartfelt expression of worship. "Why me, Lord? Here in Africa with my child? A wretch, and I'm now Your treasure. And you have brought me out here with this crowd of girls, and we are every one the same. Wretches made treasures. Praising You with all our hearts…"

On the evening before they were due to leave for home Debbie took a walk with Emily and some of the girls across to the top of a ridge from where they could look out across the plain.

They were met with a breathtaking spectacle.

The sun was setting and the sky behind the distant mountains had turned a stunning orange colour. Occasional waterholes glinted like orange-red jewels across the expanse of plain between, and orange-tinted white columns of smoke from village fires towered straight up into the windless air.

It was an idyllic, tranquil, and silent to the extent of almost being sacred, scene.

Debbie and her group of girls sat gazing at it in quiet reflection. It was making an indelible impression on each of them and no one felt bold enough to even attempt to describe the awesome beauty of the landscape before them, in words. Language suddenly seemed such an inadequate tool.

It was Shelley, who was sitting three girls across from Debbie who was first to make an attempt, and it was excellent. "I have never seen so much sky," she whispered, almost reverently. It sounded as though she was afraid that if she were to speak too loudly she would somehow crack it all up or chase it all away.

"Amazing, isn't it?" Debbie replied, equally awestruck, but annoyed at herself that she couldn't find anything more passionate or pertinent to say. A few nights before she had been praising God by the fire for the might and mystery of salvation. Now she had been rendered virtually speechless by His power and majesty in creation.

The words of the chorus of one of the first hymns she had learnt after her conversion, back in the 'tambourine church' in Wolverhampton, came into her mind. She recalled a multicultural but singularly spiritual congregation singing them with lusty voices and to enthusiastic accompaniment. As she did so she began to hum the tune. This sent the words racing from her brain down to her heart. They were,

'Then sings my soul, my Saviour God to Thee,
How great Thou art! How great Thou art!"

She revelled in the sense of worship entailed in those lines for a few minutes before standing up to announce, "Sorry girls, but it is time we were getting back. We don't want to be over here after dark."

The girls rose reluctantly, one by one, and as Debbie led the way back towards their compound, with her arm thrown loosely around Emily's shoulder, they followed, stopping occasionally to take fond and final glances back.

Africa had been a fantastic experience for all of them.

It was hard to believe they were going home in the morning.

30

I'M GOING TO KILL MYSELF

By the spring of 2002, with the heady days of her trip to Swaziland the previous summer nothing more than a pleasant but distant memory, Debbie began to think seriously and prayerfully about the direction of her life in the service of the Lord. She had discharged her responsibilities in Hope Acres as best she could during the autumn and winter, but she didn't see that as her life's work, her ultimate destination for God. Although she worked hard in her new position she felt isolated from the main activity going on in Hope House sometimes, even though she was continuing to teach her classes there in the morning. It was unsettling, for she felt that although she was active in both centres and responsible for one of them, that she didn't really belong in either.

With the condition of Audrey, her mentor and close friend, having worsened over the period also, Debbie considered it unfair to burden her with all her concerns and so kept them to herself. This helped increase both her sense of insecurity in the present and uncertainty about the future.

One Wednesday in April, she was driving a minibus full of girls back to Hope House for their evening meal. It was almost five o'clock and the roads were busy. The girls had been to an afternoon class on hairdressing and beauty therapy in Llanelli College and were having a light-hearted discussion about what they had heard, said and done during the session. Debbie was only semi-aware of the traffic, and totally switched off to the lively conversation, interspersed with occasional laughter, going on behind her, however. She was driving in mechanised mode, with her eyes on the road ahead of her, her hands on the steering wheel in front of her, her feet at or on the pedals below her, and her mind miles away. She felt downhearted. Was this really what God wanted her to do for the rest of her days?

Debbie was almost back at Hope House and was sitting, stopped, at a set of traffic lights when the rolling restlessness of her mind was suddenly soothed by the silent intrusion of a verse from the Bible. It was from Jeremiah chapter twenty-nine. Debbie had heard it quoted in meetings and had used it herself, from time to time to encourage her students.

It now seemed so reassuring in her situation. The words came as a fresh revelation to her downcast spirit. They were,

'For I know the plans I have for you,' declares the Lord, 'plans to prosper you and not to harm you, plans to give you hope and a future…'

That was it. Derrick Cole all over again, Bilston square revisited.

It was, 'Young woman… Jesus loves you and He has a plan for your life,' from the lips of 'the Lord' Himself.

Inspired by this promise Debbie returned to Hope House and when she had seen all the girls safely out of the minibus she checked the text messages on her mobile phone. It were as though she half expected God, who had given her the words of scripture as confirmation of His plans for her life, to somehow give her a second sign, a reassurance of His reassurance, as He had done to Gideon long ago. She wouldn't even be looking for a reversal of the damp fleece phenomenon, but a message on her mobile would be nice.

And there was one! It hadn't come directly from heaven, but it had originated in heaven and came through Cardiff. It was from Pastor Ray Smith and it read simply, 'We are going back to Uganda. Are you in?'

'Absolutely.' Debbie texted back. Her single-word response represented a sigh of relief from a dispirited soul. At last God was beginning to show her that He had something different for her to do.

Further texts back and forth revealed that Cardiff Elim City Temple were going out with another group in October or November. They had observed Debbie's love of Africa and her ability to relate to its people, on her first trip out, and would be keen to have her join them again. It was something for Debbie to look forward to, but it was still six months away at least. There was a long summer ahead.

Little did she know it, but God had big plans for it as well. Plans that would make the summer pass so quickly Debbie would be too busy in His service to even see it go!

Next day Debbie went to have lunch with Audrey, as she did occasionally. Although it was Audrey who was ill, Debbie always felt encouraged and enriched having visited her.

They had just finished their meal and were sitting back for a chat before Debbie returned to her duties, when Audrey enquired, casually, "Have you any plans for the future, Debbie?"

There was a short pause before Debbie replied, rather hesitantly, "Well I'm arranging to go back to Uganda with a group from Cardiff in October or November, but other than that I'm not quite sure. I was thinking of applying to Trinity College in Carmarthen. They run a teacher training course. I think that I might like to become a teacher. To be honest, though, I have no idea what I will be doing. I am just waiting on the Lord for guidance."

"What?" Audrey reacted immediately. "Has John spoken to you yet?"

"No, he hasn't," Debbie said, a bit bewildered. "Why? What about?"

"Don't worry," Audrey went on, conscious that her enquiry was causing her friend some concern. "I just thought that he might have."

That was the end of the matter and Debbie soon returned to her work at Hope acres. She was out taking charge of a work party, which was clearing up the garden, when one of the girls who had been working inside came out to her with a message. "Pastor Macey phoned there looking for you," she reported. "He would like you to ring him back."

When Debbie did as requested Pastor Macey arranged for her to call and see him at his office later. As she drove across Debbie wondered what she had done to merit receiving such an urgent call to meet the National Director of Teen Challenge UK. She hadn't a clue what this was all about, other than that Audrey had intimated that Pastor Macey had been intending 'to speak to' her.

She hadn't long arrived in the Director's office, though, until she found herself pleasantly surprised and totally shocked at what he had to say.

"As you know, Debbie, our Deputy Manager is retiring," he began. "Audrey is on long term sick leave. We need someone to take charge of the day to day running of the centre and undertake her counselling role, and we would like to offer you the job."

This came as a bolt from the blue to Debbie. She was completely taken aback. When Pastor Macey had asked to see her she had no idea that he was about to put a proposal like this to her!

"I can't do that!" Debbie stammered back at him, as the full import of what he had just offered her began to sink in. "Who? Me? Running the centre? I'm sorry, but I think you have got the wrong person."

Pastor Macey had expected a reaction something like this from Debbie. He was prepared to be patient, but also persistent. "No. I don't think we have," he continued. "We have thought about it carefully. We know that you will need a lot of support but we will be prepared to offer that in different ways."

Debbie found the prospect totally daunting. "But what about all the administration?" she asked, apprehensively. "I don't mind working with the girls, but I know nothing about the books and finance and things like that."

"Don't worry about that side of it," Pastor Macey was quick to reassure her. "Mike Rankin will oversee you from here, and Alicia will continue to do all the office administration as usual. Will you take it on?"

"Yes, I will, if you think I can," Debbie told him nervously. "But I had never expected to be asked to do anything like this. What you are saying has come as a real bombshell to me and I suppose I am a bit scared."

"You can do it, Debbie," the Pastor encouraged her. "We have every confidence in you."

When Debbie went out into the car she just sat and cried. This was totally unbelievable. She had graduated from the Teen Challenge programme at Hope House just eighteen months before, and now she had undertaken to run it! She felt so inadequate. Sitting, confused in the car, she bowed her head and prayed fervently for help. She was going to need a lot of it, both from God and the senior management team.

On taking up her new position at the beginning of May Debbie found attending to all the various aspects of the work quite challenging. Pastor Macey, Mike and Audrey were very supportive, as they had promised, and Alicia kept her right when it came to office matters in a very gentle, patient manner.

This assistance was invaluable for Debbie had been approaching the administrative responsibility of her new post with a sense of trepidation whereas she felt at least some small degree of confidence in relation to her role as a counsellor. She was soon to discover, however, that working with some of the women in her group was to prove an extremely challenging occupation. It would test her Christian wisdom and basic counselling skills to the limit.

One of the first women to be admitted to Hope House, and commence the programme, after Debbie became acting centre-manager was Brenda, a West Indian woman from London. She was in her thirties, had four children, and presented with a wide range of complex physical and mental issues.

Brenda had just been in Hope House for about three weeks when Debbie noticed the petrified look on her face one afternoon, just after lunch.

"Are you O.K., Brenda?" she asked, to allow her the opportunity to explain her anguished expression.

"I'm fine," Brenda replied, trying to brush off the enquiry. Debbie knew that she was not telling the truth. With her mouth she was claiming to be 'fine' but the look of abject fear and terror in her eyes was telling a different story.

When Brenda marched deliberately out of the dining room in the direction of her bedroom, probably to avoid any further questioning about her panic-stricken appearance, Debbie felt instinctively that she should follow.

Realising that Brenda was in deep distress, Debbie joined her in the bedroom and began talking to her. As the session continued on into the afternoon, and Brenda began to reveal the complex web of misery she had known as life, Debbie sat and cried with her.

This was a new experience for Brenda. Nobody had ever cried with her before. All she had known throughout her thirty-something years was rejection, addiction and abuse. She was moved that at last she had found someone in the world who cared enough about her to weep with her in her woe.

Eventually, after three hours of talking and crying, Brenda told Debbie of a horrific memory that had been haunting her for years. She had felt bound by it, never having been able to express it to anyone before. Now, though, in the company of a compassionate Christian counsellor, she was able to verbalise it, and sensed a burden lift from her mind as she did so.

That long and anguished sharing session allowed Debbie some slight insight into the horrendous background Brenda was trying to put behind her. She appreciated that this was going to be an extremely difficult exercise and was alarmed, but not entirely surprised to find a note pushed below her office door one evening.

It was frightening in its clarity, unmistakeable in its message.

Seven simple words were enough to send a chill chasing up and down the spine of the acting-manager of Hope House.

'I AM GOING TO KILL MYSELF' the first six announced.

The seventh was the scrawled signature of the sender, 'Brenda.'

Debbie had heard girls talk about taking their own lives before, and knew that she could talk them through it. This often happened when they were undergoing the discomforts of detox, and she could always assure them, from her own personal experience, that if they were willing to 'hang on in there,' things would appear much better in a day or two.

She sensed, however, that this situation was more sinister. Brenda was a different case entirely. Knowing the horrible inhibitions that had beset her mind, and the determined nature of her spirit, Debbie recognised at once that this was a serious matter.

Brenda's note was either a wild and despairing plea for attention or a final and ultimate expression of intention. Debbie chose to recognise it as the latter, and realised that she needed help to deal with it. This was one instance where she would have to make use of Pastor Macey's promise to 'support you in every way we can,' and summon the assistance of experienced senior members of staff.

She phoned Mike Rankin at Teen Challenge headquarters, about a mile away and when he heard of Debbie's dilemma about Brenda's note volunteered to 'come across straight away.' That was reassuring, and when he arrived Debbie's mind was set further at ease when she saw that he had called on his way and collected his wife.

Although Audrey was very ill, her interest in the affairs of Hope House never abated, and when Mike phoned her for advice on the situation confronting Debbie with Brenda, she immediately asked him to bring her over too. The three of them talked the problem through and prayed about it together, before Debbie and Audrey went to meet Brenda.

They found her in her bedroom, and it was then that Debbie willingly stepped back and allowed Audrey to take over. As she listened to the founder of Hope House counsel this severely disturbed and certainly suicidal young woman she was amazed at her skill, her gentleness and her grace, in spite of her illness. Although Debbie had been invited to run the centre in Audrey's absence it would be a long time until she could match the former manager's natural discernment and spiritual integrity as a counsellor. She learnt more about counselling, as she observed her respected mentor deal with Brenda in that practical situation, than she could ever have done in weeks of theoretical discussion in the classroom.

What Audrey had to say, and the gently persuasive way she had of putting it across, must have had an impact on Brenda as well. After they had been an hour together she had adopted a more positive attitude to her circumstances and given up any idea of taking her own life.

After that incident Brenda was to go on and complete the programme, although not without difficulty and the occasional setback. When she came to graduate, about a year later, she had come into a vital relationship with God though faith in Jesus Christ, and established an effective witness for Him.

As for Debbie, she had successfully negotiated yet another learning curve, having made a few skids and swerves in the process. Her role as acting–manger was developing into a sometimes painful but nonetheless often rewarding experience.

She was gaining even deeper and more valuable insights into the horrendous problems some of the women carried with them into Hope House, the craft of the Christian counsellor, and above all the mighty power of the God she had chosen to serve for the rest of her days to carry her through each and every situation she may be called upon to confront.

31

THAT LADY'S A GREAT PREACHER

Summer and autumn passed in a flurry of activity. As Debbie became more familiar with her new round of responsibilities she began to feel that God was leading her to devote her time and energies, at least for the foreseeable future, to the ministry of Hope House. It was rewarding but challenging, thrilling but often tiring, work, guiding women with deep problems of addiction through the dark tunnel of the trauma of detox and out into the sunshine of the spiritual light and liberty which can only be found through trusting in Jesus.

Back in the not so definite days of spring, however, she had responded both positively and enthusiastically to an invitation to return to Uganda. That call had come when she was anxiously seeking for guidance in her life, and Debbie felt that although she was now very involved in the running of Hope House, she still ought to honour her original 'absolutely,' and go.

She joined the team flying out from Cardiff on Friday, November 1, 2002, and they had a day to rest and acclimatise in Uganda before they began addressing meetings at various locations on Sunday. When Pastor Ray Smith had considered the requests he had received from different church groups to send them a speaker for the Sunday morning service he began assigning his team to cover them, as far as possible.

Debbie was quite relieved when he told her that she would be going to the church in Ntette, in Kampala district. She had been there on her first visit to Uganda, two years earlier. It had been a small friendly church, and she had taken a mid-week Bible study in it with a most appreciative audience of about 50 people present. Debbie even remembered what she had spoken about. It had been an outline on Psalm 63 that she had been taught in Hope House. The memory of the eager, attentive faces as she had read and spoken about 'souls that thirst for God in a dry and barren land' and 'lips that praise God for His lovingkindness which is better than life,' had lived with her for weeks.

'Ntette will be nice,' Debbie thought. 'It's a welcoming little place, and I've been before. I'm glad I don't have to go to one of these huge churches with hundreds of people there.'

Having consoled herself with the notion of a 'nice Ntette' Debbie was to receive a rude awakening when she arrived there, about an hour before the service was due to begin. The little building she had envisaged from her previous visit had completely disappeared and a huge arena had been built on the site where it once had stood. This new construction was like an amphitheatre with a massive tin roof covering a semicircular sea of white plastic chairs grouped around a central dais. As the roof was supported only by beams and the sides of the building were mostly open, Debbie could see that although there was still some time to go before the meeting was scheduled to start, a large expectant crowd had already gathered.

As she was being shown to her seat, directly below the central platform, Debbie was beset by a bout of nervous panic. She sat down and found that her hands, and the Bible they were clutching tightly, had all begun to shake uncontrollably. All feeling had left her legs. She only knew they were still there because of her knees, which insisted in banging into each other.

Debbie bowed her head, and although those around may have seen this as a final act of contemplation and dedication before she was called upon to speak, it was in fact to allow her to dispatch a passionate, panic-stricken prayer to her Heavenly Father. "Oh God please help me!" she begged. "Please help me! I've never seen a crowd like this before. I'm totally out of my depth here!"

She had just opened her eyes to sit up straight and try and settle herself down in preparation for what was to come, when she was conscious that the person beside her was poking her elbow purposefully into her ribs. It was Rose, a lady from Cardiff, who had been asked to give her testimony for the very first time at this meeting.

When Debbie turned round to look at Rose, in response to her prodding, the woman who had never been to Africa before appeared scared stiff. She may have felt as though she was about to be 'thrown in at the deep end,' but she looked as though she was about to be thrown to the lions.

"There are a lot of people here, aren't there?" she croaked.

Although it was just a single simple question, her pale face and fear-filled eyes gave some indication of the sheer inner terror which had prompted it.

"There are indeed, Rose," Debbie had to agree. "But don't worry, you will be all right. We will be praying for you."

Rose relaxed a little, reassured by the confident words of an experienced campaigner. It would hardly do for Debbie to confess that she was probably the more terrified of the two of them!

Following a short session of praise and worship, and then Rose's testimony, Pastor Jamiel introduced their speaker for the evening. When Debbie had mounted the platform and surveyed the vast congregation her mouth seemed to dry up all of a sudden, and her heart skipped a beat. There were shining eyes set in eager black faces gazing up at her from every angle, and for as far as she could see. The pastor had said in his opening remarks that their new auditorium held 1500 chairs, and from Debbie's vantage point above the crowd she couldn't see a single vacant one. And the chairs were only for the adults. The children, in what looked like their hundreds, were sitting on the floor!

Her theme for that afternoon was the power of God to change lives. She opened by saying that she would be basing her remarks on a story from Genesis chapter 32 in the Bible. When she had read the account of Jacob's tenacity in his desire for blessing as he wrestled with God, and the touch of God on his thigh and how this was to mark him for life, she began her address. Having to speak through an interpreter allowed her to stop at the end of each sentence and consider what she wanted to say next.

A sense of silent awe descended over the packed congregation as Debbie told them that the God who had touched 'the hollow place' in Jacob's thigh' is still both willing and able to touch the hollow and empty places in our lives, even today. He wants to fill our hollow places with His power, replace our weakness with His strength, our insecurity with His stability and our wrestling with His rest. This could only come about, though, when people were willing to enter into a personal and intimate experience with God.

To illustrate her point Debbie told them her life story. "I was once so addicted to heroin and crack cocaine," she proclaimed at one point, "that I couldn't stand on my feet for an hour. I would have collapsed into a pathetic helpless heap. Now, though, since God has touched my life I stand before you, and will be standing here for some time yet, by His grace and in His power. He has saved my soul and cleansed my body ever since I came to put my trust in Him."

She then invited the audience to compare the photograph she had arranged to have passed around amongst them, with the person standing before them, if they required practical proof of what she was saying.

When she had finished her scripture reading and begun to preach Debbie found that her initial trepidation had all melted away and she was soon expressing the message she wanted to convey in a full and confident flow of language. It was almost scary for she felt borne along by an Unseen Power that had obviously taken control of her mind and her speech. She found herself using words that she didn't even know she knew, and illustrating her address with personal incidents which she had, up until that moment, long since forgotten.

Her African interpreter entered into the spiritual and emotional atmosphere of the occasion as well. As Debbie became more intense about her subject, she raised her voice occasionally for emphasis and became more expressive with her hand and arm movements. This had an energizing effect on the naturally dramatic and demonstrative nature and temperament of the interpreter. When Debbie raised her voice, he raised his, like an echo in a foreign language, and the more she gesticulated the more animated he became!

At the close of the service many people came forward seeking salvation and asking for prayer for various life situations. As Debbie, and all the other members of the team who were present that evening, moved amongst the large group of men, women and young people assembled around the front of the building they were called upon to deal with different degrees of need.

The most common of these was a desire to know peace with God and freedom from the burden and bondage of sin through coming to Christ for salvation. Debbie was thrilled that evening to counsel many people and see them open their hearts to the Lord.

There were other requests as well. In a country where the only doctors are hundreds of miles away in the cities, and there in no such thing as a National Health Service, many came forward requesting prayer for healing.

" I have aids, will you pray for me?" one would ask.

"I have TB," or "My mother has malaria," or "My son has dysentery..."

"Would you please pray for me... or him... or her... or them?"

The pleas were all so genuine and the people were so patient, waiting quietly for someone to counsel them or pray with them, that Debbie was physically and emotionally drained by the time she had spoken to the last person waiting for her.

It was almost midnight. Although very tired Debbie felt greatly enriched having experienced such a sense of divine guidance as she spoke, and she was thrilled to see so many commit their lives to Christ or come forward for prayer in response to the message.

On Monday morning the touring group with a mission travelled northwards to Sroti where they were booked to conduct a number of meetings on successive evenings.

When they arrived Debbie was surprised to discover that many people had come particularly to hear her preach on the night of her first speaking engagement there. She was later to discover one of the reasons why. Reports of the meeting in Ntette had gone ahead of her, with Pastor Jamiel having phoned one of the senior pastors in Kampala to tell him, "This lady's a great preacher. God is using her testimony and ministry in a mighty way."

Debbie took her turn at speaking with others on the team that week and as they did so witnessed many others come to trust in Christ as Saviour. One of these was a man who showed unusual determination to have his sins forgiven and know peace with God, whatever the cost.

The meetings in Sroti were held outdoors with the large crowds being addressed through a public address system. That particular system seemed to have only two knobs that worked. One was 'Off' and the other was 'Full.' There was no halfway measure or no such thing as toning down the volume to suit sensitivities of the audience. You either didn't have it on at all, or you had it full blast.

One night Pastor Smith was speaking and in the course of his message emphasised the power of Jesus to save. He used the words "Jesus can save you" and "Jesus will save you, if you will only come to Him," repeatedly.

Neither he, nor Debbie nor anyone else in the gathering that evening, was to know the effect those words were to have on a heart and mind far away, however.

Out in a distant village the message of the meeting came floating across the still night air, boosted by the full volume setting of the PA system. A man, sitting out at the door of his hut, heard the words, "Jesus can save you," and "Jesus will save you if you will only come to Him," boom out across the African bush.

Reckoning that this salvation by coming to Jesus was probably what he had been craving for many years, he decided to do something about it. He had a swollen and infected foot, which was extremely painful, but he wasn't going to let that stop him finding out more about Jesus. Picking up the makeshift crutch he had made from the branch of a tree he set off to walk away from his village and out into the darkness.

Having struggled through the snake-infested bush, barefoot, all night he arrived into Sroti just after sunrise the next morning, and immediately began making enquiries amongst the local people. Where could he find the team from Wales who were preaching last night?

When some team members were eventually contacted and told that there was 'somebody who wanted to see them' they were surprised to find a dust-covered man with a swollen foot and tree-branch crutch waiting patiently outside.

They were even more astonished to learn that he had come forward in response to an appeal at the close of the meeting the previous evening. The only problem was that it had taken him twelve hours to reach a counsellor!

The purpose of his determined trek was astounding, too. All he wanted to know, he told those speaking to him through an interpreter, was how he could be saved. When this was explained from the Word of God he bowed his head and having sought forgiveness for his sin, accepted Jesus into his heart.

It was Debbie's turn to speak in the meeting that evening and seated happily, somewhere in the large crowd, was the man who had walked miles through the bush the night before. His face was radiant. He had found what he had come looking for. He was saved and satisfied.

Others trusted Christ at the close of that service, too, and there were to be many more conversions in the evenings that followed.

When it came time to return home Debbie was glad that she had volunteered 'absolutely' and wholeheartedly to come.

Africa had been a marvellous and maturing experience for her once more.

She had been enthralled to witness God work through her, beside her and without her in that vast continent yet again.

32

GRAB HOLD OF THE BATON

Debbie phoned Fiona in mid-January 2003. The two women who had worked together so closely in Hope House a few years before had just recently learnt, from separate sources, that Audrey, who had been such an inspiration to each of them, had passed away. Having shared their initial reaction to the sad news they both agreed that they would see one another again, for the first time in a number of months, 'on Saturday.'

That Saturday, January 25, 2003, was the day of Audrey's funeral service and Swansea Elim City Temple was full to overflowing even before it was due to begin. Fiona was there with her husband Jay and baby son, Ethan, and Debbie was sitting across at the other side of the large church in the middle of all the girls from Hope House. Although the two friends were seated some distance apart, they were united in grief at the death of someone from whom they had both learned so much, but also united in thanksgiving for a life lived solely for the glory of God.

It was the theme of rejoicing rather than mourning that dominated that unique funeral service. No one came all dressed in black. The family had requested that if those attending felt they must wear something black, to comply with deeply ingrained funeral traditions, then they ought to wear another item of light-coloured clothing to offset it. Audrey had loved the Lord, her family, and her 'girls' at Hope House, and her husband and children wanted her funeral service to reflect the vibrant Christian joy that had been such a basic element in her life.

They were not to be disappointed.

With around 700 people, many of whom were, like Debbie, grateful graduates of Hope House, packed into the City Temple, the volume of the praise and sincerity of the worship at the commencement of the service was truly amazing. Paul, Mike and Audrey's son, spoke first, giving a moving tribute to his mum. After that it was Fiona's turn. She left three-week-old Ethan, who had been brought along in his car seat, in the charge of his dad, as she rose to read a tribute that Naomi had written. When she had finished Audrey's daughter's warm-hearted reflections on her mum, Fiona went on to add a number of fond memories of her own.

One of the most comprehensive and moving tributes paid to the former manager of Hope House was delivered by Pastor Macey, National Director of Teen Challenge UK. Having known Audrey, Mike and the family well for many years, he was able to outline in detail, and extol without question, what he described as the three outstanding qualities of his former colleague. These were her devotion, her dedication and her determination.

Pastor Macey could not have anticipated at the time, though, the effect that a phrase he was set to use was to have on a member of the vast congregation. As he drew his remarks to a close he revealed his vision for the future with the words, 'Let us be inspired by her life, by her commitment and by her courage. I pray that God will give Teen Challenge more

Audreys, more people who will grab hold of the baton and continue the race from where she was forced to stop...'

It was the phrase 'grab hold of the baton' that set Fiona Fallon off into a strange and sudden emotional and spiritual spin. A sense of nervous tension, having been called upon to address such a large audience in such an emotionally highly-charged situation would have been understandable in the circumstances, but this was something entirely different. Those five words had sent her heart thumping so hard that Fiona thought it was going to bang its way out through her ribcage.

Why should this happen? What does this mean, she began asking herself, conscious that Pastor Macey had now resumed his seat and Pastor Phil Hills had stepped forward into the pulpit to deliver the funeral address.

'Grab hold of the baton. Could that phrase possibly be a voice from God to her? And if it wasn't, why had it affected her in such a peculiar way? Could it be that she was supposed to 'grab hold of the baton' that Audrey had laid down, and carry on the work?

When the funeral service in Swansea was over the cortege proceeded to Gorslas where Audrey was buried in the village graveyard, just behind Hope House. It seemed so fitting that her body was laid to rest less than five hundred yards from the rear of the centre which had been so dear to her heart, and in which she had seen God intervene in a marvellous manner in the lives of dozens of woebegone women like Debbie and Brenda.

Those who attended the final committal at the graveside were entertained to tea in Hope House late that January afternoon, and as Fiona walked about amongst the large group of former residents and staff members she felt unexpectedly at ease. She knew them, and they knew her, and it was as though none of them had ever moved on. It was back to the old days, back to belonging. As a number of these former residents recounted their memories of how Audrey and she had cooperated in the uphill work when the centre was still in its infancy, and in the expansion of later years, Fiona found a series of vivid images of the former manager flashing up onto the screen of her mind. And each one of them seemed invisibly overprinted with the title, 'Grab hold of the baton.'

Within weeks of returning home, Fiona had a telephone call from Pastor Macey. He was ringing to enquire if she would be interested in coming back to manage Hope House. He explained that although Debbie was running the centre at that time she was more interested in one-to-one work with the girls than administration, and would be quite happy to assume the role of deputy manager if a new, and suitable person, like herself, were to be appointed manager. Pastor Macey was convinced that Fiona would be an ideal person to fill the position with her background of work in Teen Challenge

Fiona thanked him for his call and the confidence that he seemed to be willing to place in her, but asked for time to consider his suggestion. There was so much to be taken into account. The work in which Jay and she were currently involved in Whitchester House, in Scotland, caring for a tiny baby and the upheaval of having to move house once more, were some of her main practical concerns.

Then there was the spiritual aspect. Could this possibly be the will of God for her? Had the heart flutter at the huge funeral been a physical alarm bell to alert her to God's plan for her life? Or had it been merely her imagination?

Having given the matter long and prayerful consideration during the spring and early summer Fiona eventually submitted to what she had come to believe was God's purpose for her. In July she applied for the post of manager of Hope House, Teen Challenge, and was appointed, with an agreed starting date of September 1, 2003.

Debbie was extremely pleased to learn of Fiona's decision to come back to Hope House as its manager. She was happy to recognise that in the capacity of deputy manager she would have more time to devote to the aspect of the work that she most loved, the teaching and counselling of the increasing number of students.

The bond of mutual respect that had grown up between the two most senior figures in Hope House was very evident one morning in late September when Debbie was conducting morning chapel. Fiona, who had taken up her new position with a wealth of counselling experience behind her, and was rapidly 'finding her feet' as an administrator, was sitting at the back.

Speaking about the parable of the talents, in Matthew chapter 25, Debbie was endeavouring to illustrate the truth of verse 21, which states, 'Well done, good and faithful servant. You were faithful over a few things. I will make you ruler over many things…'

"It is easy to complain about doing the menial tasks," she began, " but it is in those little things that we can prove our faithfulness to God. When I was in the programme my job was to do the laundry. It was not perhaps the most classy of callings, surrounded day after day by washing machines, driers and piles of dirty washing, but I did it to the best of my ability. And I tried to go the extra mile with it, too, folding everybody's underwear and returning it to their rooms when I could. I learnt to look upon it as something I was doing for Jesus.

When I moved on from that I was asked to assume responsibility for the work schedule at Hope Acres. One day there, when I was out with a group of girls scraping dog pooh off the garden, I received a telephone call to offer me the position of acting-manger of Hope House!"

Realizing that her down-to-earth examples were being readily received and easily understood by her audience, Debbie went on to elaborate further. "I can give you another case of being faithful in little and being put in charge of much," she told them. "I have a photograph at home of a young woman, down on her hands and knees, scrubbing the floor of this chapel with a wire-brush to smooth down the surface of it after the concrete had been laid. Audrey Rankin, the lady who started Hope House had just taken her on as her assistant, but there was no pay in those days. There were only six girls in the centre then and that woman came here because she had a vision for working with women with addictions, and she felt that it was God's calling on her life. She offered her services voluntarily and looked to God to supply all her needs."

There were a few eyebrows raised in amazement, and sensing this, Debbie pressed home her point. "I can see that you are wondering who would come here to work so hard with no guaranteed income," she continued. "Well I can tell you who it was. And in fact you know her, all of you. She is sitting right behind you. Her name is Fiona Fallon, the new manager of Hope House."

Debbie was forced to pause in her talk for a moment, for her audience had suddenly turned their backs on her, instinctively and en bloc. They were anxious to see how the lady they were just getting to know, and learning to appreciate, would react to Debbie's disclosure.

The width of the smiles, and the warmth of the little waves, that were exchanged between Fiona at the back and Debbie at the front had a reassuring effect upon them all.

These two women knew each other well and understood each other completely.

The girls turned back to Debbie again to allow her to continue her lesson, just as happily, eagerly and automatically as they had turned away from her to look at Fiona behind them.

They found it comforting to be in such caring, capable, Christian hands.

33

MAD ALI

One of the stiffest challenges to face the new leadership partnership came in late November when a wild-looking and apparently half-crazy young woman applied for admission to Hope House. A Christian group had found Alison Kavanagh virtually destitute on the streets of Newport in south Wales. Recognising that she was so far gone on drink and drugs that she needed urgent attention or she would soon die, they arranged for her to visit the centre for an interview.

When the young woman in her late twenties, with the fierce, faraway look in her eyes arrived on the appointed afternoon it was Debbie who showed her around. As she moved from room to room, pausing occasionally to take another sup of the yogurt she was slurping straight from the tub, and then wipe her mouth with one deft stroke of the back of her hand, the newcomer appeared overwhelmed. It was obvious that Alison hadn't lived in anywhere like this for years, perhaps even in her life.

She kept exclaiming in her strong Welsh accent, "Oh this is a lovely place! I would love to come 'ere! How beau-u-u-utiful!"

Debbie and the prospective resident were to meet other members of staff on their tour of the building and each time they encountered someone new Alison greeted them with the same light-hearted half-baked abandon.

It was "Nice to meet you, Fiona! Lovely place you've got 'ere, eh?' or "Hi Julie! Great spot this, isn't it? I could 'ack it 'ere real good!"

All those whom Alison met went away shaking their heads. That girl would be 'a handful' they thought. She was either 'freaked out' on drugs or else completely 'out of her mind.'

When Debbie came to interview Alison for admission all the false euphoria of the walkabout had gone and the applicant for a place fell asleep and had to be awakened three times. When the interview was over Debbie consulted with other senior members of staff about Alison and they expressed some reservation. "We have had girls like this before and they quit the programme after a month or two. They never seem to quite make it somehow," they said, quite rightly.

There were a number of things about her, though, that appealed to Debbie. The first of these was a telltale sign that would have been particularly evident to an ex-addict. This young woman was the first person she had ever come across whose fingertips were as black as her own had once been. When Debbie noticed the calloused black tips to Alison's fingers on both hands she realised how deep this person had dropped into her addiction. The blackened fingertips had come from repeatedly lighting crack cocaine pipes and burning heroin on foil.

Her sincerity was appealing too. Debbie, who had conducted Alison around the centre, could sense that the constant torrent of inconsequential chatter was merely a mask to conceal a deeper desperation. This became evident when she asked her during one of her waking moments in the course of the interview, "Why do you want to come in here, Alison?"

"I need 'elp," came the pathetically candid reply. "Please 'elp me. If you don't take me in I'm going to die!"

This anguished appeal for instant aid struck a chord in Debbie's heart. She felt an affinity with this pitiful little wisp of humanity with her frighteningly pale face, her skinny body and burn-blackened hands. It was a mixture of sympathy and empathy that prompted her to advocate giving Alison 'a chance.' Debbie felt sorry for her, that was true, but there was more to it than that. She had been where Alison was now and realised that her plea for help was the frantic cry of a perishing soul. Her prediction had been painfully accurate. If they didn't take this girl in she would probably be dead in a matter of months.

Above all the human elements and considerations Debbie also had an unusual, instinctive conviction that there was something 'different' about the girl she had met for the first time just a few hours before. Hidden in the fluent flow of language and tucked away in the depths behind the frightened eyes, she spotted what she believed could possibly be an untapped talent.

Audrey Rankin had felt the same way about her when they had first met. Could it possibly be a divinely-influenced intuition that somehow 'God had His hand on this girl's life?'

When it came time to make a decision as to whether or not to accept Alison on to the programme Debbie put a very strong case in her favour, assuring the others that she would be quite happy to accept her into her counselling group. Although she had only been in Alison's company a short time, Debbie recognised that they had probably come from similar backgrounds, and that there was a good chance they would understand each other and get along well together.

The other senior staff members accepted that Debbie's reasoning was possibly sound. Her conviction about the applicant's slim chances of survival if refused entry to Hope

House was certainly both sincere and sound, and taking all into consideration they decided to shelve their misgivings and offer her a place.

It was early December 2003 when a bed became available and Alison Kavanagh, or 'mad Ali' to the drug dealers and users of Newport, entered the Teen Challenge programme at Hope House.

The Christian atmosphere in the centre had an immediate effect upon her. She felt, from her very first day, that 'there is something good in here,' although she could not identify quite what it was. She reached the conclusion that it must be something to do with the fact that the staff always seemed to be talking about Jesus. Everybody, including the women who were well advanced in the programme seemed so happy when they were singing about Him in the chapel, too.

Recognising that there was a peace about these people that she had never seen before, and certainly didn't possess herself, Alison began to enquire about it. Was it, she wondered, their obvious relationship with God that had made them into such a content and caring community?

Julie Murray, the nurse in charge of detox, is the person with whom the women entering the programme at Hope House have most contact at first. In this position she has to deal with the new residents' queries of all kinds. Sensing that Alison had been impressed by the Christian ethos of the centre, Julie told her why the staff were so committed to seeing the women cleared of their addictions, released from self-reproach and returned to their homes and families. It was also important to emphasise what they believed to be the best method by which to achieve this aim.

She explained to Alison that she needed to be liberated on three levels, physical, emotional and spiritual. The physical element would come through a carefully monitored medical programme of detox and the emotional part would be dealt with in a series of one-to-one consultation sessions with specially trained Christian counsellors. It was the spiritual factor, though, that made the Hope House approach different from that of many other rehab centres. This was where the relationship with God, which had been such an unmistakeable feature of the centre to Alison, came into play.

"We believe that people can never be totally liberated in body, mind and spirit until they know their sins forgiven," Julie told her. "The Bible teaches us that Jesus Christ loved everybody in the world so much that He died on the cross to bear the punishment for the sins of all mankind. When a person trusts in Him then he or she can have their sins forgiven and be made a totally new person.'

This was fantastic news to Alison's ears. When she heard God's rescue plan for sinful souls so clearly outlined she responded eagerly. "That's exactly what I need," she confessed without hesitation or reservation. "That's what I have been looking for all my life!" In a matter of seconds she bowed her head, and with tears flowing down her cheeks, a broken woman, Alison poured out her heart in prayer to God asking Him to forgive her sins, and committing her life to Him.

Having come into a living relationship with God, she had established a solid foundation from which to launch her physical and emotional recovery.

It wasn't going to be easy, though.

Alison had appalling problems.

Ridding her body of her deep addiction to heroin and crack cocaine was the first obstacle to be overcome. Although not having to undergo the trauma of the 'prayer and paracetemol' panacea, she found detox extremely difficult. Her body seemed to be falling to bits and her mind was in a mess. It seemed to want to think about a million things at once, flitting from something to everything and focusing on nothing.

She felt sick all the time, too.

It was hard to pray. Debbie and Julie encouraged her to place herself in the hand of God and keep talking to Him in prayer. That was O.K. in theory and theology but when your mind was splintered like a shattered windscreen it was hard to concentrate on framing a prayer and difficult to place yourself anywhere.

On one of her most despondent days she called out to Debbie from the depths of physical agony and mental frustration, "I can't do this any more. I have been using heroin and crack for nine years now and I have tried 'cold turkey' nine times and it hasn't made any difference!"

"Only nine times!" her counsellor retorted, in mock surprise. "I put myself through it fourteen times before the Lord eventually set me free. Stick with it, Alison.

Remember that photograph I showed you? That was me less than five years ago. And what God has done for me He can do for you."

Alison liked Debbie. She was so positive and encouraging. Nor could anyone argue with the evidence. She was definitely a different woman now from what she once had been.

The physical presence of a now perfectly healthy but once deeply-drug-addicted Debbie proved inspirational to Alison. Perhaps it was true. If she could make it so can I, she began to reason.

It worked, too. Alison persisted and two weeks after beginning the induction part of the programme she began to feel slightly better. The effect of the drugs she had been depending upon for years gradually diminished in her body, and she started to take an interest in life as it was being lived around her.

Although there were many issues yet to be addressed in her life, since she was a still a long way from being either physically or emotionally restored to anything resembling normality, Alison began to find her incentive for living where many of the others on the programme appeared to have found it. That was in God.

She began to read the Bible and as she heard various speakers in morning and evening chapel explain its teachings through the application of its stories she developed an appetite for it. Everything she heard she read all over again as soon as she returned to her room. Alison had begun to explore a realm she had never even known existed on planet Earth up to a month before. It was the exciting sphere of the revelation of amazing scriptural truth to the eager new believer.

Her spiritual growth was undoubtedly assisted in her early days as a Christian by listening to the CD of 'Cleaned Up' by 'Living Hope.' Residents in the induction stage of the programme are permitted to listen to Christian music on specially provided Walkman sets. Alison had only been in Hope House about three weeks when she discovered the CD. It was supposed to be kept in the lounge so that it was available to everybody, but she often paid the lounge a visit last thing in the evening and if 'Cleaned Up' was still sitting around she sneaked it out with her to listen to late at night and early in the morning.

Alison just couldn't get enough of it. Debbie, her counsellor, had begun to minister to her in song. One of her favourite tracks was 'Joy in the Morning.' Debbie found it infinitely encouraging to hear one day, from round a corner in a corridor, the girl whom she had advocated bringing in, singing happily in a husky voice. Alison's throat was still cracked and dry from the constant use of drugs but that did not in any way deter her from rasping passionately, "And there'll be joy in the morning,

Joy in the evening, joy all day long."

When Debbie turned into the corridor where Alison was they met face to face. The singer paused only to greet her counsellor with a cheery, "Hi Debbie," before walking on, singing away, "joy in the morning, joy in the evening, joy all day long."

The extent of Alison's physical problems was highlighted in the early months of 2004 when, although she had progressed to another level of the programme and had left detox behind she was still constantly tired. She had begun to eat a normal diet again but remained extremely pale, and fearing that she may have other health problems Debbie arranged an appointment for her with a local GP.

The doctor arranged for a number of tests to be carried out and the cause of Alison's anaemic-looking appearance was soon revealed. Her blood count was extremely low. When he began to investigate the possible cause of this, including asking about incidences of 'severe blood loss in the past' Alison told him about something that she had not yet dared to share with anyone. She was too scared.

Six months earlier she had been attacked by a drug-crazed boyfriend to such an extent that, as she confessed to the doctor, "When I had a shower after it the water was red. Blood was flowing from my nose, my mouth and cuts all over my body. I thought I was going to die."

Having conceded that she was indeed 'lucky to be still alive' the doctor was able to arrange a course of treatment that would, in time, see her blood count restored to normal levels.

The psychological scars that the violent incident, which had caused the problem in the first place, had left, required treatment also, however. And that was where Debbie's skill as a counsellor was tested to its limit yet again.

As she sat with Alison in their counselling sessions Debbie realised that she had been right in thinking that their backgrounds had been very much alike. Guilt complexes, stemming from lack of self-esteem, triggered by early abuse. Trying to drown out the disappointments of life with drink and obliterate reality with drugs. From dabbling to addiction, from using to dealing, the downward slide was common to both. It was all there. When Alison eventually disclosed the details of the tempestuous relationship that had almost ended in disaster, Debbie could empathise as well. She had been in one too.

Alison was often overtaken by guilt when the sheer mountain of sin seemed to pile up endlessly as she talked through her unhappy and turbulent past. When this sense of shame surfaced in their discussions, Debbie had the answer. It was usually something like, "Take it to Jesus, Alison. Look hard at the cross. Calvary covers it all." Occasionally she would expand the theme by relating how Jay Fallon had explained to her in one of her bouts of guilt-ridden depression that God saw her 'cleansed as white as snow, as a pure and spotless virgin in Christ Jesus.'

This worked well when Alison was in listening mode, but when she was in loquacious mode it was different. The woman who had talked her way around Hope House on her initial visit, and who sang her way around it, with or without a Walkman ever since she discovered 'Joy in the Morning,' liked to have her say about most matters. And that would possibly have been O.K. too, if she had learnt to put her point across in a few words and leave it there, but she didn't. Alison had a habit of going on, and on, and on, and when she did Debbie found it most exasperating and when pressed beyond measure reacted instinctively. It was like putting up an umbrella to protect herself from the deluge of words.

When members of staff approached Debbie's counselling room along the corridor one afternoon they heard high-pitched screeching and automatically assumed that 'mad Ali' was at it again.

"Shut up will you!" the voice was yelling. "Will you just shut up and listen to what I am trying to tell you!"

As they came nearer the door, however, they were able to identify the voice. And it wasn't Alison's. It was Debbie's!

Her Christian patience had snapped, her counselling psychology had been forgotten and she had decided to adopt a more definite and direct approach with this chirpy little character!

Such instances were rare but they helped shock Alison back into sense when they occurred. The more common scenario was the considerate counselling session and as these consultations continued Alison's mentally crippling complexes gradually disappeared and were replaced by a rapidly maturing spirituality.

By the time she was six months into the programme Alison was proving an inspiration to others. The new life she had received in Julie Murray's office on December 10, 2003 was beginning to manifest itself, not only in the relish with which she read and studied the Bible but also in the heart of love and compassion she showed for others.

When she saw someone struggling Alison seemed to be always at hand to encourage her. Whether it was a written assignment she was having difficulty with, a broken relationship that had led to a broken heart or just the overwhelming urge to 'pack it all in' during the distressing days of detox, it didn't matter. Alison was soon by the anxious woman's side with an encouraging, "Come on then, you can do it!" or "Let's find somewhere quiet where we can have a chat about it!"

The staff at Hope House had not told Alison to assume this role. She had been with the others on the programme in class and in chapel when they were exhorted to obey the scriptures and be 'kind to one another and help one another,' that was all. It just seemed to come naturally to her, this spontaneous manifestation of practical Christian care.

Her caring attitude, plus her positive approach to anything she was asked to do whether big or small, upfront or backstage, did not go unnoticed, however. So much so that the staff considered that her unique blend of determination and dedication, and of tenacity and tenderness, should be tangibly recognised.

This happened in October, when, just ten months after she had been admitted to the programme, Alison Kavanagh was awarded the Hope House Teen Challenge Resident of the Year Award 2004.

34

THEY WANT SAVED!

Following the presentation of her award and the completion of phase three of the programme Alison spent the winter in the Teen Challenge School of Ministry. Here she was introduced to more intensive Bible study and undertook courses in effective Gospel witness and Christian living.

Debbie still maintained close contact with her and the relationship between them developed from that of counsellor and counselled to close Christian friends. When invited to speak at meetings in the south Wales area Debbie often took Alison along to tell of the change in her life, how that God had made a new woman out of her. This was a valuable element in her training in evangelism but it also proved interesting for audiences. Alison's flow of language, coupled with her patent sincerity in presenting what many classed as an 'almost unbelievable story,' had a habit of holding them spellbound.

A church in Dowlais, near Merthyr Tydfil had a vision for reaching out to the drug addicts in their community and the pastor contacted Debbie with a question. If they were to arrange an informal meeting for the local addicts could she bring a team along to speak?

The response was an enthusiastic affirmative. Debbie was delighted to hear of this initiative and forwarded a set of her 'before and after' photographs. A committee used these to produce striking advertising material which was then displayed or distributed in the district.

The church worked hard on promotion and on Monday, March 7, 2005 a large crowd, including many addicts, arrived for the meeting and the meal that was to follow.

Debbie had planned carefully for that evening. She had invited Becky, Christine and Nadine, all of them former heroin addicts and women who were well advanced in the Teen Challenge programme, to take part in the outreach presentation along with Alison and herself.

They were a collective modern-day miracle, five of them, prepared to witness as individuals to what God had done in their lives. Becky and Nadine gave short accounts of the emptiness and despair they had experienced before conversion and how they now felt fulfilled in the Christian faith.

When Alison stood up to recount her life story her rich Welsh accent seemed to have a hypnotising effect on the audience. As she recalled brief incidents from her unsettled childhood, uncontrolled teenage and the exploits and escapes of her early twenties, the crowd appeared mesmerised.

This was a different atmosphere in which to speak than that of a normal church service. Although this gathering was being held in a church building there were no impromptu 'Hallelujahs' or heartfelt 'Amens.' The organisers were anxious to ensure that the atmosphere created would make their especially invited audience feel particularly welcome without being specifically 'churched.'

They needn't have worried. Although Alison found it unusual to tell of God's intervention in her life without the backing of an enthusiastic Christian chorus, the climate her testimony created proved compelling to that particular crowd. Any member of an addict audience would identify with some aspect of her earlier life. If they had done it, whatever it was, so had she.

The awesome silence that had descended over the gathering remained unbroken as Alison continued to describe her admission to Hope House, her awareness of the presence of God in there, her personal commitment to Christ and the physical healing and spiritual satisfaction of the past year.

Conscious at one point that she was perhaps going on too long she looked down questioningly at Debbie, while saying aloud, in the course of her talk, "I must hurry up and finish." Recognising that Alison's graphic account was making an indelible impression on her audience and setting the scene for her address to come, despite the speaker's misgivings about being too longwinded, Debbie happily whispered up, "Go on. Go on."

When Alison did conclude what she had to say all five women assembled on the platform. People listened attentively as they sang a number of pieces to the accompaniment of Becky on the guitar. One of these songs, ' Beautiful One I Love,' was to prove particularly appealing.

Debbie introduced herself briefly as 'the woman on the posters.' She was yet another person whose life had been transformed by the power of God. Turning to the Bible she then read aloud the story of 'blind Bartimaeus' from Mark chapter ten.

Everyone appeared to be listening intently as Debbie summarised the deep problems in the life of Bartimaeus, and how these were resolved when he came in contact with Jesus. He was, as Debbie pointed out, blind, and although he was on the road to somewhere he was going nowhere. As a result of his disability he was also forced into becoming a beggar, which meant that he had neither guaranteed income nor future prospects.

She proceeded to outline the three steps which marked his determination to get to Jesus and ask Him do something about his situation. Initially he did not let the crowd hold him back, and then he threw away his begging cloak. Finally, when the Saviour stood still before him he admitted his need in humility and faith.

Sensing that the message was being well received Debbie went on to apply the story to the lives of all present in the form of a very personal challenge.

"When Bartimaeus was brought to Jesus our Lord asked him, 'What do you want Me to do for you?'" she said. "The Saviour is with us tonight and His question to each of us is still the same. It is, 'What do you want Me to do for you?' Jesus has the power to forgive your sin and clean up your life. Look at us. If He can do it for a Debbie, or an Alison or a Nadine, He can do it for you. All He asks is that you open your heart to Him and accept Him into your life. The Bible says that all those who call on the name of the Lord shall be saved."

Having pressed home the point that she had come to make, to an audience, some of whom were like what she once was, Debbie prayed briefly and went on to make an appeal. Recognising that these people would probably find a church-type invitation to 'come out to the front,' too embarrassing, she varied her approach.

"I can see that there is some lovely food waiting for us down at the back," she began, "and we want everybody to stay and share it. If there is anyone who wants to learn more about anything we have said please speak to any member of the team. We will not be rushing away and would be glad to spend time with you, possibly answering any questions, or talking over any concerns, you might have. Above all we would be delighted to tell you what Jesus can do for you."

During the supper that followed the people who had helped themselves to the tempting fare that was laid out on a row of tables at the back, stood or sat around in pairs or small groups chatting. The topic of conversation seemed to be, as far as Debbie and her team could gather from those who approached them, 'the wonderful evening' they had enjoyed.

Christine, Debbie and Nadine were standing together at the front of the church, reflecting on what had happened that evening so far when Alison approached them. She had paid a visit to the food table and on her way back had noticed a young couple who were sitting in the chairs they had occupied during the meeting. It was obvious that they hadn't moved across to the table or helped themselves to any food.

"What about that pair down there?" Alison asked Debbie, when she had joined her friends. "They haven't moved up for anything to eat yet. I wonder if they are they waiting for some of us to come and speak to them."

"They could be," Debbie replied. "You could go over and see, Alison."

Nothing was too much trouble to the 'new person' from Newport, especially when it was in the service of the Lord, and Alison crossed to where the young man and woman were sitting. She spoke to the couple for a few minutes and then came back to report her findings to Debbie and the others.

Her message was both short and sweet.

"They want saved!" she announced, her once-frightened eyes now alight with the love and joy of the Lord.

Debbie smiled at her. "Well then, Alison, why don't you go over and counsel them?" she suggested. "Your testimony has probably been a factor in bringing them to this point. I can't think of anyone better qualified to speak to them than you."

Alison didn't need to be told twice. As soon as Debbie had proposed that her friend should undertake the counselling of the two young people who seemed more concerned about finding salvation than eating sandwiches, she was away.

When she reached the pair, Alison pulled a chair up in front of them, sat down, and began to talk. Soon her Bible, which she had gone across to pick up from the seat where she had left it earlier, was open in her hand.

It wasn't long until Debbie excused herself from the other women to whom she had been speaking, and found a vacant space on the otherwise crowded floor. She wanted to be on her own as she watched what was happening in the little group huddled together ten yards away. Alison's former counsellor was afraid that she might be overcome with emotion as she witnessed the woman she had counselled for almost a year counsel someone else.

Five minutes later Debbie saw Alison reach forward and place her right hand on the man's left shoulder, and her left hand on the woman's right shoulder and all three of them bowed their heads.

When Alison began to pray it was time for Debbie to turn away.

She swung around sharply to face the wall and began to cry.

Tears of joy flowed down her cheeks unchecked.

What a sight!

How good God was!

He had saved her, and given her power and purpose in her life.

Then He had done exactly the same for Alison.

Now she in turn had been used to lead others to Him.

A third generation of drug addicts had been cleansed 'as white as snow.'

TEEN CHALLENGE UK
is a registered charity with a proven cure for drug addiction.
They are committed to helping hurting people in a caring
Christian environment.

For further information contact

Teen Challenge UK
Hope House,
6 Church Road,
Gorslas,
Llanelli
Carmarthenshire,
Wales.
SA14 7NF

Tel: 01269 844114
Fax: 01269 844069

Email: tcuk@globalnet.co.uk